Kangaroos
Myths and Realities

Maryland Wilson and David B Croft

'The papers in this book were refereed by the editors and at least one
other reviewer.'

Published by:
The Australian Wildlife Protection Council Inc.

First published 1992: Kangaroos - Our Wildlife
Heritage - Not an Exploitable Resource.
By The Australian Wildlife Protection Council Incorporated

Second edition 1999: The Kangaroo Betrayed.
Published by Hill of Content Pty Ltd.

This Third Edition: Kangaroos - Myths and Realities
Published 2005 by
The Australian Wildlife Protection Council Incorporated

Publication of this edition has been supported by a grant from
Voiceless, the fund for animals.

Co-Edited by:
Maryland Wilson, President of the
Australian Wildlife Protection Council,
David B Croft, School of Biological, Earth and
Environmental Sciences, University of New South Wales.

Designed by: Neil Williams
moocreative graphic design studio
www.moocreative.com.

Cover design - Brian Sadgrove - Sadgrove Design
Cover illustration - Peter Nicholson
AWPC logo - Brigitte Charron
NKPC logo - Deb Barnden

National Library of Australia
Cataloguing-in-publication entry
Kangaroos : myths and realities.

3rd ed.
Bibliography.
Includes index.
ISBN 0 9586178 1 3.

1. Kangaroos - Australia. 2. Wildlife conservation -
Australia. 3. Kangaroo hunting - Australia. I. Wilson,
Maryland. II. Croft, David, 1950- . III. Australian
Wildlife Protection Council.

333.959222

Distibuted in Australia by:
Envirobook, a division of Trekaway pty ltd.
38 Rose Street, Annandale.
Tel. 02 9518 6154

**Australian
Wildlife
Protection
Council**
A voice for wildlife

envirobook

247 Flinders Lane, Melbourne, Vic. 3000 Australia.
Tel. (03) 9650 8326 Fax. (03) 9650 3689
email: kangaroo@peninsula.hotkey.net.au
www.awpc.org.au   (Registered Charity A12224)

A 2005 year of the Kangaroo project for
the National Kangaroo Potection Coalition
www.national-kangaroo-coalition.org
(Co-ordinator - Pat O'Brien)

2005
The Year of the Kangaroo

This book is dedicated with grateful appreciation to our beloved matriarch Elsie Quinn for her devotion and passionate love for all animals, but especially her dedication, hard work and determination which has been an inspiration to us all.

and

In memory of the late Hans Fischinger whose devotion and love for all animals, especially Australia's kangaroos, endeared him to the World.

ACKNOWLEDGMENTS

With grateful thanks to Voiceless.

I want to thank my husband Doug for his unfailing love, and support. I thank him also for seeking the talent of his long time friend and colleague, Brian Sadgrove, arguably Australia's finest graphic artist, who designed the cover. Brian selected the multi-talented artist Neil Williams to then design the book.

Thank you to all our contributors for their courageous, moral and principled stand and their dedication to research and scientific integrity.

Special thanks to David B Croft my respected friend and Co-editor for his scientific expertise, commitment and guidance.

And finally my love and thanks to all those, too numerous to mention, who care as deeply and passionately about Australia's kangaroos as I.

CONTENTS

4.5 million kangaroo young-at-foot were left to a cruel death in the last decade. If you feel compelled to eat kangaroo meat or wear kangaroo hide or support the lethal control of kangaroos, then how many young-at-foot have to die from abandonment to satisfy you?

(Photo: Andrew Chapman - www.vicnet.net.au/~bigcheez)

INTRODUCTION

BY ONDINE SHERMAN

Director and Co-founder, Voiceless, the fund for animals.

Cows, sheep, pigs, chickens and turkeys are considered 'food products'. We therefore find it acceptable for them to be physically mutilated, kept in cages or confined for life and generally treated in a manner in which we would find abhorrent (and illegal) for our 'companion animals'. Introduced species such as foxes, rabbits and feral cats are considered to damage the country and are therefore hated and 'justifiably' shot and poisoned. Primates, who we know are remarkably intelligent, as well as dogs, rabbits and the humble mouse suffer greatly in the name of scientific experimentation despite many available alternatives. Polar bears are perfectly adapted to survive in the harsh conditions of the Arctic in temperatures of -45 degrees Celsius. What are they doing in the heat of an Australian summer? 'Educating our children', is the common answer to why it is acceptable for zoos to imprison wild animals in man-made constructions with only a fake tree or simulated ice berg as a reminder of where they belong.

Ask an average Australian why the Kangaroo is killed. The answer will be simply because they are a 'pest'. This term justifies the annual slaughter of millions of kangaroos and the suffering of hundreds of thousands of joeys taken from their dead mothers' pouches and shot or clubbed to death, and older, but still dependent joeys, often left to starve or die from hypothermia.

The power of the label, 'pest', is really quite remarkable.

Aussie kids curl up to stories of kangaroos at night while cuddling their soft toy kangaroos. They dress up as kangaroos for birthday parties and recite 'kangaroo facts' at school.

Kangaroos are part of our national identity, the Qantas emblem, our coat of arms, and our sporting life (e.g. North Melbourne Kangaroos, Socceroos, Qantas Wallabies etc). Kangaroos are also the subject of international curiosity and pride for anyone Australian who has travelled overseas.

This book brings together esteemed scientists and animal advocates, to argue that the kangaroo is not in fact a pest. If this is indeed the case, how then will we Australians continue to justify their slaughter? Perhaps we will simply transfer the kangaroo from the category of 'pest' to that of 'food'.

We might, however, recognise the beauty and complexity of these unique animals. We may acknowledge that they were, in fact, here millions of years before us and have adapted and evolved to our land which we sing 'abounds with natures' gifts of beauty rich and rare.' We could decide that there is in fact no justification for killing kangaroos, that kangaroos are actually a national treasure, something that tourists travel thousands of kilometres to see and that many adults and children find truly amazing.

FOREWORD:

THE ETHICS OF COMMERCIALISING WILDLIFE

By Professor Peter Singer

Patron - Australian Wildlife Protection Council

Professor Peter Singer
Ira W. DeCamp Professor of Bioethics,
University Centre for Human Values,
Princeton University
(Photo: Denise Applewhite/ Princeton University)

Two radical ideas have become significant, both politically and philosophically, animal liberation and biocentrism (concern for the environment). Both question the right of our species to assume that our interests must always prevail. For virtually all of the history of western civilisation, the right of human beings to trample over all the other species on this planet, and over nature itself, has been taken for granted.

When Europeans first came to Australia, they saw our continent's wild animals much as we now see its coal and iron ore; as a resource for the taking. So they shot kangaroos and koalas for their skins, meat or for sport, slaughtered seals for their fur, harpooned whales for blubber and oil, and even boiled down the penguins of Macquarie Island so that their oil could be used in cosmetics. (I am staggered that anyone could really think that the meager amount of oil obtainable from a penguin could justify seizing these birds and boiling them down).
The Australian animals that were not exploitable in this way were pests, and better eliminated.
So there was a bounty on the head of Tasmania's marsupial "tiger", the thylacine, and grazing kangaroos and wallabies had to make way for more useful animals imported from Europe, like sheep, cattle and even rabbits.

The Europeans who did this to Australia's animals brought with them attitudes to the natural environment that were a legacy of more than two thousand years of Western civilization.
These attitudes ruled with very little challenge until the 1970's; and it could be argued that they are still the predominant force in decisions about the environment.

According to the dominant Western tradition, the natural world exists for the benefit of human beings. God gave human beings dominion over the natural world and God does not care how we treat it. Human beings are the only morally important members of the world. Nature itself is of no intrinsic value, and the destruction of plants and animals cannot be sinful, unless by this destruction we harm human beings. Something is of intrinsic value if it is good or desirable in itself; the contrast is with "instrumental value", that is value as a means to some other end or purpose.

Now consider the issue of killing wild animals to profit from their meat, or skins. Should the decision be made on the basis of human interests alone? Those who exploit kangaroos, for example, seek to show that the "resource" is being " harvested" on a "sustainable" basis. Kangaroos then, only have value if they can provide commercial profit and the exploiters want to ensure that the kangaroos survive so that they can continue to be exploited.

Those who see kangaroos only as a resource, overlook the ethical aspects of how we are treating other sentient beings. Several hundred thousand kangaroos die inhumanely every year. There is also the suffering of joeys, who are orphaned when their mothers are shot and upon whom they depend for their survival.

In the light of this suffering, whatever views one may have about the rights and wrongs of eating other animals, it should not be too difficult to see that there are special reasons for not eating kangaroos or supporting the kangaroo trade in any other way.

Non-human animals are capable of feeling pain, as humans are; they can certainly be miserable, and members of many mammalian species can suffer from separation from their family group. Pain is pain, and the extent to which it is intrinsically bad depends on its duration and intensity, not on the species of the being that experiences it. The entire mindset that lies behind talk of "sustainable use" and "harvesting a resource" is derived from this Western tradition that makes animals merely of instrumental value. It is therefore fundamentally wrong.

To drive a species to extinction is a crime against the ecology of our planet, and against all who will come after us, inheriting a world that has lost something irreplaceable. The same is true of the death and suffering we inflict on individual animals. The fundamental problem is one of attitude: are this planet and all its non - human inhabitants to be regarded as the rightful possession of those humans who presently live on it?

At least since Darwin, we have known that the forests and animals were not placed on the earth for us to use. They have evolved alongside us. Once felled, the virgin forest can never be restored. The animals we kill for their skins or for pet food have similar nervous systems to our own, and can presumably feel pain, or enjoy life as we do.

When we remember that the attitude of the first European settlers to the Aboriginal inhabitants of our continent was little better than it was to the animals they so ruthlessly slaughtered, it is not surprising that many of us still do not question what we are doing to Australia's wildlife. One day Australians will look back on what we are doing to wildlife in horror, as we now look back at what the first Europeans to land in Australia did to the aboriginal people who were living here.

We need a Mabo decision for Australia's wild animals, a legal recognition of their special status as original residents of Australia, alongside its original inhabitants. The only ethical approach is one that gives their interests equal consideration alongside similar human interests.

PROLOGUE

By Maryland Wilson

President of the Australian Wildlife Protection Council Inc. and served from 1996 – 2003 on the NSW Kangaroo Management Advisory Committee.

The tragic news came in a phone call April 13, 1991, from a Herald Sun Reporter, that my valued friend and mentor of nine years was dead. Peter Rawlinson, La Trobe University zoologist, sage of our wildlife protection and welfare movement died aged 48, while on a scientific expedition in Krakatau. Would I give a statement please? Leith Young wrote in 'The Age' a few days later, that "this courageous campaigner had publicly condemned commercial kangaroo killing as scientifically indefensible, morally unjustifiable and commercial nonsense."

Following his death, it was full steam ahead for the kangaroo industry. Not one Australian scientist publicly condemned its rapid expansion or lauded the intrinsic value of kangaroos, as Rawlinson had done. He had travelled to the United States in **1983** with Richard Jones and Marjorie Wilson (OAM), where his testimony to the US Fish and Wildlife Service, in Washington, D.C. was crucial in stopping Australian Government moves to de-list kangaroos from the US Threatened Species List.

Predictably, after intense lobbying by Australian interests, on March 7, 1995, Patricia Fischer of the US Fish and Wildlife Service issued a News Release *that kangaroos were removed from the U.S. Threatened Species List and United States protection.* Few comprehended the disastrous ramifications that this action would have for kangaroos and the seriously detrimental effect Rawlinson's death would have on the fabric of kangaroo protection in Australia.

From 1995, government kangaroo *'management'* killing programs have been **without international scientific scrutiny.** With no obvious scientific opposition, a group of self-serving scientists, regulators and industry lobbyists combined to create an industry that artificially manipulates kangaroo populations to breed next years' crop.

Dr Stuart Cairns of the University of New England is quoted by Andrew Hoy in 'This farm offers a roo with a view' (1999) "All of Mulyungarie is easily accessible to a professional shooter. This means that the Mutoroo Pastoral Company is turning the roo into something resembling a domestic animal, culling any surplus males and topping up each night with a few does. Essentially, they are lifting the food resource base for new recruits - animals just leaving the pouch and young at foot. It is certainly a sustainable harvest". This 'kangaroo farm' scenario ignores the importance of natural selection, embraces gross cruelty, is cavalier about sustainability, and dictates an uncertain future for kangaroos, a group of a species in crisis.

Female red kangaroo with young at the stage of making excursions from the pouch. As a commercial product, the mother would be shot, gutted and decapitated and the young bludgeoned to death and discarded. (Photo: Neil McLeod)

The myth that kangaroos can be farmed was " debunked" by the Australian Conservation Foundation in the 1991 publication 'Recovering Ground' where it is pointed out that 'the amount of meat obtained from a kangaroo could only amount to 0.5% of Australia's present meat production. Only about 10% of the kangaroo carcase is fit for human consumption. As many as 50% of kangaroos shot for human consumption are rejected in the field as they were not head shot or because the meat was possibly contaminated for other reasons such as the carcase being dropped, becoming soiled, the gut contents being spilled or the carcase not getting to the chillier.'

Professor Michael Archer, who commands considerable media attention, preaches that "farmers can get filthy stinking rich" killing kangaroos. The net economic benefit of allowing farmers this privilege would appear to be negligible.

Narrow media ownership has played a significant role in ensuring that most Australians are kept unaware of the true nature of the slaughter. An unchallenged coalition of scientists have been allowed to turn a protected species into a 'renewable resource', which they say, "if managed in an ecologically sustainable manner, can provide a perpetual source of economic benefits for all Australians."

Senator George Georges, Chairman of the Senate Inquiry into Animal Welfare 1983-1987, said in his minority report:

"The industry was established as a clever means of kangaroo management for the benefit of farmers, but took on a life of its own with its own monstrous agenda, and sought increased quotas to supply market demands. Add to this the illegal killing of kangaroos, and Australians must accept that they are responsible for the greatest killing of wildlife on earth.

The nature and method of slaughter cannot be ignored; it is barbaric and inhumane.
Each night thousands of animals are butchered, many are maimed, the young in pouch are cruelly dispatched and the young at foot are left to fend for themselves. Any reasonable person would not wish to be a party to this slaughter by purchasing kangaroo products."

Prof Gordon Grigg from the University of Queensland says kangaroos are undervalued as a 'harvestable resource' and killing them for profit is the panacea to farmers' woes and ills. Grigg, with former student Dr Tony Pople, also from the University of Queensland wrote the "Commercial Harvesting of Kangaroos in Australia" in 1992 which is the foundation of Environment Australia's policy. It was revised in 1995 and again in 1999. Together Grigg and Pople shape scientific policy towards management of kangaroos in Australia with the following premise:

"To harvest a sustained yield from a population at steady density, it first must be manipulated in some way to promote the rate of increase. Rates of harvest may be raised to levels at which they can cause the extinction of the population.

Arguments will be confounded when there are non-consumptive values attached to the resource such as for tourism."

Scientists saw it was in their interests to support and promote the kangaroo industry to gain consultancies and funding from the government.

The scientists advising the various Commonwealth Environment Ministers on wildlife use over this period may be expert in their field, but they are biased in favour of the commercial harvesting of kangaroos. Furthermore, their expertise is not necessarily in terrestrial and population ecology as Griggs' outstanding reputation is built in animal physiology and the fundamental understanding of thermoregulation in vertebrates. In 1999, three of the scientists advising on terrestrial vertebrates were from the same Queensland Institution (University of Queensland) and two of these, Grigg and Pople were from the same Department and held the same views. All support commercial killing of kangaroos.

There is no voice for the welfare of kangaroos, no voice for Tourism and related non-consumptive use, no voice to say that kangaroos have intrinsic value and no voice to speak against the largest and fittest males being singled out by the commercial industry, leaving kangaroo populations a teetering pyramid. This disregard for important stakeholders like the $6 billion nature-based tourism industry, and breaches of ecological and scientific oversight, are indeed very serious.

With the severity and duration of the 2002-3, (continuing into 2005) drought across the Australian rangelands, dire concerns emerged about the continued onslaught of the kangaroo industry on the remnant population and the ability of regulators to manage this. And on November 16, 2003 Dr. Judy Messer of the NSW Nature Conservation Council wrote to Nicole Payne, NSW NPWS Kangaroo Program Manager as follows:

"We believe that it is critical that the commercial quota for red kangaroos be assessed only on populations within the commercial zones.
The assessment should exclude populations that exist within National Parks. Currently the red population count for NSW includes red kangaroos existing within national parks that are not available for commercial shooting. The final count to establish the quota should exclude those reds in Protected Areas, otherwise 'objective science' cannot be argued when monitoring the relationship between red kangaroo populations and the commercial harvesting quotas."

Posters from one of the many campaigns against the commercial killing of kangaroos.
(Photo: Marjorie Wilson OAM)

"The current assessment practice generates the assertion that a larger population exists than is the reality in terms of reds commercially available to industry. This gives rise to inaccurate percentage figures and Maximum Sustainable Yield (MSY) calculations as they are based on inappropriate Total Population figures."

"Kangaroo populations suffer dramatically during drought. Australians have been convinced (since childhood) that the species is indestructible and in fact, continues to reproduce, even during drought. This is a fallacy. Though red kangaroos can breed continually in good seasons, females cease to breed and pouch-young die in drought." (Newsome1965). Contrary to media reports, kangaroos do not keep reproducing and suffer greatly due to poor body condition and associated stresses.

Only 25 of the past 100 years have been drought free. To their shame, State and Commonwealth Australian wildlife authorities sanction the killing of drought survivors, the biggest and best kangaroos left standing, those essential for the genetic strength, and biological fitness of remaining populations, those very kangaroos that are absolutely critical, to sustaining the species.

Ecologist Bryan Walters, Ecoplan Australia wrote in 'The Kangaroo Betrayed': *"What a bonanza. What a harvest. What a marketplace. We are harvesting our future. We are doing it with such momentum and conviction that we have swept aside the knowledge and wisdom that exists to show us how it might be done, for us all. For the animals. For the plants. For ourselves to find the harmony in an all-sustaining planet."*

Such sentiments are ignored by regulators who allow the kangaroo industry to roll on through natural disasters like severe drought that have been intensified by Government failures to control natural resource disasters like unsustainable pastoralism, land clearing and degradation, and greenhouse effects on climate. We are supposed to trust their 'wise' policies on kangaroo management.

From time immemorial, in this ancient land of the kangaroo, alpha males have fought for the right to mate while younger males practiced, waiting to challenge. Only the strongest, the best, survived the challengers, droughts, disease, bushfires, and flood. Females selectively chose these dominant males to pass on the best genes, the inherited genetic strengths of the mob. They nurtured and educated their young, according to the laws of nature. Then everything went terribly wrong! Kangaroos went from being a 'protected species' to a commodity - a 'renewable resource' to be killed for profit!

Shooters destroyed the rich, complex, hierarchical society of kangaroos for the commercial 'harvest'. They killed the alpha males, immediate rivals and mature females, the educators of the mob. With the dominant males killed, females mated with younger males. 'The real danger in this has been a drastic change in the social and biological make-up of these wild populations.' Doug Reilly warned, 'Precedents have been set in other parts of the world where large populations of a species (bison, wolves etc) have faced extinction after widespread and destructive 'culling' programs. In any wild animal, if you disrupt in a short period of time the normal reproduction processes that have evolved over tens of thousands of years, you are in danger of putting the species at risk. Other species have suffered incursions of exotic bacterias and viruses when their populations contained a critical and unsustainable gene pool'.

Of all Australian wildlife, it is the maligned and misunderstood kangaroo which evokes the greatest emotion. A long and sustained program of misinformation within Australia has convinced an apathetic and ill-informed community that kangaroos are in plague proportions throughout the country. Wildlife authorities issue permits to kill kangaroos within Australia's wall-to-wall agriculture zones, at times fast-tracking them to assist supposedly overwhelmed farmers and graziers.

Kangaroo habitat in the inland has been severely eroded and on the coasts, kangaroos are trapped in fragmented areas of suburban sprawl. Everywhere, kangaroos are at the mercy of land holders, agri-businesses, politicians, government wildlife bureaucrats and shooters. Kangaroos are a stress-prone, free ranging species that needs space afforded by continuous, connecting safe wildlife refuge areas, free from the nightly attacks on their mobs. The Australian Government not only subsidises the killing, but actively promotes kangaroo meat and hide products.

The various state and federal wildlife authorities apparently conserve kangaroos in the rangelands through the acquisition of flogged out and discarded pastoral properties, so degraded that the owners and managers were at the point of walking off. They then suffer relentless criticism from agri-business lobbies for harbouring kangaroos within these supposed havens. How do they respond? Not with programs of habitat and community restoration leading to the re-introduction of lost species and support for the remnants left after pastoral mismanagement but rather by investment in the exemplars, like old wool sheds, of the very industry that caused a swathe of extinctions and natural disasters across the continent.

Species loss is not just a thing of the past. Most Australians concerned about endangered species think that lost, extinct species are a result of past lack of concern, that numbers are a sure guarantee against extinction but the reality is that most of this country's modern extinctions have occurred within the last 50 years. **With the aid of modern technology, our expanding population is hastening the rate of extinction.** Today, we have pesticides, insecticides, fungicides, aerial spraying of 1080 poison or 1080 poison baits, chainsaws, bulldozers, land clearing, introduced plants and animals, exotic diseases which add to the effect of the traditional axe, plough and gun, to ensure the demise of species. Australia has been responsible for the extinction of more mammal species within the 200 years of European occupation than any other continent on Earth.

Australians support the largest and most cruel slaughter of wildlife on earth, yet we condemn other nations that exploit wildlife.

We write letters to the Canadian Government to stop the seal hunt and bitterly complain to the Norwegians and Japanese for killing whales. We cannot see our own hypocrisy when we cruelly slaughter kangaroos and brutally bash their joeys to death, with no policing or monitoring at the point of kill. Our record for wildlife conservation is woeful, so what gives us the right to condemn others, until we get our own house in order!

The bridled nail-tail wallaby was once widespread across the inland of eastern Australia. It is now one of the most endangered kangaroo family.
(Photo: David B Croft)

Through this book we hope that 2005 will herald a new era of change. We hope for wisdom, and an acknowledgement of the recent advances in our scientific knowledge of kangaroos, securing their health, well-being and the next generation of joeys. 2005 and beyond is a time for wildlife to live their lives wild and free, unmolested and protected in safe habitat across Australia's 'Dead Heart'. It is a time long overdue.

It is time to maximize the limitless potential of wildlife tourism and to embrace the non-consumptive use of our betrayed, maligned and misunderstood kangaroos. Let us finally rid ourselves of 19th and 20th Century views about wildlife as simply a novel source of meat, fur and feathers, and comic entertainment.

The red kangaroo is symbolic of Outback Australia and its presence authenticates the tourism experience there. (Reproduction of a painting by Rosemary Woodford Ganf)

KANGAROOS MALIGNED

- 16 MILLION YEARS OF EVOLUTION AND TWO CENTURIES OF PERSECUTION

By David B Croft

BSc. Hons. (Flinders), PhD (Cambridge).
Fowlers Gap Research Station School of Biological, Earth and Environmental Sciences,
UNSW Sydney.

Kangaroos bound onto the Australian landscape

The likely ancestor of the great Super Family of kangaroos and their kind, the Macropodoidae, was an arboreal possum. Angela Burk and Mark Springer (2000) used a molecular clock based on a phylogenetic analysis of the mitochondrial and nuclear DNA of living Macropodoids to date this ancestor to around 38-44 million years ago. There is always some uncertainty about the relationships amongst fossil and living taxa but Tim Flannery (1989) identified eight sub-families in the Macropodoidae. The relationships between these have most been recently described by Bernard Cooke and Ben Kear (1999) to provide the simplified kangaroo family tree of seven sub-families (Fig. 1). Lack of skeletal material creates uncertainty as to the position of the extinct Balbarines and the Propeopines.

In general, the branches represent the basic grades of forage in the diet - mixed invertebrate and non-fibrous plants (omnivore), low fibre leaf (browser) and high fibre grass (grazer) – and the dentition to match.

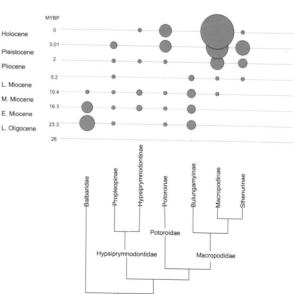

Fig. 1. The evolutionary history and relationships amongst families and sub-families of the Macropodoidea – the kangaroos and their kin.

Musky rat-kangaroo (*Hypsiprymnodon moschatus*)

Of the living sub-families, the hypsiprymondontine Musky rat kangaroo of the Queensland rainforest is omnivorous and bounds rather than hops. Thus this species is perhaps reminiscent of what the ancestor of the kangaroos looked like. The Potoroines and the Macropodines are the hoppers and they also have complex foreguts that have allowed them to ferment plant material. The latter adaptation has enabled the largest species to forage on high fibre grasses like their ruminant mammal counterparts elsewhere.

Two interesting macropodoid noses: Long-nosed potoroo *(Potorous tridactylus)* a potoroine on the left, Antilopine wallaroo *(Macropus antilopinus)* a macropodine on the right.

The diversity of species in the fossil taxa are clearly underestimated because most will not be found, but in relative terms we are in the era of the Macropodines with the Potoroines in a holding pattern and the Sthenurines in steep decline. The latter are represented by the diminutive 1-2 kg banded hare-wallaby *(Lagostrophus fasciatus)* now marooned on some off-shore islands in Western Australia. This is an insignificant remnant of the 3-m tall Sthenurines or broad-faced kangaroos of the Pleistocene when they and other megafauna roamed the Australian continent. Tim Flannery (1994) has argued that their demise is evidence of the first of many conflicts between people and wildlife on the continent. Aboriginal hunters engaged in an unsustainable over-kill of the megafauna reducing them to extinction in what Flannery called a 'blitzkrieg'. Others see evidence of co-existence of people and the megafauna with the latter's demise the result of climate change – Mary White's (1994) 'browning of Australia'. Most recently Mike Archer and Bob Beale (2005) argue against blitzkrieg but accept the possibility of a synergy between climate change and human hunting in the extinction process. Australia was a tough place as the Pleistocene drew to a close. The climate was more arid and the tropics colder at the last glacial maximum of 18,000 years ago than previously and these effects persisted for several thousands of years. Peter Kershaw and his colleagues (2003) describe a long-term trend towards a drier and more variable environment, as those experiencing the droughts from 2002 will attest. People had a secondary role in creating this environment but now rapid greenhouse warming is only likely to exacerbate environmental challenges for people and wildlife alike.

Most of the modern kangaroo fauna have their origins a million or more years ago. But through the climatic challenges of the Pleistocene, the Macropodines, which include the large kangaroos and wallaroos, emerged to clearly dominate the modern fauna with 61 species in Australia and New Guinea. In comparison, the Potoroines number 9 species (or ten if the recently re-discovered Gilbert's potoroo is elevated to specific status), the Sthenurines one and the Hypsiprymnodontines one. They co-existed with aboriginal peoples over many millennia and apparently survived the introduction of the dog a few thousand years ago. Then they all met another challenge – European colonisers, their land management practices and their livestock, especially sheep.

In recent times the relationship between people and the kangaroos has been one of conflict, persecution, ignorance and indifference founded on myths about the numbers and distribution of a few large and conspicuous species. Few celebrate the outstanding diversity of this guild of browsers and grazers which far outnumbers that of the antelope of southern Africa (a mere 34 species). This is truly a magnificent wildlife heritage for Australians to conserve through careful stewardship. We and the rest of the world's peoples can take an unparalleled journey of discovery across the vast Australian continent and its offshore islands to see supreme athletes such as one of the four species of plains dwelling kangaroos, rock climbers who seem to defy gravity such as one of the fifteen species of rock-wallaby, and one of the best noses for truffles in the world, the long-nosed potoroo.

Sadly we squabble over how many blades of grass a red or grey kangaroo apparently steals from the mouth of a sheep or cow. We execute management plans for (or against) the few large conspicuous species with grand sustainability visions and tasty meals that really are about population suppression. The agents and benefactors of these plans are best served by keeping the populace ignorant about the rest of the kangaroo mob lest their eradication from much of the agricultural and pastoral lands too becomes a problem and clarion for change. Let's take a brief journey to see how it has come down to this.

PEOPLE MEET KANGAROOS: CHANGING PERCEPTIONS

The term 'kangaroo' is used with varying degrees of precision. Strictly it is applied to the six largest species of the Macropodinae – the red, eastern and western grey kangaroos and the common, antilopine and black wallaroos. More generally it refers to those marsupials, the Macropodoidea, with a common body plan of large muscular hindlimbs and large feet, shorter forelimbs, and a long, thick muscular tail, who progress with a saltatorial (hopping) gait, and whose females bear their young in an anteriorly-opening and all-enclosing pouch for most the young's pouch-life.

Young male red kangaroo (Macropus rufus) hopping along a fence line showing basic body plan of kangaroos.

Given that 19 species of tree-kangaroos and wallabies are found in New Guinea, people undoubtedly first met kangaroos there. Kangaroos were first encountered in Australia when these Aboriginal peoples migrated across to this continent. Much later, European explorers on voyages of discovery and commerce to the Antipodes encountered them. Naturalists accompanying these voyages and the early European colonists avidly depicted and collected these odd-looking mammals and revealed them to the European (Old) world. The curious nature of their body form, gait and reproduction engendered much debate among eighteenth and nineteenth-century scientists about their affinities. With the development and expansion of pastoral and agricultural enterprises in Australia after colonisation, what had been an early source of game and food became a pest and a period of their destruction commenced. Many species were successfully extirpated from urban, agricultural and pastoral lands through direct destruction often aided by bounties or indifference to loss of habitat compounded by the introduction and lack of control of exotic competitors and predators. A history of the concerted effort to kill off the large kangaroos was provided by Bill Horndage in 1972. Some graziers in the western division of NSW publicly rue the failure 'to finish the job' with bullets and poison in the 1960s drought. Contemporary attitudes are founded on myths, models and management plans. From the veil of the bulldust, sustainable nature-based tourism may now be the brand that reveals a more benign and supportive attitude towards kangaroos.

TOTEMS AND TUCKER TO ABORIGINAL PEOPLES

The Aboriginal peoples colonised Australia 50,000 years ago or earlier. At this time, they would have been contemporary with the largest kangaroos known, the Sthenurinae, as supported by fossil evidence discussed by Gorecki and his colleagues (1984). Members of this now extinct Pleistocene fauna are probably represented in the Aboriginal art of Arnhem land studied by Murray and Chaloupka (1984). To the extent that Aboriginal hunting and habitat alteration played in the contentious causes of the demise of this fauna, the first relationship between people and kangaroos was certainly negative from the kangaroos' perspective.

The Aboriginal diet includes a wide diversity of animal and plant matter, but kangaroos have probably always been an important and valued source of meat. The reward of many kilos of meat for the hunting effort certainly makes the large species worth it. Altman (1984) found that the Gunwinggu of western Arnhem Land consume some 90 species of animals and 80 species of plants. Mammals provide up to 84% of energy intake in the mid-wet season and 91% in the late dry. Of the mammals consumed, seven of the fourteen species are kangaroos. Kangaroos also provided the Aborigines with other valued resources in addition to meat. O' Connell (1980) describes the manufacture of kangaroo-skin water bags in central Australia. Meagher and Ride (1978) list the use of skins for cloaks and water bags, bones for personal decoration and awls, sinews of the tail for sewing and binding, and teeth for making scrapers.

Anthropologists frequently cite the Aboriginals' acute knowledge of the behaviour and ecology of the species they used. This is not supreme wisdom but a necessity for a successful hunt. Louis Liebenberg (2001) has in fact argued that the origin of the scientific method may reside in the principles of tracking followed in our hunter-gather past. From his observations mainly of San people in the Kalahari, he determined that trackers classify and interpret their target's spoor and formulate speculative hypotheses that they test through further observation. Thus they pursue a scientific method and Aboriginal peoples, known for their exceptional tracking abilities, no doubt do the same. Aboriginals also differentiated species and sexes and size classes of prey much as a behavioural ecologist would classify the population. For example, in the Gunwinggu language we find *Kandakeet* (male) and *Kandite* (female) for the antilopine wallaroo and *Kalperrt* (male) and *Wblerrk* (female) for the closely related common wallaroo (Altman 1984).

Solitary and communal hunting techniques were employed against kangaroos and included ambush, traps, simple stockades, leafy screens to hide solitary hunters, beaters and fires to assist communal hunts. The killing of the animal was effected by spearing or clubbing but Michael Terry (1974) records the Warramullas maiming individuals when food was plentiful, for preservation until they were consumed. David Bennett (1991) discusses the notion of animal rights and cruelty in Aboriginal concepts. He makes several pertinent observations. Firstly, the Aboriginal peoples were many groups with as many different viewpoints, thus he cautions that there is no single Aboriginal formulation of rights. Secondly, Aborigines had an intimate and materialistic relationship with the natural world. They did not farm or herd and drew directly upon nature for their necessities. Rites had a material endpoint - securing an adequate supply of species like kangaroos to eat. They may have kinship with other species but this did not preclude eating them for their own survival. For example, William Beatty and Marian de Lacey Lowe (1980) record that breaking the legs of kangaroos so that they would keep was common practice in north-western Australia even though the people shared a 'bond' with the kangaroos.

There is some debate as to the degree to which Aboriginals managed their prey populations as needs and opportunities no doubt varied across the continent. For the Tiwi of northern Australia, Stevenson (1985) proposes that resource management was de facto rather than explicitly intellectualized. In effect, actions maximized resource reliability and range productivity.

The resources utilised were extremely broad but preferences for some were exercised and so the optimal strategy was to maintain a mosaic of habitats in the ecosystem. The role fire plays in such 'management strategies' is also arguable and the concept of 'fire-stick farming' may be oversimplified. However, there is general agreement that firing of certain habitats had beneficial effects on kangaroo prey populations and these benefits were perceived by the Aborigines.

For example, Gould (1971) describes the firing of spinifex in Western Australia prior to expected rain and the return to such areas when green shoots attracted kangaroos. Likewise cattle graziers in northern Australia fire rank dried-off grasses to stimulate new growth for enhanced productivity of their livestock. In southern Australia, Aborigines maintained open forests and grasslands through repeated and deliberate firing to stimulate green pick for kangaroos (Hallam 1975). Fire was also used to drive small wallabies from cover into ambush by hunters (Finlayson, 1945). Thus Tim Flannery (1994) concludes that these 'Sons of Prometheus' used fire to increase the productivity of medium-sized mammals (like modern kangaroos) favoured for hunting but in the process disadvantaged the larger and now lost megafauna.

Generalised kangaroo in petroglyph (rock carving) on Mutawintji National Park.

Kangaroos are important in the art and mythology of Aborigines. Eric Brandl (1980) identified the fauna in Arnhem Land rock art. He notes that kangaroos were a special animal to the Aborigines and that they were very familiar with them through the hunting, butchering, cooking, and eating of many species. Of the fauna in the Mimi art style of Kakadu, kangaroos and fish are most frequently portrayed (Brandl, 1982). Likewise, kangaroos are the major mammalian component of the Laura art site in North Queensland (Rosenfield, 1982). The significance of this art is not fully understood but several reasons for the prolific art of the Kakadu region have been proposed by Edwards (1979). Some paintings helped illustrate stories, some depicted evil spirits and warned of danger, some involved sorcery or magic, and others simply recorded events. The depiction of kangaroos probably related most often to the latter two reasons: the belief that by drawing a kangaroo it came under the will of the hunter and thus could be speared more easily, and the illustration of a successful hunt.

Charles Mountford (1976) relates myths about the hunting of kangaroos from the Pitjandjara of central Australia. At the Muluindina site, Aborigines invoke hot winds through ceremony in the belief that kangaroos under these conditions are more easily hunted. At a site in the Tomkinson Ranges, Pitjandjara performed a kangaroo increase ceremony that involved blood-letting from the veins of the arms and deposition of the blood on a group of rocks which represent the transformed bodies of a mythical group of kangaroos. Through this ceremony the life-essence or *kuranita* of the kangaroos was released from the stones, impregnated the females, and thus increased the prey population. Stories about the red kangaroo, *Malu*, the euro, *Kunjula*, and their companion, the fairy-owl (spotted nightjar), *Tjulki*, are a central part of the philosophical and ceremonial life of these Aborigines. Alan Newsome (1980) has examined the relationship between the Aranda mythology of the red kangaroo and this species' ecology.

He found a close correspondence between the movement patterns of the mythical kangaroos (Ara) and the behaviour of the actual animal including discontinuities in their range.

He concluded that "the coincidence of myth and reality indicates an underlying ecological base to the mythology" (p. 333). Thus an important aspect of such mythology may be the teaching of adaptive strategies in the exploitation of prey, such as the red kangaroo.

This should not be confused with a conservation ethic. John Morton (1991) examines totemism in both aboriginal and non-aboriginal societies in Australia. The central Australian Aranda totemic system where a man may be of the kangaroo group generally precludes him killing or eating his totem, the kangaroo. This has been equated to a conservation strategy that prevents over-exploitation of a species but the rule is not absolute. The totem may be killed and the hunter will express remorse and might eat the least desirable cuts of meat. The system is more akin to modern agriculture with an explicit business-like quality about increase rites relating to prey.

The difference is that farmers are less likely to be sorry about producing domestic animals to be killed and eaten in our industrialised systems. However, it is not so long ago that Europeans shared their habitations with their livestock, enduring the cold winters together.

Thus where a degree of intimacy between livestock and the producer is retained, we should not so quickly dismiss a farmer's respect for the animals that form his or her livelihood or the affection that might be displayed towards an especially tractable and productive animal.

Jared Diamond (1997) discusses the development and nature of the bond between many peoples of the world and the very few species that became livestock, and the key role this bond has played in the last 13,000 years of history.

CURIOUS KANGAROOS AND THE EUROPEAN EXPLORERS

In1606, the Spaniard Diego de Prado y Tovar describes an animal shaped like a dog, smaller than a greyhound, with a bare and scaly tail and testicles hanging from a nerve like a thin cord. The animal, a wallaby, was killed somewhere on a landfall in the Torres Strait and was promptly eaten. Later Francisco Pelsaert made landfall on the Abrolhos Islands in Western Australia in 1629. Here he encountered the tammar wallaby *(Macropus eugenii)* and described them as a very strange species of "cat" drawing analogies from civet-cats, hares, monkeys, and squirrels in his description (Whitley, 1970). Unfortunately, Pelsaert was to inaugurate the falsehood that the kangaroo young formed and developed out of the nipple.

Tammar wallaby *(Macropus eugenii)*: one of the first kangaroos to be described by Europeans. The species has become extinct on mainland Australia but re-introductions from off-shore islands are in progress in Western Australia and South Australia.

Another Dutch seaman, Samuel Volckertsen described the quokka *(Setonix brachyurus)* in 1658 as a variety of cat resembling the civet-cat. Better remembered is Willem de Vlamingh who visited and named Rottnest Island in 1696 where the quokka remains abundant today. He described them as a "kind of rat as big as a common cat." Cornelius de Bruijn published the first picture of a kangaroo, the New Guinea pademelon *Thylogale brunii*, in his Travels into Muscovie published in 1698. William Dampier in the 1703 edition of 'A Voyage to New Holland' describes two further species sighted in 1699. The banded hare-wallaby *(Lagostrophus fasciatus)* on Dirk Hartog Island is "a sort of Racoon different from those of the West-Indies chiefly as to their legs; for these have very short Fore-Legs, but go jumping upon them as others do (and like them are very good Meat)." In Dampierland he sighted the burrowing bettong *(Bettongia leseur)*, likening it again to a raccoon.

James Cook's voyage in the Endeavour in 1770 (Hawkesworth, 1773) brought 'kangaroo' into the English lexicon. At the Endeavour River on June 22, 1770, Joseph Banks saw "an animal as large as a greyhound, of a mouse colour and very swift". Cilento (1971) argues that what was to become the English word 'kangaroo' entered the vocabulary from the aboriginal term 'gangaru' at this time. Muller used a plate of this painting from Hawkesworth's account of Cook's voyages to describe the species and name it *Mus cangaru* (i.e. a type of mouse). Zimmerman from the same material proposed the name *Yerboa giganteus* and Erxleben, the name *Jaculus giganteus* in 1777 inferring a giant hopping mouse. Shaw in 1789 provided the now accepted generic name of *Macropus*.

Thus the taxonomic affinities of kangaroos were confused for some time but by the mid-nineteenth century, a further 35 species from Australia and New Guinea had been described. This dramatic increase in the knowledge of kangaroos was the result of further expeditions of discovery by the French and English, the establishment of the penal colony in New South Wales and subsequent colonisation of other states, the exploration of the interior of Australia, and the work of naturalists and collectors visiting the colonies.

During much of this period, kangaroos were of considerable scientific curiosity. Joseph Banks remarked: "To compare it to any European animal would be impossible as it has not the least resemblance of anyone I have seen" (Beaglehole, 1962, p. 94). Watkin Tench (1789) provides some biological notes on the eastern grey kangaroo *(Macropus giganteus)*, assigning it to a species of opossum, but accurately describing aspects of its morphology, reproduction, and locomotion. A notable observation was that "the testicles of the male are placed contrary to the order of nature." De la Billiardière in 1790, in referring to a kangaroo, noted: "His stomach was full of vegetables and divided by three very distinct partitions, which seem to approach him to the class of ruminant quadrupeds" (1800, p. 101). Dr. John Hunter described the mammals in an appendix to John White's Journal of a Voyage to New South Wales (1790). Hunter is also puzzled by the kangaroo, especially the teeth, which he classes as an amalgam of the dentition of rodents, the horse, hog, and other ruminants. He is intrigued by the kangaroo's morphology: "The proportions of some of the parts of this animal bear no analogy to what is common in most others." The first live kangaroo - "The wonderful Kanguroo, from Botany Bay" - was exhibited in London about 1790 (Hornadge, 1972).

Two male red kangaroos sparring: The left individual shows how the scrotum lies above the genital opening, the cloaca. This is the 'contrary to the order of nature' that Watkin Tench refers to (Photo: Ulrike Kloecker)

KILLING KANGAROOS FOR FOOD, FUN, AND PROFIT:

COLONISATION AND THE EXPANSION OF PASTORALISM:

The novelty of kangaroos quickly waned as colonists turned their interest to the more mundane but pressing need of acquiring food. Thus surgeon Arthur Bowes Smyth commented in 1788: "There are great Nos. of Kangaroos but so extremely shy that 'tis no easy matter to get near enough to them even to shoot them. . . . As there is a most exact print of this uncommon Animal in Capt. Cook's Acct. of this Country I shall not take the trouble to describe it" (Smyth, 1979, p. 58). On the culinary value of kangaroos, Watkin Tench writing in 1778 remarks: "Of the flesh we always eat with avidity; but in Europe it would not be reckoned a delicacy: a rank flavour forms the principal objection to it. . . . The tail is accounted the most delicious part, when stewed" (Tench, 1961, p. 268). More than two centuries later, kangaroo meat likewise rates very poorly against beef (and ostrich) for taste, texture and storage in a German study by Watkinson and colleagues (2004). Even so some found favour with the meat, Cunningham writing in 1827:

> Our largest animals are the kangaroos, all of which are fine eating, being clear of fat except about the tail, tasting much like venison, and making the most delicious stews and steaks, the favourite dish being what is called a steamer, composed of steaks and chopped tail, (with a few slices of salt pork), stewed with a very small quantity of water for a couple of hours in a close vessel. (p. 309)

When the colony became established and more reliant on domestic stock, kangaroos were hunted more for recreational than culinary reasons. A special breed of "kangaroo dog" was selected from the greyhound and a more powerful breed such as the mastiff. Of the sport, Oxley (1820) enthuses: "I think that most fastidious sportsmen would have derived ample amusement during our day's journey. He might have seen the truest coursing .from the commencement of the chase to the death of his game without moving, and tiring of killing kangaroos he might have hunted emus with equal success." The sport was given Royal favour when members of British royalty such as the Duke of Edinburgh in 1867 and the Princes Edward and George in 1881 joined kangaroo hunts while touring Australia.

Hunting likely had a lesser impact on kangaroo populations than the killing that followed the identification of kangaroo species as pests to the pastoral industry. As squatters followed in the tracks of explorers and established pastoral enterprises grazing sheep and cattle, the conflict began. In 1889, Neville-Rolfe writes:

> A plain, stripped of all grass by the invading hordes, brown, too, with the figures of four or five hundred of the enemy, who, on first appearance of a human being, dispersed in all directions, and with rapid bounds passed away into mere specks on the rolling downs. The poor starved sheep, wondering where all the grass had gone, and why it did not come after the rain as of yore, were unable to copy the hardier kangaroo, who, if he never grows fat, can live on country where the domesticated animal must die.
> (Morris, 1978, p. 312).

By the 1880s, all eastern Australian states had enacted legislation that encouraged eradication of kangaroos. Kangaroos and wallabies were declared vermin in NSW in 1880. Neville-Rolfe (Morris,

1978, p. 312) states that "a price varying from one shilling to threepence was put on the head of each grass-eating marsupial, of which the Government pays one half and the district in which the marsupial is killed the other half." The targets were certainly not just the large kangaroos that are shot under current management plans. Jeff Short (1998) documents around 3 million bettongs and potoroos (Potoroines) were shot for bounties in NSW between 1883-1920. Three of the five species are now extinct in NSW although Short postulates that the introduction of the red fox not over-hunting caused the coup de grace. The brush-tailed rock-wallaby fared even worse because of its attractive pelage in the skin trade. Jeff Short and George Milkovits (1990) analysed the historical distribution of the brush-tailed rock-wallaby and found that between 1884 and 1914, the Pasture Protection Boards in NSW paid at least 640,000 bounties for this species. In the 1890s they record 66,152 presented as bounties but the killing of this species was much greater. Dan Lunney and colleagues (1997) analysed the fur trade in Sydney for the same decade and found a further 144,000 skins in this trade. The brush-tailed rock-wallaby is now absent from most of its former range in NSW, listed as vulnerable and subject to an expensive recovery plan.

One of the last of two female brush-tailed rock-wallaby *(Petrogale penicillata)* in a colony near Goulburn NSW. Two males were introduced from a captive colony at Tidbinbilla and one survived to breed with the females. The location of the site is not made public due to the strong likelihood that a hunter would shoot the wallabies for the novelty of the kill.

Thus in the space of a century, the perception of kangaroos had moved from one of scientific curiosity, to utilitarian value as game, to enjoyment as sport, to vilification as a pest. Commercial exploitation through markets and bounties was added in the 1840s. Skins were available at auction in Sydney from this period and meat could obtain up to a shilling a pound at market. In Tibooburra, John Gerritson (1981) summarises records that show skins fetched from one shilling and threepence to one shilling and sixpence per pound in 1898. The peak price for a brush-tailed rock-wallaby skin was 52 pence in 1913 (Lunney et al. 1997) and demand apparently outstripped supply. The trade continued through to 1927. Skins of the large kangaroos were exported in large quantities to the United States where they were regarded as making a fine leather, especially for footwear (Wilson and Daub 1926). The remaining commercial return on kangaroos was the paying of bounties for scalps by governments and landholders.

CONTROVERSIAL KANGAROOS: CONSERVATION AND CONTROL

In the twentieth century, scientific interest in the Macopodoids burgeoned. Zoologists like Troughton and Le Soeuf (1928) sought to inform and stimulate interest in the native fauna through scientific and popular articles. Troughton in particular was ardent in dispelling misconceptions about kangaroo biology, especially the nature of birth (Troughton, 1942). As the academic community in Australia matured, biologists started to focus their research on the native fauna. Professor H. Waring at the University of Western Australia was particularly influential in the 1940s and 1950s (Waring, 1956). The body of research produced by his successors was reviewed in a landmark conference in 1988 with proceedings edited by Gordon Grigg, Ian Hume and Peter Jarman (1989). By the time that this accounting of scientific knowledge was made, John Calaby and Gordon Grigg (1989) report that of the 50 species reviewed, 60% (30) had substantial declines in range and/or abundance, while 28% (14) remained stable or had increased in the prior 200 years. Six species had declined to extinction and ten (20%) were extinct on mainland Australia. Most species could not sustain the anthropogenic changes, hunting and pest management introduced by European colonisation. A concern for conservation and management were added to the perception of kangaroos as agricultural pests. Even the large kangaroos which we regard today as common were under threat. For example, Saville-Kent states:

Being essentially vegetarian in their habits, the larger species of the kangaroo family, where abundant, so seriously tax the resources of the Australian pasture lands as to necessitate the adoption of stringent measures to keep them in check. This untoward necessity, combined with the high value set upon kangaroo skins, has contributed towards the complete extirpation of the `Boomer' throughout a large extent of the prairie-like tracts of Australian pastoral land on which it abounded previous to the advent of the settler. (1897, p. 21)

Killing as vermin continued including poisoning campaigns like that executed against euros in north-western Australia as reported by Ealey (1967). Added to this was a meat and hide industry directed mainly at red and grey kangaroos and common wallaroos. Saville-Kent's concerns were again echoed the 1960s with severe drought causing high kangaroo mortality and kangaroo harvesting seemingly out of control as unemployed station hands sought alternative income. The conservation voice was heard stridently for the first time. Articles such as "Is it too late to save the Big Red?" (Montgomery, 1969) appeared in popular international journals such as Animals.

Montgomery lamented that "Australia's national emblem is in danger." Readers were confronted with photographs of massed kangaroo carcasses. If Montgomery's article is emotional and lacked verifiable data, the same view was expressed by scientists leading research on kangaroo populations. Harry Frith and John Calaby (1970, p. 33) sound alarums with: "If any large species of kangaroo is endangered it is the Red Kangaroo, the symbol of the inland plains.... We have already seen Red Kangaroos in N.S.W. reduced to a fraction of their former numbers in only seven years of uncontrolled meat hunting and drought." These concerns culminated in the first comprehensive review of the relationships between people and kangaroos in 'Kangaroos and Men' edited by Basil Marlow (1971). This was to be followed by a second review – 'Kangaroo Harvesting and the Conservation of Arid and Semi-arid Lands' - edited by Dan Lunney and Gordon Grigg in 1988. The title of the second volume is in itself revealing of how attitudes had further changed in the intervening two decades.

Skinned red kangaroo carcasses left by commercial shooters beside a main road in Outback Queensland.

Recognition of species endangerment through declines in range and abundance placed kangaroos on the political agenda and the states enacted legislation to protect wildlife and manage kangaroo populations (Poole, 1984). As the legislatures of the United States and Europe questioned Australia's kangaroo management programmes, the fate of kangaroos moved into the foreign affairs arena and the Commonwealth assumed some control over State management plans to commercially harvest and export kangaroo meat and hide products. In the new millennium these plans have come under greater public scrutiny and more frequent challenge (e.g. Administrative Appeals Tribunal 2003, 2004). The continued government-sanctioned killing of kangaroos has fermented argument as to what are the true numbers of kangaroo populations; what is the cost of kangaroos to pastoral enterprises; how effective is the management system in enforcing legal quotas; and what is the morality of exploiting wildlife as meat and hides when these resources are readily available from livestock. Ron Hacker and his colleagues (2004) recognised this divergence of opinions (or aspirations) about the nature and goals of managing four species exploited in a meat/hide industry in the Murray-Darling basin. Through a workshop with some representatives of parties concerned with kangaroo management, they identified four stakeholder groups – pastoralists, non-government conservationists, kangaroo industry members and government wildlife management agencies – and defined their somewhat divergent viewpoints. The orthodoxy of kangaroos as pests in no longer accepted by government in current kangaroo management plans. We have entered the era of kangaroos as sustainable resources – the small ones to be conserved, recovered and reintroduced in public-private 'partnerships' and the large one to be eaten, worn and evaded (on roads).

The only common theme is that all kangaroos, small and large, can be enjoyed either vicariously through a television wildlife documentary or directly through a wildlife tourism experience from zoo to wilderness. Even so wildlife needs to pay to justify expenditure on continuing its existence since we are arrogant enough to believe that this is under our control. Michael Conover (2002) reviews the positive values provided by wildlife. Amongst these are: physical utility (meeting human needs like food and clothing), monetary (benefits that can be exchanged for money such as products, licences to exploit, services to support hunting or tourism), recreational (wildlife in nature-based tourism), scientific (advancement of knowledge, indicators of environmental health), ecological (role in ecosystem services), existence (potential for future value), and historic (human satisfaction and well-being gained from maintenance of wildlife in 'natural' ecosystems).

Kangaroos easily provide all of these values but perhaps what can and does bind Australians is their iconic or totemic value or in the modern lexicon their incomparable value as a 'brand'. As John Morton (1991) observes, an aboriginal person may state to a non-aboriginal interrogator that 'I am a kangaroo' – the person's totem. This was a metaphor. The person imitated a kangaroo to recount the mythical deeds of persons who could turn into kangaroos. Today a non-aboriginal Australian may likewise say 'I am a kangaroo [or wallaby]'; i.e. a member of an Australian Football League team or national rugby league side. The symbolism here is one of athleticism and place. Kangaroos take centre stage in the marketing of Australia as researched by Hill and his colleagues (2002). Where once we 'culturally cringed' at the perceived backward notion that aspiring sophisticated urbanised Australia had kangaroos hopping down the main street, we now have the nation's capital with eastern grey kangaroos apparently doing just that in abundance. Tim Flannery (2004) reminds us again in his autobiographical book 'Country' of Justice Barron Field's 1819 eulogy:

'Kangaroo! Kangaroo!
Thou spirit of Australia,
That redeems from utter failure,
From perfect desolation,
And warrants the creation
Of this fifth part of the earth;
....'

With federation and the emergence of an independent Australian nation in 1901, the populace started to reflect on an Australian identity. Faunal symbols, such as the kangaroo, must have been part of this identity – it props up half of the coat of arms. Thus when the debate on the conservation status of the kangaroo heated, we read of threats to the national symbol, the symbol of the outback and the bush, among others. Australians continue to be confronted with questions about how best to exploit this symbol if they care at all. Do we offer kangaroo on every Australian table to enjoy the benefits of low-fat game meat? Do we give back the outback to its native herbivores and remove the exotic sheep on whose back we for so long rode since the wool industry is now a minor economic driver? How do we cope with the tourists' laments that when drawn to the Australian wilderness and its wildlife, they drive all day and never see a (live) kangaroo? How do we address blaring headlines that we are engaged in the greatest wildlife slaughter in the world? How does the most urbanized society in the world measure the realities of the bush against these demands for a new relationship with kangaroos?

We need to redeem our most potent symbol, turn away from further persecution, celebrate our faunal heritage, and all stand up and say 'I am a kangaroo'. The lesson we can learn from the Aboriginal peoples is that we are part of the land and, if we are lost in the urban jungle, then we should follow the kangaroo mob and re-establish our relationship with it.

KANGAROOS: CONSUMATE AUSTRALIA

Australians like to contend that they are free spirited, athletic and resilient to the hardships that 'the wide brown land' throws at them. My vision is that at the next citizenship ceremony, flag-raising event, singing of the national anthem, prancing on the national (or international) stage, opening of parliament or other celebration of being Australian we are moved to shout 'I am a kangaroo'. If we did this we would be celebrating diversity, the successful occupation of most of Australia's terrestrial ecosystems, resilience to our climatic extremes, athleticism, careful conservation of energy and water needs, and individualism in a rich social life. We could also reflect on vulnerability to rapid environmental degradation and change of our own (anthropogenic) making. These qualities conveyed to us by understanding and observing the kangaroo mob might cause us to think about our own ecological footprint and how to tread more lightly on the Australian continent. And for those who wish to kill kangaroos for monetary gain or consume and wear them, perhaps they might recapture the compassion of our distant hunter-gather past by reflecting on the continuity between kangaroos and themselves. So come on, stand up, be imbued with the spirit of Australia and declare 'I am a kangaroo'. Then think about the 30 million killed in the commercial industry in the last decade, and the many more outside this industry that are shot, bludgeoned and fatally hit on our roads. Isn't it time to stop maligning and persecuting them?

A young red kangaroo male in hopping stride: a supreme athlete and consummate Australian.

Kangaroo

I was your living symbol - south, through mist
Of primal morning, in the lonely dawn,
I came to you ... bright fortress of the sun,
Wild continent of colour - the Yaraandoo,
Whose winged outriders beat against the night
And, at the last day's ending, they will know ...
White birds, my spirit follows in their flight.
I am your dying emblem - broken here,
Whose blood, more ageless than this timeless land,
Gushes for gold across the plundered plain
And floods my country ... at the gun's command.

(Poem by Nan Ingleton, from her book 'Shores of Dusk'. Photo: Bill Corn)

THE KANGAROO
– FALSELY MALIGNED BY TRADITION
By David Nicholls

Former commercial Kangaroo shooter

Consecutive Australian Federal and State governments have failed to consult with the Australian people in the process of classing the shot at species of Kangaroo as a resource, they have failed to inform the Australian people of the implications of that decision and failed to utilise the best possible science and common sense in forming the "opinion" that commercial kangaroo shooting is, necessary, sustainable and does not infringe on acceptable and accepted community standards of animal welfare. Kangaroo shooting for commercial purposes is widespread, relentless and driven by financial interest.

The Environment Australia publication, The Commercial Harvesting of Kangaroos in Australia by Pople & Grigg (1999), supposedly a justification of this practise, is nothing of the sort. Nowhere in its 134 pages does it state that kangaroos are a significant and widespread problem other than a perceived one to the grazing community. It does however, on many occasions point out that the unsustainable use of land by sheep and cattle producers is a real problem.

Figures show conclusively that the "cull" is not necessary on the grounds of large numbers interfering with grazing business. Figures show that the grazing community is driven by tradition rather than fact in vilifying the kangaroo as some kind of wrongdoer.

For kangaroo "culling" to be necessary, scientific method requires that significant, widespread and continual damage to rangelands and infrastructure is actually happening. IT IS NOT and no such inkling of evidence exists and because of the proportionally smaller number of kangaroos than stock, for it to exist, would mean that kangaroos would have to be far greater destroyers per capita than introduced stock.

The kangaroo has lived on this continent for tens of thousands of years and has developed characteristics to suit the environment. It requires less water, has soft feet, is on average smaller than sheep, seeks shade in the sun, has no need to grow wool or fat, is efficient in travelling and not limited by artificial boundaries but rather follows its food requirements, which are in most instances, different to that of the introduced animals.

It is of some note that in the publication The Commercial Harvesting of Kangaroos in Australia, there are over 40 references to the perceived "pest" status of kangaroos.

Kangaroos have never been in widespread pest proportions and they are not now.

In every other situation throughout the civilised world where there is widespread and relentless killing of animals, due consideration is given to the alteration of the genetic structure of those animals. Kangaroos are shot at in every place a kangaroo shooter can get with a vehicle. The areas that are safe to the kangaroo are generally hilly, boggy or too dense with forest or inaccessible for some other reason. Kangaroos and humans have one thing in common. If the area is no good for humans then it is no good for the shot at species and these areas are small, not evenly distributed and may not have feed. National Parks are also credited as a refuge but the same story affects them.

The biggest (alpha) males are continuously and relentlessly hunted down. They may escape being shot this year or the next, but kangaroo shooting will get them sooner or later. A proper study is near impossible, as the genetic structure has been altering since European invasion.

Let it be made clear to the reader that the biggest and most genetically fit kangaroos are the target animals. Even this is being disguised as the program is called culling.

Culling is popularly understood to be the weeding out of the weak, the infirmed and the old. Australia is weeding out the strong and the bold. Common sense has taken a huge dive into the highly speculative chasm of self-interest on this point alone.

Large Alpha male in an eastern grey kangaroo mob - the prime target of the commercial industry. (Photo: Glen Carruthers)

Kangaroos are not magically separated from the laws of evolution and with the preferential emphasis on killing the Alpha males they have been and are being genetically altered to a degree that puts their very long-term healthy survival at stake.

If the kangaroo were in such numbers as to be an actual threat to landholders by way of causing overgrazing and damage to infrastructure, then the present system of "control" would not only not suffice, but it would not be acceptable to Australians and the world, purely on the grounds of the cruelty involved, if the full story of that cruelty were to be come more widely known. A system of large-scale immuno-contraception, or some other humane action would have to be undertaken.

That the kangaroo has become a resource after decades of ignorant perception as pests should be no surprise to anyone. That proper public education has not been undertaken, whereby Australians should have been deprogrammed from that sorry state of thinking, is an indictment against those that are now in support of this transition.

Most Australians think that Kangaroo numbers are far higher then they actually are. It is in the interest of Governments, the kangaroo Industry and thoughtless landholders to uphold this myth.

The cruelty comes in two forms. Shooting is not an exact science because of the many variables and the result does cause horrific non-fatal injuries. To quantify the wounding rate is near impossible. To imply that a certain wounding percentage is "acceptable" only begs the question. "Acceptable" to whom? Acceptable to the kangaroo shooter? Acceptable to the Australian citizenry? Acceptable to the world at large? Acceptable to the mutilated kangaroo?

It is not acceptable to a civilisation that prides itself on how it regards other creatures and which goes so far as to give a mandate to the Royal Society for the Protection of Animals to stop such excesses.

Apart from the wounding rate, the other form of cruelty is straight out of the annals of our brutish past and is a blight on all we hold to be decent and fair. This cruelty is so extreme that the publication, The Commercial Harvesting of Kangaroos in Australia, steers well away from anything but mere mention. And well might it, as it is the stuff of nightmares.

Young joeys are unceremoniously dragged out of their previously secure world (the pouch) by the hind legs and swung against a purposed hard object. One swing may be followed by another and yet another if the prior does not complete a death. Otherwise healthy young animals are killed for no reason than there are no other choices. Even hardened kangaroo shooters are often sickened by this never-ending process. If this unsavoury, to say the least, part of kangaroo shooting were to be graphically filmed and widely televised to a public made aware that killing kangaroos was not even necessary, then the industry would fold overnight. As it should!

Possibly an even worse cruelty is inherent in shooting kangaroos. A very large proportion of adult female kangaroos also have a joey-at-foot (see chapter by Ingrid Witte in this volume).
This joey is not only psychologically dependent on its mother but also it feeds off one of the multiple nipples in the pouch. The publication, The Commercial Harvesting of Kangaroos in Australia, again makes very small reference about this offspring. It does however acknowledge the strong bonds between mother and joey.

When the mother is killed, this joey is left to fend for itself, and any zoologist with knowledge of kangaroo habits would have to admit that its chances of survival are at the best minimal. Panic, fear, starvation or

CO-OCCURRENCE

OF HUMAN VIOLENCE, CRIMINAL BEHAVIOUR
AND ANIMAL ABUSE:
IMPLICATIONS FOR HUNTING BEHAVIOUR.

By Eleonora Gullone

Department of Psychology.
Monash University.

(Illustration: Mark Wilson)

In the last decade there has been an increasing awareness of the significant links between violence toward humans, animal cruelty, and criminal behaviours (e.g., Arluke, Levin, Luke, & Ascione, 1999; Ascione, 1998; Flynn, 2000a; 2000b; Gullone & Clarke, in press). Related to this, animal cruelty has been proposed to be a potential indicator of subsequent or simultaneous violent criminal behaviour. Prominent examples of this link in Australia are seen in anecdotal evidence of notorious violent adult offenders. For example, mass murderer Martin Bryant was known to RSPCA officers in Tasmania in relation to animal cruelty offences. Similarly, serial killer Ivan Milat was known for being cruel to animals prior to murdering seven victims in New South Wales.

By far the greatest number of studies looking at the co-occurrence of the links between abusive behaviours of human and non-human animals comes from the body of research examining the association between family violence and animal abuse. However, in recent times, increased attention has been given to the association between criminal behaviours and animal abuse. Hunting behaviours have also begun to attract some research attention. Ascione (1993: 51) has defined animal abuse as "socially unacceptable behaviour that intentionally causes unnecessary pain, suffering, or distress to and/or death to an animal". Similarly, Felthous and Kellert (1986: 57) have defined cruelty to animals as a "pattern of deliberately, repeatedly, and unnecessarily hurting vertebrate animals in a manner likely to cause serious injury". Both definitions incorporate an element of intent to harm and Ascione's definition incorporates an element of "social acceptability". Further, as with child abuse, animal abuse can include physical abuse, sexual abuse, and neglect.

Ascione *et al.* (2005) also assessed the experiences and behaviours of children and found that over 61.5% of the shelter women reported that their children had witnessed pet abuse. This contrasted with only 2.9% for the community sample. A total of 38 shelter group children were also directly interviewed. Nearly two-thirds of these children (61.5%) reported that they had witnessed pet abuse incidents as perpetrated by their father, stepfather, or women's boyfriend. As many as 51% of the children said that they had protected one of their pets to save it from being hurt.

In the only Australian investigation carried out to date to determine the extent of co-occurrence between animal abuse and human-directed violence, Gullone and colleagues (2004) surveyed 104 women recruited through family violence refuge or outreach services and a comparison community sample of 102 women from neighbourhood houses and community centres. The inclusion criterion for participating women was that they owned at least one pet during their current or most recent relationship. For the community sample, there was the additional criterion required that there be no current or past experience of family violence. The findings were highly comparable to those of past similar studies as reported above. Specifically, it was found that 46% of women in the family violence sample reported that their partner had threatened to hurt or kill their pet compared with 6% of women in the community sample. Similarly, a markedly larger percentage of family violence group women (53%) reported that their partner had hurt or killed their pet compared to 0% of women in the community sample. Out of the 104 family violence cases, 17.3% reported that their pet(s) had been killed.

A total of 34 women in the family violence sample were living in a refuge, crisis accommodation or transitional housing (as opposed to outreach services). Of these women, a total of 33% reported that they had delayed leaving up to 8 weeks. Also, consistent with past similar studies, Gullone *et al.* (2004) asked the women in the family violence sample about their children's experiences. With the comparison sample percentages given in parentheses, it was found that in 29% (1%) of cases, children were reported to witness threats of abuse and 29% (0%) were reported to witness actual abuse. A total of 19% (1%) of the women reported that their child had abused their pet. Further, a total of 5% (1%) of the children were reported to have threatened to hurt or kill their pet(s).

The outcomes of the research reviewed above leave little room for doubt that a relationship between intimate partner human violence and animal cruelty exists. At the very least, this research suggests that the detection of animal abuse should be of significant concern to professionals and researchers. The research outcomes also suggest that when children are found to be abusing animals, there is a significant probability that they have witnessed and/or directly experienced abuse themselves. Thus, children's abuse of animals should be taken very seriously as it may well be a marker of other sinister crimes. Also of importance are research outcomes suggesting that animal abuse is predictive of other types of criminal behaviours. On the basis of these research outcomes, it can be concluded that animal cruelty constitutes an important marker of antisocial or criminal behaviour. Therefore, it appears that the same underlying factors that predict or increase the likelihood of an individual engaging in animal abuse, may also increase the likelihood that the same individual will engage in other types of criminal behaviour. Providing further support for this proposition are Australian Victoria Police data. These data are considered below...

Out of four categories of offence for all alleged offenders, the data clearly show that the largest proportion of offences was consistently that against property, ranging between 79.52% (number = 344,905) of total offences in 1998 and 80.85% (number = 354,785) in 1999. Over the eight year period, offences against property constituted an average of 80.8% of the total 3,364,078 crimes committed in Victoria. Drug offences consistently constituted the smallest proportion and ranged between 2.84% (n = 12,838) in 2001 and 4.23% (n = 18,354) of total offences in 1998. Of note, offences against the person also constituted a relatively small proportion of the total number of crimes at an average of 7.71% of all crimes over the eight year period with the lowest percentage of 7.98 recorded in 2000 and the highest percentage of 8.01 recorded in 2001.

The equivalent statistics relating to criminal offences for alleged animal abuse offenders only, classified in the same way show some interesting trends. Specifically, for animal abuse offenders, the average percentage of offences committed against the person was found to be substantially higher compared to the percentage for all alleged offenders (25% compared to 7.98%). The category of offences against the person included such crimes as homicide, rape, assault, abduction/kidnap, and harassment.

Where does hunting behaviour fit in the co-occurrence hypothesis?

As noted above, animal cruelty can, in part, be explained by compromised empathy development. Low empathy levels constitute a central characteristic of Conduct Disorder and Anti-Social Personality Disorder. Given such findings, it is not unreasonable to argue that killing animals in the form of hunting for purely recreation purposes is a demonstration of compromised empathy since deriving enjoyment from a behaviour that causes suffering and harm must be devoid of compassion. It is also likely that children's witnessing of such behaviours by their significant others (e.g. parents, older siblings) is conveying a message that harming and killing sentient beings for pure sport is acceptable. Following from this, it is likely not a coincidence that hunting is performed predominantly by males who, as a group, have also been consistently demonstrated to have lower levels of empathy compared to females.

Despite the fact that hunting is a legal behaviour, in both the US and Australia, there has been a significant and steady decline in numbers of licensed shooters. In the U.S., in the last quarter of a century, the number of adults holding paid hunting licenses has declined from 17.1 million in 1975 to 15.1 million. Support for hunting has also significantly declined (Irwin, 2001 cited in Flynn, 2002). A similar decline has occurred in Australia. For example, the number of licensed duck shooters in Victoria, Australia has declined from 95,000 in 1986 to 17,609 in 2003 (The Victorian Shooter Newsletter, December, 2004). In Australia, duck shooting, once commonly regarded a legitimate form of recreation, is now seen by the majority of the Australian population as outright animal cruelty. This has been most clearly demonstrated by animal rescue programs focusing on saving injured birds and by the continued campaigning against duck hunting by the Royal Society for the Prevention of Cruelty to Animals. That hunting is a behaviour engaged in by the minority of the Australian adult population is reflected in the numbers of license holders. As reported by the SSAS (2005), the proportion of license holders in Australia as a percentage of the adult population is 5.2%. Further, not all licensed gun owners actively engage in hunting. Thus, hunting is a behaviour representing a clear minority of the Australian adult population. The defensive position taken by the SSAS suggests that shooters themselves are aware of changing community attitudes and feel the need to justify and protect their position.

As noted by Flynn (2002), contrary to perceptions of shooters that hunting is a sport, many animal activists and feminists consider hunting to be another form of violence and male domination. Indeed anecdotal data suggest that there is a co-occurrence between domestic violence and hunting (Adams,1995 cited in Flynn, 2002). Others have argued that legal violence (e.g. hunting) can generalise or "spill over" into illegal violence (e.g. domestic violence).

To systematically investigate the associations between violence, animal cruelty and hunting behaviours, Flynn (2002) obtained self-reports from a sample of 236 university undergraduate students regarding whether or not they had engaged in hunting during childhood or adolescence and asked about their involvement in violent behaviours toward humans and other animals. Additionally, Flynn examined whether hunting behaviour was predictive of lower levels of empathy.

Consistent with the trends reported above in the Victorian data, one of the main findings was a consistent gender difference with males far exceeding females on almost all cruelty and violence variables. For example, 45.7% of males in the sample reported that they had hunted at least once in their youth compared to only 9.5% of females. Males were also significantly more likely to engage in violent acts compared to females. Consistent with most literature on gender-related empathy differences, females scored significantly higher than males on empathy.

Of most significance, those students who reported that they had hunted were approximately twice as likely to engage in violence toward animals as non-hunters. Hunters in Flynn's sample were also more than twice as likely compared to non-hunters to report that they had damaged or destroyed someone else's property during their high school years. Although these associations were only significant when hunting was defined as "killing an animal", just "going hunting" was found to be a significant marker of destructive behaviour during adolescence among the male participants in the sample.

Flynn concluded that his study findings provide evidence of a relationship between hunting and illegal aggression or violence and killing stray or wild animals and damaging the property of humans. Also, gender was found to be an important variable with males being markedly more likely to engage in hunting, animal abuse, property damage, and fighting with others. As would be expected, males reported significantly lower levels of empathy compared to females. Related to this, it can be argued that the endorsement of hunting through its legal status provides societal endorsement to engage in acts of cruelty and violence. Such endorsement is likely to manifest in a circular manner both by being acted upon by those with compromised levels of empathy and by increasing individuals' levels of desensitisation to others' suffering through such legally endorsed acts of cruelty.

Kangaroo Shooting

Definitions of animal cruelty vary but there is an implicit assumption, consistent with Ascione's (1993) definition, as given above (i.e. "socially unacceptable behaviour that intentionally causes unnecessary pain, suffering, or distress to and/or death of an animal"; p.51), that if behaviour is legally endorsed, monitored and controlled, then it is acceptable. Kangaroo shooting in Australia is one such "industry". As summarized by the Australian Government's Department of the Environment and Heritage (2002), on mainland Australia there are five species of kangaroo and wallaby that can be legally killed by commercial shooters for commercial use. These species and others can also be legally shot by non-commercial shooters. Annually, large numbers of kangaroos are shot. For example, in 1999 the recorded number was 2,654,496 and in 2000, the number was 2,747,491. This is a conservative number since there is no accurate record of kangaroos shot by non-commercial shooters, recreational shooters, or kangaroos shot illegally. An estimated 95,686 kangaroos were killed in NSW, Queensland and South Australia for damage mitigation or recreation (Australian Government, Dept of Environment and Heritage; RSPCA report, 2002).

Under the Code of Practice for the Humane Shooting of Kangaroos, in most Australian states (Australian Government, Dept of Environment and Heritage, 2002), there are training requirements that commercial shooters (in some states this also applies to recreational shooters) must undertake. There are also tagging system requirements for the tracing of carcasses. The Code also requires that kangaroos are shot in the head to ensure a quick death. An additional cruelty concern relates to the fate of pouch young and young at foot. In this regard, the Code requires that the pouch young of a shot female are killed by decapitation, a heavy blow to the skull or by shooting.

According to a report prepared by the RSPCA (See Australian Government, Dept of Environment and Heritage, 2002) on the extent of compliance with the requirements of the Code of Practice, Western Australia differs most from the other states through its Restricted Open Season for the shooting of both red and Western grey kangaroos. This enables landholders and others to shoot kangaroos without a license. Although a condition of this Restricted Open Season is that all shooting be carried out in accordance with the Code of Practice, monitoring of such is for all practical purposes impossible. Indeed, the RSPCA (2002) report states that, despite concerns being expressed by representatives from NSW and Queensland, "none of the states could provide information about [the] extent of illegal kangaroo harvesting, or compliance with the Code during such activities." (Section 2: p. 11 of 15; Australian Government, Dept of Environment and Heritage, 2002).

Additional concerns regarding compliance with the Code summarized in the RSPCA report included the following:

- Reports that damage mitigation licences have led to the selling of tags by the holder of the licence resulting in 'shooting parties' by people who then shoot the kangaroos as a source of recreation.
- 'Kangaroo drives' resulting in kangaroos being injured with knives, snares, bow and arrows, dogs and iron bars.

- Kangaroo carcasses at processors being found to have pellets and projectiles under the skin or in the muscle.
- Reports of farmers who deliberately shoot kangaroos and wallabies in the body so that they travel off their property to die and thereby decrease the chances of their detection and prosecution.
- Reports that for young who were highly mobile, given the time required to capture them, it was more likely that they would be left alone, and would thereby die by natural causes (e.g. dehydration, starvation).
- For larger young, it was considered by some shooters that they were too big to club to death and it would be too dangerous to shoot them at close range resulting in the method of 'disposal' being to simply release them into the bush.

Whilst it was made clear in the RSPCA report that the major welfare concerns regarding kangaroo shooting come from the non-commercial sector given the greater difficulty of monitoring adherence to the Code for this sector, it remains the case that serious welfare concerns cannot be ruled out for the commercial sector. Given the large numbers of kangaroos involved, even 95% adherence to the Code leaves very large numbers of kangaroos not being shot 'humanely' (in the head). As stated in the RSPCA report, statistics regarding adherence to the requirement that kangaroos only be shot in the head are limited in that the data available are those from processors and many processors will not accept kangaroos unless they are 'head-shot'. Secondly, evidence suggests that a regular occurrence during a shoot is that many kangaroos are injured but not retrieved by shooters.

Therefore, the number of kangaroos that die a slow death remains unknown. Further, the argument that a head shot is humane and results in a quick death can also be questioned given the small brain size of the kangaroo relative to its skull size. There remains a significant chance that even head shot kangaroos do not die quickly.

And then there is the major issue of the fate of joeys whose mothers are shot. The line so conveniently drawn between the commercial and non-commercial sectors with regard to welfare concerns disappears when considering the young kangaroos whose mothers are killed since the fate of young kangaroos is something the Code has clearly failed to adequately address. Indeed, in their report RSPCA recommend that in order to avoid the cruel fate faced by pouch young or young at foot, female kangaroos should not be shot at all. Given the evidence, the kangaroo 'industry' is clearly an inherently cruel one and there remain too many unresolved issues. Among such issues are the unknown numbers of young kangaroos that die a slow and painful death from dehydration, starvation or predation. There are also unknown numbers of kangaroos who die slow and painful deaths from being wounded by gunshot but not killed. In addition, there are unknown numbers of kangaroos who are hunted down and likely killed inhumanely for recreational purposes as is supported legally particularly in Western Australia. Other issues have relevance beyond individual animals. For example, if the largest kangaroo in the group is systematically selected for shooting, what are the sustainability consequences? Despite these significant issues, the kangaroo industry remains a legal and legitimate source of individual employment and revenue.

Conclusions

There is increasing evidence that a significant co-occurrence between animal cruelty and human violence exists. It has also been reported that deriving pleasure from killing or causing suffering to other sentient beings is predictive of low empathy levels, as has been shown to be the case in hunting behaviour. It is also true that whilst hunting was once considered to be an acceptable recreational activity by a significant proportion of the population, such a position is now held by a small minority of the Australian population as has been seen through the significant decline in numbers of adults who are licensed gun owners. That only 5.2% of the adult Australian population hold such a license clearly shows this.

Given that such a small proportion of the population choose to hunt or to kill animals either for an income or for "fun", is it appropriate for it to be considered a "socially acceptable" behaviour. Who are the individuals attracted to such an industry or such a source of recreation? Are we as a society, unintentionally promoting "criminal" behaviours through the continued legal status of industries such as the kangaroo industry and hunting as a source recreation. Equally, where is the logic or sense in a society criminalising only certain very specifically defined behaviours as constituting cruelty toward animals yet legalising others? Given that engaging in cruel or abusive behaviours toward animals (and that the witnessing of such behaviours by children in particular) is not only associated with engaging in those behaviours toward humans but also with desensitization to the suffering of others generally (including that of humans), it would seem that the only logical, and indeed responsible, position for a society to take would be one that eschews all behaviours deliberately intended to bring about the suffering and/or death of sentient beings.

The diminutive quokka of Western Australia. Some people find it amusing to kick it in what is known as 'quokka football' on Rottnest Island. (Photo: Jan Aldenhoven)

KILLING FOR KICKS

By Juliet Gellatley

Zoologist and founder & director
of Viva!, examines why Australia
continues its assault on kangaroos
and how other countries can help
stop the slaughter

Juliet with young red Kangaroo

It's easy to be emotional about the killing of
Australia's national symbol because death,
injury, bereavement, pain and suffering are
the very stuff of emotion – and they are the
products of this slaughter. However, Viva!'s
campaign to end the sale of most kangaroo meat in Britain, which saw all 1,500 big supermarkets
empty their shelves of the stuff, was a product of logic, scientific research, persistence and
determination.

A culture of blame has become entrenched in Australia which results
in video footage of farmers engaging in 'pest' control, whooping and
shouting with glee as they plough through a mob of terrified kangaroos
at high speed in a fourtrack, shooting indiscriminately with shotguns,
injuring more than they kill.

It is blame which encourages a smiling, 12-year-old boy to swing a baby
joey around his head by the legs and repeatedly smash her head against
a rock then laugh and punch the air like a champion for the camera.

Of course, we're told that these images have nothing to do with the 'humane', 'well regulated'
and 'rigidly controlled' commercial killing industry, even though it shares the same roots and has
been fertilized by this savagery. Which is why, in a 60 Minutes programme on which I appeared,
a professional killer was able to admit that he feels nothing when he takes a helpless baby
from his or her mother's pouch and beats it to death. It's what enabled an industry vet in a
radio debate with me unemotionally maintain that to repeatedly club a joey with an iron pipe is
humane.

To support the kangaroo industry you have to subscribe to this culture
of blame – and how can this be possible in a developed country like
Australia?

But then you look across the world and see what happens to whales and wolves, rhinos and tigers, elephants and seals and some 70 per cent of all the wild creatures who are struggling to survive or are facing extinction. Whether you mean to or not, your focus inevitably moves on to Auschwitz and Rwanda, Bosnia and Iraq and you can see the common threads that bind all these together.

It is power, economics, self interest and the suspension of truth which increasingly drives society – all societies – and Australia is no different.

To exploit or destroy humans or animals en masse you first have to demonise them and present them as a threat or create an artificial need, as in the case of livestock farming. It then requires only a small, additional step to begin the slaughter but once it starts it develops a momentum and a life of its own. It is this which results in a 12-year-old seeking approval by cruelly killing a creature. He isn't yet aware of it but it is his lifestyle not the kangaroo's which poses the real threat to Australia and the rest of the planet.

Monitoring the massacre and listening to the excuses which drive it is like watching a Greek tragedy unfold in slow motion. As a nation, the course Australia has chosen is based on short-term financial and political expedients which will eventually lead to disaster. The same is true for most other countries but because of Australia's unique and fragile environment, it will be one of the first to hit the buffers. Eventually, it will not be just the kangaroos who pay the price. If kangaroos were a genuine threat, the industry would have had no need to manufacture excuses in order to justify the slaughter.

The original excuse for kangaroo killing was 'damage mitigation' – polite words for pest control. However, it wasn't helped by the nation's own scientists. First, CSIRO showed that wheat crop damage was a myth and that kangaroos aren't keen on any farm crops and can't thrive on them (Arnold 1980). A study of the kangaroo killing zones quickly revealed that kangaroos are largely commercially shot in areas which produce almost no crops and account for only 10 per cent of Australia's meat production. Despite this, the excuses shifted to grazing – kangaroos have to be killed so that sheep can prosper.

A study by Steve McLeod (1996) knocked the legs from beneath this one by showing there is no competitive effect for grazing between sheep and kangaroos even during drought. 'Competition' only occurs in the most exceptionally poor conditions. He even showed that sheep can negatively impact on kangaroos, not the other way round. So the focus shifted again – to artificial watering points (AWP) and the argument that this unnatural water supply had caused kangaroo numbers to explode, causing serious overgrazing.

No sooner was the claim established than a study in Sturt National Park destroyed it. It reveals that kangaroo distribution is not related to 'water-focused grazing patterns' but is mainly determined by the best grazing and resting spots (Montague-Drake & Croft 2004). Researcher Rebecca Montague-Drake showed that because kangaroos prefer to drink at specific times of day, they may be seen in high densities around watering holes, but the animals quickly disperse to the best grazing or resting places. Montague-Drake & Croft (2004: 87) state "Low vegetation biomass near artificial watering points in Sturt National Park may be more correctly attributed to past sheep grazing pressure, than to any current (kangaroo) grazing pressure."

Research on red kangaroos by Amanda Bilton and David Croft (2004) was even more disturbing when it revealed that far from numbers booming, few joeys survive. The average number of young weaned in a lifetime is only 3.7 (41 per cent less than their potential). Half the females weaned less offspring than expected and a quarter left no offspring at all. Only about seven per cent reach adulthood each year and, even worse, red kangaroos are being slaughtered three times faster than they can breed. Without showing concern, other scientists stated at a conference in July 2001 that the average age of red males, who can live for more than 20 years, has collapsed from 15 to just two years old, caused by the industry's practice of targeting the largest animals.

This might not be of concern to the killing industry but it is to macropod expert, Doug Reilly. "In any wild animal if, in a short period of time, you disrupt the normal reproduction processes that have evolved over tens of thousands of years, you are in danger of putting the species at risk." Seals, bison, wolves and other animals have faced extinction after similar destructive 'culling' programs.

Extinction? It's certainly a possibility, remembering that Australia has an appalling record for wildlife – the worst in the world. Eighteen species of mammals gone and another 45 threatened; six species of kangaroo exterminated in Australasia as a whole and four more on the mainland and 17 now classified as endangered or vulnerable. Not bad going in a couple of hundred years!

And it may not be over yet, according to vet and kangaroo expert, Dr. Ian Gunn (Animal Gene Storage Resource Centre of Australia): "..the current situation will ultimately reduce the mature

Red kangaroo male in a sea of green pick after rain on Sturt National Park supposedly in a population out of control and degrading the landscape. (Photo: David B Croft).

weights and sizes of future generations and could lead to a decrease in the ability of the population to survive. (Gunn 1996) ...the continued slaughter of kangaroos has the potential to cause the extinction of a number of remaining species. (Gunn 1999)"

If there was any doubt left that kangaroos are pests and compete with sheep, it was finally laid to rest by Gordon Grigg, the man who first encouraged the slaughter with his bible, The Commercial Harvesting of Kangaroos in Australia. It had previously been claimed that one kangaroo equalled one sheep in its grazing demands, forgetting to add that at about 100 million, the actual number of sheep far outstrips even the most ambitious estimate for kangaroos.

Grigg finally did some research and discovered that one sheep equalled almost five kangaroos - so estimates of their grazing pressure had been 500 per cent out and the excuse for killing kangaroos was therefore also 500 per cent out. Unsurprisingly he concluded: "The hope of getting a significant improvement in wool production by pest control of kangaroos is probably doomed to failure." (Grigg 2001)

Toolache wallaby (*Macropus greyi*) last seen in 1924. Joan Dixon (1973: 43) comments "...this example of rapid extermination of a harmless and beautiful species illustrates the destruction of civilisation" (Illustration from John Goulds' The Mammals of Australia)

If you were naive you might think that this demolished the last excuse of the industry and killing would be ended. Governments are much more duplicitous than this, particularly when a few votes are at risk in remote rural areas. They simply removed the need to prove damage mitigation at all – in other words, anyone can now kill kangaroos simply because they're there.

Those of us who oppose the slaughter warned that once an industry is started it has its own imperatives and would kill increasing numbers of kangaroos, even if populations crashed. Even the Queensland government can claim full marks for its farsightedness on this score despite its questionable reasoning. It said in 1984:
 "It is important to recognize that while the kangaroo industry was originally a response to the pest problem caused by these animals it has now come to exist in its own right as the user of a renewable natural resource and thus serves its own interests".

The safeguard against these interests dominating and resulting in over exploitation, we were assured by the industry, was a failsafe scientific model which would show when numbers were under pressure. It fell at the first hurdle.

No sooner were the words out then drought struck and kangaroo numbers crashed – red kangaroos by more than 50 per cent. The Kangaroo Industry Association of NSW sent an impassioned plea to Government (NPWS) asking it to curb the numbers still being killed as pests. It included these words:

"I'm sure I need not remind you that extensive computer modeling has suggested that the one strategy most likely significantly to depress kangaroo populations to extremely low levels in the long term, is heavy culling immediately before the breaking of a long-term drought... We believe that any such cull is not necessary ... unless of course it is the intention to place the population under an unsustainably high level of culling pressure."

Culling was not curbed but the NSW Government extended commercial killing into new areas previously seen as unproductive simply to keep the number of carcasses flowing. It was condemned even by some who had previously been gung ho about the industry. We can only assume that the intention was to place kangaroos under unsustainably high pressure. So much for scientific models, which are now doing for kangaroos what they have done for fish - encouraging extinction by pretending to have scientific rigour.

Having been stripped of all other excuses, the final and most crass claim is increasingly being pushed – kangaroos are destroying the country's environment! A primary school kid could demolish this one. Unique animals with long, soft feet flit over the delicate scrub – an environment with which they have evolved over millions of years and are an essential part of. Their toe nails make small holes in the ground – holes into which salt bush seeds are washed to germinate and be protected. They are animals which nibble at vegetation rather than tug at it, pulling out the roots and are finally attuned to the native vegetation.

There are two alien animals, of course, which do none of these things and which are inexorably turning the outback into desert – 160 million sheep and cattle. Those who enhance their careers out of the exploitation of Australia's wildlife – people like advocate Michael Archer – is laughable. Eat kangaroos instead of sheep and cows they say – the industry even received a $120,000 grant from government to help them say it (Kelly 2003). About 1,700,000 tonnes of farmed meat is produced each year.

(Photo: Viva Library)

To provide this amount of meat from kangaroos, their total population would have to be 566 times bigger than it is and every one of them would have to be killed every year.

Without State and Federal government support, the kangaroo industry would be a shadow of what it is and far more vulnerable to attacks by groups such as Viva! Not only does it receive grants to increase its kill quota, the Government is prepared to fight its battles for it. As the Australian meat industry stated in the food press:

"When Viva! successfully lobbied Tesco in the UK to remove kangaroo meat from sale, the deputy Prime Minister contacted the chairman of Tesco to plainly state that kangaroo meat production meets every required standard. But despite the intervention Tesco still pulled the meat from sale." (Williams 1998)

The important point is that David can still take on Goliath and win! But there have to be more victories because if a rich country such as Australia can ravage its wildlife for export, it shows a massive green light to every impoverished country in the world. So this is not just about saving kangaroos - but all wildlife. Ironically, it is also about saving Australia!

Australia lies firmly in the belt of semi-arid land that girdles the globe making up one-third of its surface area. These are amongst the most fragile of all rangelands and grazing pressure, land misuse and clear felling of tree cover is inexorably turning them to desert – nowhere more so than Australia. The environmental disaster caused by the hard hooves and destructive eating habits of cattle and sheep is already well advanced. Scapegoating the kangaroo is simply a way of pretending to people that action is being taken. Sadly, it is entirely the wrong action.

The fate of Australia is being determined by butchers and bakers and candlestick makers who have traded sustainability and long-term ecological survival for a fist full of foreign dollars today. When the question is finally asked – "Who was responsible for this catastrophe?" the culprits will have disappeared and no one will even remember their names.

The KIAA (Kangaroo Industries Association of Australia) issued a statement on its website when Viva! targeted Adidas for its use of kangaroo skin in football boots. It said:

"A United Kingdom based radical animal liberation organisation (sic) has launched a campaign targeting Adidas... This (soccer boot) market is vital to the kangaroo industry. Without it underpinning kangaroo skin prices the entire industry would be at risk.... Adidas have received to date over 10,000 emails complaining about their use of kangaroo leather...and are obviously concerned about damage to their image.... The Kangaroo Industry is under attack and needs your help." (KIAA 2002)

You bet your sweet life it is and everyone in Australia should fervently hope that we win.

RED PLAGUE GREY PLAGUE

THE KANGAROO MYTHS AND LEGENDS

By John Auty

Auty J, 2004. Red plague grey plague: the kangaroo myths and legends. Australian Mammalogy 26: 33-36. (Reprinted with the permission of the editor).

The conventional wisdom is that kangaroo (*Macropus* spp.) numbers have increased in Australia since European settlement due to cessation of predation by Aborigines and dingoes (*Canis lupus dingo*), as well as increased availability of water. The historical record shows that at the time of first European contact the kangaroo was numerous and abundant over the continent and Tasmania. The Aborigines were at best poor hunters of kangaroos and quickly incorporated the Europeans' large hounds into their hunting methodologies. *C. l. dingo* was a solitary hunter and scavenger. Its lack of capability as a hunter of kangaroos was recognised by the Aborigines who appear to have not used *C. l. dingo* for this purpose unlike their early use of the Europeans' kangaroo dogs. Water supplies were largely unimproved by 1860 when Australia de-pastured domestic livestock equivalent to 110 million kangaroos. In 1880 when there were 240 million kangaroo-equivalents, water supplies had been upgraded only in closely settled areas. It seems probable that at the time of settlement kangaroo numbers exceeded the present population at least threefold.

Key words: kangaroos, numbers, predation. Aborigines, dingoes.
J. Auty, 3/400 Latrobe St., Melbourne, Vic 3000, Australia.

EXAMINATION of the historical record reveals that kangaroos (*Macropus spp.*) were widespread in their distribution at the time of European exploration and settlement of Australia and are usually described as being numerous or abundant. This paper reports on a review of records from the 18th and 19th centuries and provides information about the possible numbers of kangaroos during the early years of European exploration and settlement. A previous study by Denny (1980) has shown that kangaroo numbers in New South Wales (NSW) were not as low as commonly assumed. This paper confirms these conclusions.

John White, Chief Surgeon at Sydney (NSW) in 1788 saw kangaroos during local exploratory

Adult and juvenile eastern grey kangaroos seen in abundance by early explorers. (Photo: Bill Corn)

journeys (White 1962: 129). By 1794 John Macarthur was taking 300 pounds of kangaroo meat a week using one hunter and six greyhounds at Parramatta (Onslow 1973: 43). At Sutton Forest to the west of Sydney James Macarthur saw kangaroos in immense flocks in 1821 (Onslow 1973: 371). In Van Diemens Land (Tasmania) kangaroos were harvested for human consumption as early as 1804. The usual means was to hunt them with suitable sight hounds, apparently crosses of the greyhound. Kangaroos were in "abundance" (Historical Records of Australia 1922a: 380). By 1808 hunting pressure had driven the kangaroo into the interior. Hunting and loss of habitat reduced populations to such an extent that in Tasmania the kangaroo was in danger of extinction by 1850. In 1814 G.W. Evans was sent by Governor Macquarie to open a road over the Blue Mountains in NSW. Hoping to victual partly on kangaroos he took hounds. Although he saw numerous kangaroos in his passage the dogs, after suffering wounds, became shy. (Historical Records of Australia 1921: 167). Three years later Evans saw numerous kangaroos on the Lachlan (Historical Records of Australia 1921: 614).

During 1829-1832 a series of explorations were made in the south-west of Western Australia. The explorers recorded "numerous herds of kangaroos" (Cross 1833: 67), "kangaroos and birds in abundance" (Cross 1833: 93), "kangaroos and birds in great abundance" (Cross 1833: 96), "heard kangaroos in the night and found numerous traces of them" (Cross 1833: 113), "saw many large kangaroos on the plain" (Cross 1833: 125), "great numbers of kangaroos" (Cross 1833: 143), "plenty of kangaroos" (Cross 1833: 188), "numerous impressions of the feet of natives and kangaroos" (Cross 1833: 190), "kangaroos ...seemed abundant traces in all places" (Cross 1833: 198), "plenty of kangaroos here without going out of our tract we saw at least twenty" (Cross 1833: 216), "The kangaroo must be very numerous in the interior if we may judge from the quantity seen in

kangaroos. Grey lists six methods of hunting kangaroos (Grey 1841: 268-274) to which we can add a seventh, hunting with dogs which Grey, and Grey alone and somewhat ambiguously, describes in the Kimberley. Later authors describe two principal methods of hunting: the surround on burnt ground, and the stalk. Both needed large inputs of energy and the former required a substantial gathering of hunters. The burning of scrub and grasslands may in fact have encouraged the growth of kangaroo populations.

That the Aborigine was not wholly satisfied with his own methods of hunting the kangaroo is shown by his eagerness to take up European methods both on the continent and in Tasmania. On the Tasmanian Aborigine Jorgen Jorgenson is worth recording at length (Plomley 1991: 52) "the natives had no dogs for hunting ... but when they succeeded in stealing dogs ... or otherwise obtained them, the chase became neither so laborious nor so uncertain. They displayed great natural capacity in the training of their dogs, and they treated them more like children than brutes. They were taught not to bark ... in pursuit of game".

Reporting from Westemport in Port Phillip (Victoria) in 1826, Hovell states the Aborigines "look strong and healthy and live well by means of very fine kangaroo dogs, for which they have plenty of employment, which not only provide them with food but raiment also" (Historical Records of Australia, 1922b: 856). Mitchell (Mitchell 1839: 204) on the Bogan (NSW?) in 1835 comments on the attempt of the Aborigines to steal his dogs after observing their ability to kill kangaroos. He later presented a greyhound pup to the "king" (Mitchell 1839: 241). A year later Darwin on a visit to Bathurst (NSW) wrote that the Aborigines are "always anxious to borrow the dogs from the farmhouses to hunt kangaroos, the kangaroo ... has become scarce ... the English greyhound has been highly destructive" (Darwin 1889: 321). Inland from Shark Bay in Western Australia Gregory in 1858 saw "several large white dogs which were evidently of Australian breed" (Gregory 1884: 42). Whether these were used to hunt kangaroos is unknown.

A group of antilopine wallaroos, the large kangaroos seen by explorers in northern Australia.
(Photo: David B Croft)

Protector Thomas of the Victorian Aborigines Protectorate in 1839 was "much struck" by the care with which the Aborigines at Momington in Victoria cared for their guns (Historical Records of Victoria 1983: 538). Their camp looked like a "butcher shop" (Historical Records of Victoria 1983: 541).

Predation by dingoes

Aborigines at the time of first contact had domesticated dingoes *(Canis lupus dingo)*. Mitchell (1839: 347) wrote, "The Australian natives evince great humanity in their behaviour to these dogs. In the interior, we saw few natives who were not followed by some of these animals, although they did not appear to make much use of them". They were not used in hunting of kangaroos. The reason is not difficult to find. The kangaroo was a redoubtable fighter. The first European experience of this ability to fight off dogs was a report by White (1962: 147) on a mauling given to a large Newfoundland.

Lieutenant Bradley reported that a kangaroo had taken to the water and tore the pursuing dog so much that the kangaroo had to be despatched. Henderson (1832: 138) records the ability of the large kangaroo species to inflict severe wounds. Dogs which had been bested by a kangaroo were reluctant to be set on thereafter unless in superior numbers. Such reports are commonplace in the literature.

Although the historical record appears to demonstrate that the dingo was the universal dog of Australia, Grey recognised another breed in the Kimberley and described it as follows: "The new species of dog differs totally from the dingo. ... Its colour is the same as that of the Australian dog in parts having a blackish tinge. The muzzle is narrow, long, thin, and tapers much, resembling that of a greyhound, whilst in general form it approaches the English lurcher. ... I cannot state that I ever saw one wild, or unless in the vicinity of natives" (Grey 1841: 239-40). "The dogs they use in hunting I have already stated to be of a kind unknown in other parts of Australia, and they were never seen wild by us" (Grey 1841:252).

Clearly *C. l. dingo* might cut off immature, weak, or injured kangaroos but as predators they were outclassed by the ability of the larger macropods to defend themselves. It has been suggested that recent work on canine predation of kangaroos shows that at the present day *C. l. dingo* is a successful predator of kangaroos (Newsome and Coman 1989: 998). The historical record is unambiguous. I have sighted no observations of the hunting of kangaroos by *C. l. dingo*. On the other hand the failure of the Aborigines to utilise *C. l. dingo* to hunt kangaroos whilst quickly availing themselves of the demonstrated ability of the Europeans' hounds to successfully pull down kangaroos, suggests that Aborigines had little regard for *C. l. dingo's* ability as a kangaroo hunter.

Kangaroo numbers at the time of European settlement

Having demonstrated that kangaroos were abundant at the time of European settlement and that Aborigines and *C. l. dingo* were at best of little consequence as predators, I now address the question of kangaroo numbers in 1788. My base is the capacity of native pasture and scrublands to support introduced herbivores, cattle, sheep, and horses. I allow ten sheep-equivalents to each large stock, and 0.7 sheep to each kangaroo. In 1860 based on the population of introduced herbivores (Chisholm 1963) the kangaroo-equivalent is approximately 110 million, in 1880 240 million. In 1860 settlement had not extended into western Queensland, central and northern Australia, and the central and northern regions of Western Australia (Chisholm 1963). Water conservation was in its infancy, as was cropping and pasture improvement (Chisholm 1963). In 1880 settlement had barely commenced in western Queensland, central, northern, and north western Australia, some surface water storage and wells had been established, but the artesian and sub-artesian basins were untapped, and pasture improvement and cropping as known today had hardly commenced (Chisholm 1963).

Conclusions

At first European contact, kangaroos were widely distributed in large numbers over the continent and Tasmania. The Aborigines' hunting methods were wasteful of energy when compared with those based on hounds as used by the Europeans. Because of this superiority European techniques were quickly copied by the Indigenes. *C. l. dingo* was a poor predator on kangaroos and for this reason was not used by Aborigines in hunting them. The numbers of kangaroos present in Australia at the time of European settlement can be estimated on the basis of the number of introduced herbivores supported on unimproved pasture and browse.
The population was probably of the order of one to two hundred million.

Red kangaroos aggregate in loose groups where water runs on to sustain green grasses and herbs. (Photo: David B Croft)

PUCKAPUNYAL MILITARY AREA

VICTORIA'S KANGAROO KILLING FIELDS

By Rheya Linden

Department of Political Science, University of Melbourne and
Campaign Director for Animal Active: The Australian Animal Rights Network

Between May 2002 and November 2003 a sustained massacre of eastern grey kangaroos took place at Puckapunyal Army base (PMA) in Central Victoria.

In total five destruction permits were issued to the federal Department of Defence (Defence) by Victoria's Department of Sustainability and Environment (DSE), approving nineteen months of continuous killing and accounting for the death of between 36, 000-40,000 healthy adult kangaroos. Mother kangaroos with in-pouch and at-heel young were gunned down in thousands their joeys clubbed to death. (Sarah Hudson Joeys decapitated in cull: Painful death from clubbing, Herald Sun June 18 2002).

The financial cost to taxpayers, estimated at the end of the first year of killing, was $1.8 million "equivalent to $120 a head". (Fia Cumming, $1.8m to shoot Army base kangaroos, Sun Herald October 6 2002).By the end of 2003 the cost, in dollars, must have topped $5m. No public consultation took place.

No Environmental Management Plan was produced by Defence in order to identify long term management strategies for PMA's wildlife or indicate whether any non-lethal management strategies had been put in place to resolve the perceived 'kangaroo problem' prior to the onset of the massacre. Nor is there evidence to suggest that DSE sought an Environmental Management Plan from Defence even though a failure to do so contravenes conditions for activating authority to destroy wildlife that, under the provisions of the *Wildlife Act* 1975, states: *"the destruction of wildlife should be used only to reinforce other, non-lethal means"*.

Why did the PMA kangaroo massacre take place?

Ostensibly, and with the collusion of the RSPCA, Defence's stated reason was 'roo starvation'. At first, by means of a massive public relations exercise, the community was hoodwinked into accepting that this was going to be a regrettable but necessary exercise in the interests of animal welfare. It wasn't long however before the truth of the statement that "you can fool all of the people (only) some of the time" became manifest. Questions began to emerge. Why were so many apparently healthy animals being sacrificed? As it is well known that kangaroos do not produce

Juvenile mortality (especially around weaning) is high when eastern grey kangaroo populations are under food limitation. (Photo: Jan Aldenhoven)

young until food sources are available, if the Kangaroos at PMA were indeed starving how was it that joey numbers were so high ?

If Defence, DSE and the RSPCA were truly motivated by animal welfare concerns how could the cruel treatment of joeys have been acknowledged but not prevented? Above all, if the PMA kangaroo massacre was indeed motivated by animal welfare concerns why the immense pressure on the Victorian Government from farmers and representatives from the Kangaroo Industry Association of Australia, the Army and various Members of Parliament to commercialise the PMA kangaroo slaughter?

The RSPCA's executive officer, Richard Hunter, did state that the preferred method of joey destruction by 'decapitation or a blow to the head did not guarantee a quick death' (**Herald Sun** 18/6/2002). However, with its customary toothless tiger responses to animal cruelty, RSPCA failed to protect the joeys from clubbing or affirm humane alternatives such as the removal of orphans to the care of wildlife carers for rearing and relocation or, at the very least, insist on veterinary attendance at PMA to perform euthanasia by lethal injection on site.

Commercial pressure

The greatest imperative driving the PMA kangaroo massacre appeared to be to demonstrate commercial viability: to kill as many kangaroos as efficiently as possible over a sustained period of time, using teams of commercial shooters, in order to demonstrate to the State Government that a kangaroo industry in Victoria, being the last stronghold of resistance to the commercial utilization of our national icon, was both feasible in practice and commercially viable

The pressure was on from the start. Documents obtained through FOI included an undated letter from Sharman Stone, Federal Member for Murray and then Parliamentary Secretary for the Environment and Heritage, addressed to Premier Steve Bracks (received September 6 2002) noting that the "culling of kangaroos from Puckapunyal was at a considerable cost to the Defence force" and urging the Premier to consider the financial benefits "if these animals had been processed at a knackery for pet food, other by-products and leather".

It is to the Victorian Government's credit that it did not venture down the commercial path on this occasion and hopefully will not do so in the future.

Commercial enterprise at PMA was not without historical precedent. Previously Defence had used the PMA site for commercial ventures involving cattle and sheep -a factor that explains the environmental degradation at PMA for which the kangaroos are blamed as well as the over-abundant presence of phallaris grass one "of these non-preferred grasses" found to be "toxic to kangaroos and subsequently caused them to become distressed." (Puckapunyal Environmental Management Plan 2002 Update-Summary Of Kangaroo Management Strategies)

Current situation

Kangaroos are hardly to be seen at PMA these days; other than that, nothing much has altered. The sacrifice of so many has yet to guarantee a safe future for the few remaining kangaroos.

Towards the end of 2002, well after the kangaroo killing at PMA was firmly established, public outcry forced Defence to address the lack of an Environmental Management Plan. The result was in the form of the already-cited Summary of Kangaroo Management Strategies that appeared on the Defence website (http:// www.defence.gov.au).

Minimal as it was, the content of the Summary made it abundantly clear that as far as Defence was concerned the kangaroos at PMA were being slaughtered because they were in the way: "The maximum long-term population density will never be permitted to exceed 0.9 animals per hectare. It is likely that for range conditions in 2002/03, the optimal kangaroo density that will *enable the sustainable management of the PMA to support ADF training will be significantly lower than this number."*

Further, the starvation myth was finally put to rest, having outserved it's usefulness, by Defence's admission that: *"The animals themselves were suffering because the unnaturally high population could not be sustained by the food resources available on the PMA. Kangaroos had eaten all preferred grasses and were subsequently turning to non-preferred food sources"* Hardly reason for a massacre. When survival is at stake, a kangaroo would surely find a non-preferred food source more preferable than death by firing squad!

For the kangaroos that survived... the guns didn't finish them but the 'death trap' fences will.

The PMA is entirely surrounded by electrified and barbed wire "sheep" fencing that neither keeps kangaroos in nor people out. Both rows of fencing are low enough to tempt kangaroos to jump them. Some manage; others are caught by their back legs and end their days as "fence hangers". Kangaroos, sometimes with dead joeys still visible in their pouches, endure unacceptable levels of suffering as they writhe and die slowly over a period of days, their struggle to escape only wrapping the wire tighter around their ankles and feet, cutting through the flesh to the bone. After the guns fell silent it became clear that the suffering of "fence hangers" remains a permanent and chronic cruelty at PMA, a visible testimony to Defence's mismanagement of the site and indifference to the fate of its resident fauna..

Kangaroo mortality through entanglement in fences. (Photo: Pam Ahearn)

Conclusion

Non-lethal wildlife management options represent realistic, humane and long-term solutions at PMA. Such options include:

Interconnecting wildlife corridors leading into surrounding Crown Land at Greytown and adjoining areas would prevent the implosive population expansion of wildlife currently contained by perimeter fencing and provide access to additional food sources that have not yet been degraded by army manouvres and poor management practices.

The immediate replacement of Puckapunyal's "killer fences" by non-electrified kangaroo-proof fencing, high enough to deter the resident kangaroos from jumping onto main roads and surrounding farmland. Kangaroo-proof fencing would provide effective, humane and non-lethal containment to complement the free movement facilitated by interconnecting corridors. It could also be safely erected around the residential area within the PMA to alleviate anxiety amongst residents about kangaroo proximity to housing.

Ultimately, Defence must implement strategies consistent with its responsibilities as custodian of designated Land for Wildlife at PMA. A Land for Wildlife Agreement was signed off by a Defence representative at PMA on 16 July 1996 and ratified by Regional Manager of Land for Wildlife on 26 July 1996 PMA's Land for Wildlife status entails making" a reasonable effort on that land to pursue the maintenance and enhancement of native flora and fauna and/or to integrate nature conservation with other land management objectives."

As things stand the cycle of kangaroo population explosion and massacre is destined to be repeated at PMA. It is clear from the terms of reference and limited objectives informing Defence's Kangaroo Management Summary that the idea of non-lethal long-term management strategies has not entered the discourse about kangaroo management.

Post Script

On the basis of legal advice provided *probono* by Peter Seidel of Melbourne legal firm Arnold Bloch Liebler through Victoria's Public Interest Law Clearing House three wildlife protective organizations - *the Australian Wildlife Protection Council, the Wildlife Protection Association of Australia and Animal Active: The Australian Animal Rights Network* - have initiated a formal Application for Review of DSE's role in the destruction of PMA's kangaroos. The Application for Review, addressed to Professor Lindsay Nielson, Secretary Department of Sustainability and Environment, argues that the granting of the 2002-2003 destruction permits by DSE and their activation by Defence at PMA contravenes (a) the Conditions of Authority (b) the *Wildlife Act 1975* (Vic) and (c) the *Prevention of Cruelty to Animals Act 1998* (Vic). To date the Application for Review has not yielded a response from DSE.

Reproductive success in eastern grey kangaroos is high with a short green grazing lawn. These are of high quality and often floristically diverse and not indicative of 'over' grazing. (Photo: Jan Alderhoven)

AND WE CALL OURSELVES CIVILISED ?

By Pat O'Brien

Co-ordinator for the National Kangaroo Coalition Organisation

We all know that land degradation and salinity are two of the biggest environmental problems that Australia faces. What can we do about it? Plant trees? Promote Landcare? In Australia, we clear many times more trees than we plant. So that's not the answer, and a study has shown that a decade of Landcare - which has spanned three Federal governments and cost taxpayers hundreds of millions of dollars - has failed to make farmers any greener. The University of New England study found farmers who were members of Landcare had no greater increase in pro-environmental attitudes than those outside the program between 1991 and 2000.

So what about getting rid of the hard hoofed animals that do so much damage to the soil, and farming or harvesting kangaroos instead? Some people think that's a good idea, but is it? There is plenty of information now to show that the hoary old fairy tale about replacing hard hoofed animals, with soft hoofed animals like kangaroos, is just that, nothing but a fairy tale. In fact, it is a theory that is used by some people to avoid facing up to the seemingly insurmountable problems of land degradation. "If we only farmed kangaroos instead of cattle and sheep, everything will be all right!" But in reality this theory is more full of holes than a kangaroo painted on a road sign.

One academic dreamer, Gordon Grigg, has campaigned for years to have his 'sheep replacement therapy' implemented by farmers, and thus all rural environmental problems would be solved! One of the problems with this fairy tale is that our overseas markets want wool and sheep meat, not kangaroo fur and roo meat, and it fails to explain what we would replace our billion dollar wool clip with.

The reality is that our export markets demand beef and sheep meat, not roo meat, and if we didn't supply it, Argentina, the US, or someone else would. The economics also don't add up. It can take 12 years or so for a kangaroo to become full grown and then it produces only 10 kg or so of useable meat, worth at most only a couple of dollars per kilogram. A bullock at only two years of age produces 200kg or so of useable meat worth $8 or more per kg, while a lamb produces 20 or so kg of useable meat at 3 to 6 months.

It's not hard-hoofed animals 'per se' on our fragile soils that cause land degradation; it's too many hard-hoofed animals on too much marginal land. There are quite a few Australian farmers who manage their farms intelligently, do not overgraze, do not clear fell, who plant trees, allow some regrowth, use cell grazing and water retention techniques, diversify, fence adequately, and who don't kill the wildlife. These blokes don't have land degradation problems, and they are doing quite nicely thank you.

The 1998 Executive Summary of the Inquiry into Commercial Use of Wildlife and Chaired by Former Senator Woodley proposed 'trial' wildlife farms in the rangelands, supporting the view that the Government should examine the South African model, where ownership of wildlife is transferred to local land owners. They recommended that State and Federal Governments together review all administrative procedures relating to commercial utilisation of wildlife in Australia, in order to increase their efficiency so as to ensure that there are no unnecessary hindrances to Industry.

Killed Kangaroo Meat as a "kangaroo management option"

Early in 1990, a campaign was undertaken without a public process to encourage the human consumption of paddock killed kangaroo meat as a "kangaroo management option".
The campaign even went to the extent of surreptitiously changing legislation to allow the kangaroo meat to be sold in butcher shops and delicatessens. The known risk to human health from kangaroo meat was ignored and industry proponents went to great lengths to try to justify the human consumption of native animal meat. Even the Heart Foundation, who should have known better, came on board and recommended kangaroo meat as a "lean healthy product".
Kangaroo meat was classified as 'game meat', along with wild pig, so both could escape the rigorous inspection programs currently in place in export meatworks.

In 1988 the Commonwealth celebrated 200 years of settlement by serving kangaroo meat in Parliament House Canberra, ACT, the nations' capital.

In 1989, Dr Gerry Maynes, from Environment Australia, who was attending a Game Meat Working Party, sanctioned the use of 'protected wildlife' (kangaroos) for human consumption. No animal welfare or wildlife protection organizations were represented, only the kangaroo industry, government bureaucrats and vested interests. Kangaroos were classified as 'game meat' because they could not meet the strict hygiene standards of domestic animals killed in an abattoir, and the double standards for kangaroo meat was then established. Then in 1992 the NSW Parliament passed a law by ONE vote from the Reverend Fred Nile making kangaroo meat legal and it remains on the NSW Parliamentary Dining Room menu.

There are double standards under which kangaroo meat is obtained as compared to the strict and extensive hygiene, health standards and regulations for domestic meats. Australia has rigid and expensive export standards HACCP (Hazards Analysis at Critical Control Point) and meat hygiene standards (via ANZFA) for the processing of domestic stock. The World Trade Organisation (WTO) rules relating to international trade in meat products, has considerable inconsistency in the application and the level of these standards as applied to domestic animal-derived meat industries (beef, sheep meats, pork) and those applied to 'game' meat products such as kangaroo.

According to Des Sibraa, a lawyer and former NSW chief food inspector, the biggest problem with kangaroo meat is that "there is no ante mortem inspection so the kangaroo is not inspected for disease before death, which is a legal requirement in countries like Canada that do not import kangaroo meat".

Thus as Mr Sibraa further states. "What meat inspectors can't pick up, because they do not look at the animal before it is killed, is whether the kangaroo was suffering from disease."

AQIS Inspector Slams Macro Meats for breaches of hygiene standards

Contrary views to the quality of kangaroo products, and the sustainability of the industry have been expressed. For example, in the 5 November 1998 Minutes of the South Australian Kangaroo Management Program Public Meeting, Eddie Andreissen, a Meat Inspector for the Australian Quarantine Inspection Service (AQIS) reported "My primary responsibility is ensuring that export requirements are met....I have been in the field over the last few days looking at field operations and field chillers to see if there has been any improvement in two years. We've compared them against the Australian Standard and mainly looked at Macro Meat's chiller boxes but also a few other processors." Andreissen concluded:

- there is not a single chiller box that is clean, with most being unclean or uncleanable.
- a big incidence of fly-struck meat is going down to Adelaide,
- airflow floors are not being cleaned thoroughly
- and there's still congealed blood and muck,
- most of the dirty water is washed out from the front with the bones, instead of being plumbed to a drain,
- no connection to potable water, only one chiller box had chemicals for cleaning,
- there were still kangaroo feet in the surrounds from two years ago.

It is a myth to say that meat hygiene standards are adequate

There are several basic requirements which always must be carried out in order to ensure that meat is safe. Simplified, these are: independent ante-mortem inspection to ensure animals are not carrying a disease process which may render meat unsafe; strict hygiene during the slaughtering process which guarantees freedom from airborne contamination; an impervious killing floor; adequate supplies of potable water; provision for ablution on the part of the slaughtering person. None of these standards are met in bush killed kangaroos.

Ante-mortem inspection is 'carried out' by the shooter himself, the slaughtering process is done on the ground in the dust cloud that surrounds all vehicles in the bush. The slaughtering vehicle carries only 20 litres of water for the washing down of 20 or more kangaroos carcases, and shooters urinate and defecate in the bush. The acceptance of these standards by the authorities could only occur if there is corruption in the system. If people wish to eat kangaroo meat, that is their decision, but they are entitled to know that it is obtained under conditions which would never be accepted for meat from domestic animals. And the excuse that kangaroos do not carry the disease organisms carried by domestic animals is pure humbug. "All meat is capable of spreading the principal food poisoning organisms" according to Dr John Auty, Veterinarian and Historian

As a former butcher and meatworker, I can tell you that kangaroo shooters are not competent to judge disease in animals. AQIS inspectors inspect kangaroos only after they are transported to coastal or distant boning establishments i.e. after they have been eviscerated in the field. Such meat hygiene standards are not acceptable for domestic animals, nor should they be. Whereas the diseases that affect domestic animals are well understood and form the scientific basis for modern hygiene, the diseases affecting kangaroos are virtually unknown and there are virtually no veterinarians based in the areas in which kangaroos are shot.

In spite of this taxpayer funded campaign to put paddock-killed kangaroo meat on our tables, and considerable propaganda to make the killing of kangaroos appear to the public to be a necessary farm management practice, most Australians show little enthusiasm for wildlife meats. Few butcher shops will undertake the health risks of handling the meat, and few Australians will eat it.

Overall the kangaroo meat regulations have been so spectacularly unsuccessful that for at least a year, kangaroo meat from blinded, virus stricken kangaroos was sold for human consumption, including export, in at least three states. A number of cases of toxoplasmosis from kangaroo meat occurred, including a child born blind in Queensland because the mother contracted toxoplasmosis from under-cooked kangaroo meat consumed in a restaurant.

After these incidents the kangaroo Industry went into damage control, pointing out that cats carry toxoplasmosis too. Well, sure they do, but we don't eat cats!

then progressively declined, as kangaroo populations dropped, to 3.9 million in 2005. They allow 14% of grey kangaroos and 20% of red kangaroos to be killed, claiming this to be a sustainable figure. However, even under Courtroom cross-examination, no scientist, and no-one from the government, can explain how they arrived at this estimation. Nor could anyone explain how illegal kills and road kills are taken into account when setting a quota.

We believe that the whole quota process is calculated on several errors. One, that kangaroos have increased in numbers since white settlement, another that dingoes and Aboriginals were substantial predators of kangaroos, that kangaroos are major competitors for grazing and cropping; and that commercial killing reduces kangaroo numbers.

Nobody knows for sure how many kangaroos were here before European settlement, but there are many references in early writings from settlers and explorer, to show that large kangaroos were widespread and abundant over the whole of Australia including Tasmania. Models based on the available grazing resources and livestock numbers in 1890 have shown that Australia was capable of sustaining over 400 million large kangaroos pre-European settlement (Auty 2004 reprinted in this volume). Environment Australia currently estimates red and grey kangaroo populations at between 20 and 30 million, although drought is believed to have reduced that number.

Another misleading statement is the one about having more waterholes now than in 1860. Yes, there are certainly plenty of farm dams, but most have been dry or half dry for years, and are full of mud, silt, and cow manure. Many farm dams are salty, as are many bore drains. The clean flowing creeks, so abundant in the days of early settlement, and filled by regular rain, have mostly gone. Many of them have been ploughed under and planted with crops, or eroded away because the streamside vegetation is gone. Most of the abundant pre-European freshwater lagoons have been turned into smelly cattle grazing factories. If there is more surface water available for kangaroos now than in 1860, and that's unlikely, it's mostly salty, muddy, and polluted with cow manure and farm chemical residues.

Dingoes are usually solitary hunters, incapable of pulling down a large healthy kangaroo. Historical record shows that Aboriginal hunting of kangaroos, when successful, gave status and was not a common practice when other more easily gathered protein was available.

Several accepted scientific studies show that, except on marginal land, or in extreme drought situations, kangaroos are not significant competitors to cropping and grazing.

When a commercial shooter takes out the mob patriarchs and matriarchs - the largest animals, the younger and more fecund animals escalate their breeding activities. Many graziers will not allow commercial culling on their properties for this reason. Many experts have also expressed concern about the loss of genetic strength after decades of shooting the largest animals.

In the last 10 years we have commercially "harvested" countless millions of kangaroos, yet we now have more beef cattle than ever, 29 million in fact, with beef production jumping 28% in 2004. Lamb and mutton production at the time of writing is almost at an all time high. Killing all those kangaroos didn't reduce sheep and cattle numbers at all, nor do anything to resolve land degradation. It did however, put considerable stress on kangaroo populations. Recent credible research shows that the average age of red kangaroos commercially killed in NSW is only two, (they can live to 30 years old) and the average weight is only 18kg. It's not surprising that very few non-government conservation organisations in Australia have a policy of support for the commercial consumptive use of kangaroos.

The same arguments that we now hear to support the kangaroo Industry, are the same ones that were used to support whaling. Jobs and export dollars, and there are plenty of whales left. Well, the lost jobs in whaling were quadrupled many times by whale watching tourism, as were the export dollars, and some species of whales, even 40 years later, may not recover from the slaughter.

Targets of the commercial kangaroo industry are individuals like this large male and female western grey kangaroo. The joey in the pouch is bashed on the head.

The same thing could happen with kangaroos, particularly the reds. When the commercial kangaroo kill is finally ended, the few jobs and the truthfully told amount of export dollars lost, will be many times taken up by tourism opportunities to view large mobs of kangaroos in their natural environment.

There is no independent evidence that any wildlife harvesting, anywhere in the world is sustainable. The biggest problem with the "sustainable use" theory is that there is no such thing. Eventually you run out of animals to use, because when money and jobs are involved in exploiting Nature, a driverless juggernaut is created which is almost impossible to stop. There are many examples.

According to the Federal government, tourism consumption in Australia totals between $50 and $60 billion dollars annually. The Australian Tourism Industry employs over 1/2 million people, more than 6% of Australia's workforce. The subsidized kangaroo Industry claims to be worth 200 million dollars, in reality probably very much less, and employs a few hundred mostly part-time workers.

Studies have shown that viewing large mobs of kangaroos and associated wildlife would be a world-class tourism experience, greatly enhancing the outback tourism adventure for overseas visitors (Higginbottom *et al*. 2004). And yet we shoot them, kill their babies in a very cruel manner, put them in cartons, and send them overseas to feed prisoners in third world jails.

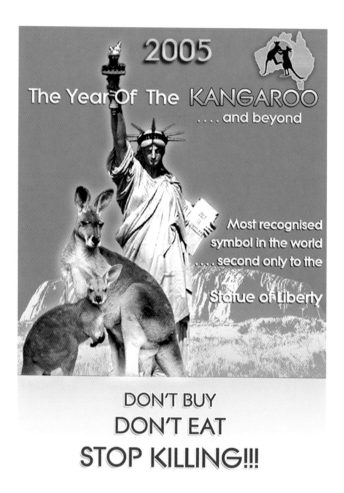

Kangaroos - Tourist icons
(Artwork - Deb Barnden - AWPC webmaster. www.awpc.org,au)

IS SCIENCE THE SEARCH

FOR OBJECTIVE TRUTH OR HAS IT SIMPLY BECOME A SEARCH FOR DATA THAT CAN BE MOULDED TO MEET PREFERRED CONCLUSIONS?

By Mary Lander

(Mary Lander is one of a growing number of Australians who are becoming increasingly concerned about the plight of our kangaroos and focuses here on the level of bias we can expect from scientists who are paid to promote their exploitation, through joint partnership arrangements between government and industry.)

We are indoctrinated at an early age, to exempt science from criticism and treat it with a degree of reverence and are taught that science is that which is proven and cannot be disputed. However, has 'the integrity of scientific research' become corrupt as a direct result of an increasing expectation by government, that scientific research is funded or at least partly funded, by the same commercial organisations that have a vested financial interest in outcomes? The influence that scientists have over public perceptions can so be easily be exploited for this purpose. Consequently, it is increasingly being used as a tool by commercial organisations for the purpose of endorsing their strategies and promoting their products.

The expression 'conflicts of interest' used in an ethical sense refers to conflicting obligations or influences confronting an individual in the course of a relationship or activity that has some moral content. Central to the issue of 'conflict of interest' is an ethical dimension, particularly when the conduct of such scientists suggests that their judgement may be affected by the financial interests of the organisations they are affiliated with which, in turn, leave their motives open to question.

At face value, it would seem quite reasonable to expect those who benefit most from research work should fund it or at least make a significant contribution towards its funding. However, in the interest of ensuring research organisations and the scientists they employ, represent themselves honestly and ethically in the course of their work, either directly to the public through media statements and articles, via publications they produce and make publicly available or in the course of their participation in public forums, it would then also be reasonable to expect they make it known they have an affiliation or connection with an industry organisation or group who have a vested financial interest in outcomes. It should be imperative that the views that they express are considered in this context.

Certainly, in the case of research organisations such as the Commonwealth Scientific and Industrial Research Organisation (CSIRO) and the Rural Industries Research and Development Corporation

(RIRDC) for whom the Commonwealth Government have overarching responsibilities and accountabilities, this should be a mandatory requirement.

As the CSIRO has been under increasing pressure over the years to source its funding from industry and become less reliant on government for this purpose it would be naïve to assume that the CSIRO remains an independent research organisation in terms of the scientific opinions they promulgate. It would also be naïve to assume that the commercial interests that provide funding to the CSIRO would not seek to obtain some form of benefit, either tangible or intangible, in return for the funding that they provide.

As scientists do not have a monopoly on the right to analyse data and draw conclusions by way of engaging rational thought processes, I take the liberty of examining and analysing the data tabled herewith, demonstrating how scientists in the CSIRO are removed from vested commercial interests. Nor are they the independent research organisations that they are publicly perceived as being, as a result.

The Kangaroo Industry Association (KIAA), for example, is an industry group that is promoted by the Rural Industries Research Development Corporation (RIRDC), which in turn, has a working partnership arrangement with the CSIRO. The RIRDC provide the CSIRO with funding for research into areas such as the development of various forms of leather (textiles) that can be produced from kangaroo skins. The RIRDC also provide extensive support to the KIAA for the purpose of 'promoting' the use of a range of kangaroo products and assist them in developing markets in the manufacturing industries both in Australia and overseas.

The extent to which the CSIRO scientists promulgate views that support the 'interests of the industry' became evident to me during the course of

Eastern grey at the Googong Dam site. (Photo: Bill Corn)

a protest against a kangaroo cull at Googong Dam (on land managed jointly between ACT and NSW governments).

By way of background, the cull was initiated by the ACT Chief Minister, Mr John Stanhope and the statement he made publicly, for the purpose of 'justifying' the cull, was that "the kangaroos posed a threat of contamination to Canberra's water supply". Animal welfare protests groups challenged him on this and demanded that he produce the evidence to support his claim. Rather than produce this evidence he became indignant about the fact that he had been challenged and even went so far as to call in the NSW police to 'control the protestors' and allow the commercial shooters access to the area to slaughter the kangaroos gathered near the Dam. Somewhere between 800-1000 kangaroos were slaughtered and we are told their joeys were 'humanely' disposed of by having their heads 'bashed' against the side of trucks, as is the 'acceptable' current practice.

During the protest action there was considerable media interest. What intrigued me was the fact that the CSIRO became involved, making a public statement about the matter, which was clearly between the ACT government and animal welfare protestors. Yet Dr Fruedenberger from CSIRO's Sustainable Ecosystems Division made the following official public comment, to support the decision made by the ACT government:
"Shooters will kill about 800 kangaroos over the next month because of concerns that excessive grazing is compromising the quality of water in the dam." (see www.abc.net.au/act/news/200407s1156067.htm accessed 1/8/04).

Information from ACTEW (responsible for water testing) reveals:
• "The conditions in Googong reservoir are within the normal range for that time of year".
• "The treatment processes at Googong are capable of treating water from the reservoir to meet the requirements of the Australian Drinking Water Quality Guidelines (1996) and the ACT Drinking Water Quality Code of Practice (2000) issued by the ACT Department of Health."

Naturally, I then became curious as to why a CSIRO scientist would support an ACT government official who had made false claims about compromised water quality, given the absence of any scientific evidence to support that claim. Is it acceptable practice for scientists from the CSIRO to promulgate false claims, in the absence of scientific evidence and to do so, on behalf of the CSIRO?

The KIAA website features several articles from Dr Fruedenberger including one titled: "Step up roo cull, urges top scientist". As the KIAA has a direct financial interest in the commercial kangaroo industry there would be no doubt that they would think of him as a 'top' scientist given his efforts to 'promote' the industry, putting considerable sums of money into their coffers.

The affiliation between the CSIRO and the KIAA has been strong for many years. The CSIRO even actively promoted the industry going so far as to encourage Australians to replace their traditional Christmas dinner with kangaroo instead. A CSIRO Media Release (94/142) dated

14 December 1994 and titled 'A Kangaroo Christmas' states:
"This Christmas, Australians could enjoy a real Australian Christmas dinner and contribute to improved land management at the same time. That's according to CSIRO Division of Wildlife and Ecology rangelands scientist, Dr David Freudenberger who is a keen kangaroo consumer and will be putting his kangaroo where his mouth is this festive season.."

To suggest that kangaroo meat is 'as safe for human consumption' as meat from farmed animals is absolutely ludicrous and I would certainly recommend that people read articles such as those at http://www.awpc.org.au/kangaroos/book_files/diseases.htm before contemplating putting kangaroo on their menu.

While the Commonwealth Government feels it is both a CSIRO and RIRDC role to actively 'promote' the industry, at the November 1998 Meeting of the NSW NPWS Kangaroo Management Advisory Committee, the NSW Farmers' nomination of Freudenberger was apparently rejected by the NPWS Chairman because he said that "Freudenberger was too pro-kangaroo industry". Questions about the level of his 'independence' in his capacity as a scientist representing the CSIRO still remain.

The RIRDC are also key players in promoting kangaroo products, including meat, to potential overseas markets. They produce reports used for this purpose which are 'endorsed by the Commonwealth Government'. Such reports can be easily recognised as they carry the Commonwealth Government Coat of Arms on the front. One such report, is titled **'Selling the kangaroo industry to the world'.** The government commissioned an 'independent consultant' by the name of John Kelly from Lenah Consultancy to produce this report (Kelly 2003), paid for by your tax dollars. The same John Kelly who is the proprietor of a Tasmanian company called Lenah Game Meats Pty Ltd has a vested interest in this company.

A better image of Australia than a supplier of cheap red meat: a beautiful male red kangaroo.
(Photo: Ulrike Kloeker)

The report contains substantial information sourced from the KIAA and also makes some very disparaging remarks about animal welfare and wildlife protection groups. Perhaps John Kelly fears these nasty animal welfare groups pose a possible threat to the 'poor helpless powerful government and commercial interests' who have a vested financial interest in the commercialisation of kangaroo products?

PARADISE SHATTERED

By Peta Rakela

It's a lovely day sitting on my verandah with the birds flying overhead; a great sense of peace and harmony exists. These types of days are not frequent enough. Nightmares are a story too. I've come to dread the nights, waiting for the guns to go off as more and more kangaroos are exterminated, and of course all the non-target species sorely affected as well.

We knew it was time to move, not enough room to rehabilitate the wildlife in our care. We found our plot of 'paradise' in the West Australian Chittering Valley. The Brockman River lined with gum trees running through undulating land and a generous dam, all backing onto a 320 acre bush block adjacent to the Julimar Forest. A superb wildlife corridor. Utopia! Little did I know that inconsolable grief would consume me and my dream of a wildlife paradise would be shattered.

Coming from the suburbs, I was naïve enough to think that wildlife demise was basically due to unfortunate acts of nature; not habitat destruction, poisoning, fire, starvation, thirst, fencing, trapping, pollution, road kill and numerous other ignorant or deliberate acts of cruelty by fellow human beings.

We revelled in our naivety and good fortune. The resident wildlife knew our motives. They told others. Our 'flock' grew. We were blessed, they trusted us. The dam, river and our planting of many trees saw to it that bird species of all shapes and sizes visited, many deciding to stay. What great joy to be lying in bed, listening to the nocturnal munchings of possums, kangaroos and others. To look out a window and see 'in pouch joeys' grazing away with Mum, ever vigilant, but sensing that this was about as safe as things got. Words can not express our delight. Our value system changed. We became 'connected' to Mother Earth, to all the creatures. The great 'at one-ness'.

But nothing lasts forever, so it seems. I would find dead birds, often close to each other, as if they had dropped out of the sky. I started to find dead kangaroos. Not a lot, but enough to take notice. Occasionally I would find the body of a dependant joey near the house. No marks or visible wounds. I suspected poisoning, with the birds. The 'roo' was a mystery. I started to think seriously then about the noises in the night. There had been shooting. We were told that there was a problem with feral pigs in the National Park. We had had a 'shooter' wander onto our property looking for his "lost" dogs. We had also had a visit from the regional Conservation and Land Management (CALM) officer informing us that permission had been given for a neighbour to shoot the occasional 'blind kangaroo'. Both claims had some legitimacy but there seemed too much shooting, I sensed something was wrong.

We realised that we were living in KILL WILDLIFE COUNTRY where wildlife is given pest/ vermin status and treated accordingly. With scant regard for wildlife species the adage "if it moves, shoot it" is almost rule of thumb in West Australia. Life here is all too often hell for us, and more importantly, hell for the wildlife. Try eating your evening meal, listening to gun blasts exploding the night air, knowing that some innocent creature has just had it's last feed. Try lying in bed, your gut in a knot, sobbing hysterically, your heart breaking hearing some sick bastard out there "getting it off " shooting yet more innocent creatures. Try waking up, your body trembling in fear, wanting to vomit, because some cretins with no respect for anyone or anything, are a law unto themselves are out there, in the middle of the night, in the darkness, murdering.

And try, when enough is enough, confronting these "low life's of the night", tooting your horn, flashing lights, yelling and screaming with all your might, only to find in the morning your gate blocked with the bullet ridden body of a kangaroo mum, no joey in sight, her head removed and conveniently placed in some sort of satanic gesture, an unwritten message sent to invoke fear. This is not just my story, it is the story of many. Those of us who dare to challenge. And so we weep. And we know that the measure of mankind's humanity is by the way we treat animals, and we know humanity is lost.

Local response to an attempt to create a wildlife protection zone. (Photo: Peta Rakela)

Calls to the authorities achieve little. Too much crime, too few police. Conservation and Land Management not worth the bother. Not a priority. Visits to our politicians elicit standard responses, letters of appeal or objection fobbed off with equal dismissive-ness.
And you wonder if there is anyone out there that cares?

And what of our health?

A recent article I read, likened dangerous stress to that which you felt when driving a car, a truck appears to be heading towards you and your subsequent reaction. The stress I feel every time I hear a gun blast is likened to a train heading towards me. My head thumps so hard I feel it will blow up, my heart races and pounds, my mouth dries, my hands and body shake, I can't think straight. Can you imagine how actual victims feel? Although not a "medico" by profession, I know that I am suffering physically. You don't need to be the "psychoanalyst" Freud to know that emotionally, psychologically and spiritually the suffering is also great.

I am no longer willing just to hope this living nightmare will go away.

Bad enough to be the perpetrator, bad enough to be the victim, but far worse to be the bystander. And so I try to be the difference, to be the change. This too, at a cost to my well being.

I network with many people involved with wildlife. What an almighty task trying to get them involved in direct action. The amount of people who say, "Look Peta, I just don't want to know - if I did I would not sleep at night." So their shutters go down, refusing to see or acknowledge. History repeats itself, over and over, just different species.

I do understand what they are saying. But there are many people like me, who are in great pain, the "connected ones", who know the animals suffer, who live daily with the knowledge that the environment and wildlife are innocent victims of a society without mercy. As fellow human beings, we all have allowed this to happen.

In "A Voice for Wildlife" the Australian Wildlife Protection Council newsletter, I recall this tribute: "Hans Fischinger leaves a legacy for reform but it is tragic that his struggle cost him is life". How many times have I heard or read similar sentiments, especially in relation to Animal Rights and Environmental activists.

A neighbour recently commented that her husband now understood why I behaved so ".....". She wouldn't finish the sentence for fear of offending me, but I'm guessing the word "crazy" might be close to the mark. Their dream purchase of 69 acres has also become a KILL WILDLIFE COUNTRY nightmare, compliments of their neighbour. They too, now know and share the pain. Another "newcomer" to the area, who came to "live with the wildlife', has kids who hide inside trembling, as the gun blasts echo through the dusk . He wanted his kids to have some "clean country living"... some welcome to "Kill Country", kids! an opportunity to see the wildlife perish before your very eyes! They can perhaps tell their grandchildren they actually saw real kangaroos once.

If we could put all this pain together, imagine the stockpile? So instead of spending lost agonising hours trying to get people on board, let's get together now... all of us who know, who care, who suffer, who weep. We live in a society where litigation is second nature. We live in a society where the almighty dollar is God, taking precedence over everything. Is it possible that we are missing a direct hit here? What about a legal Class Action? It is an idea that would require a lot of research. We could place advertisements in newspapers, on computers, in magazines and journals. We need to tell the world about what is happening in West Australia, throughout all of Australia, and that we too, are victims, that we are suffering, that we are affected, and that we too have rights.

Why should others be able to destroy all that we find fundamental to our existence, well being and happiness? Why should we have to suffer? Why should we be deprived ? Why should we be in misery? We can make a difference, we are the difference. My personal experience pulled up the shutters, and opened my heart, Maryland Wilson's brilliant book "The Kangaroo Betrayed" opened my eyes and gave me the knowledge and inspiration. The journey I have embarked upon has been one of great pain and sorrow, yet full of immense spiritual awakening and I deeply regret now, that it took so long to happen.

How enlightening it is to know your purpose, on a mission, filled with this purpose, being the difference.

I lie in bed, savouring the nocturnal munching sounds and delight in the knowledge that I am not a perpetrator or bystander and I choose not to be a victim anymore. The wildlife know this too.

We are "at one-ness".

Western grey kangaroo - target of the night killers.

KANGAROO KILLING

FOR THE FLESH AND SKIN TRADE:

NEITHER CLEAN & GREEN, NOR SUSTAINABLE

By Rheya Linden

Department of Political Science University of Melbourne & Campaign Director
Animal Active: The Australian Animal Rights Network

Introduction: If abattoirs had glass walls we would all be vegetarians...
Likewise, if we could all witness the reality of the so-called 'sustainable
harvest of kangaroos' and describe the process accurately, the task of
generating a global boycott of kangaroo products, and the consequent
demise of the commercial industry, would be achievable.

Juliet Gellatley describes, in language that does not mystify, an episode from undercover video
footage of commercial kangaroo killing that depicts the 'harvest' of a mother kangaroo:
A man takes aim, supposedly to shoot her in the head but blows a hole in her neck. She falls...
helpless to save her joey who retreats into her pouch. But there is no escape. The hunter pulls
the joey out of his mother's blood-spattered body, tosses him to the ground and stamps on his
head...The shot mother does not die instantly. She struggles as the hunter slits her leg open,
thrusts a hook through it and hangs her upside down on a truck. She is knifed, gutted, her head,
tail and legs tossed aside."

In the words of Carol Adams the mother kangaroo described above is not only shot but also
subjected to "the knife, real or metaphorical" as the chosen implement of "the aggressor seeking
to control/consume/defile the body of the victim". The process of her transformation from subject
to object is complete. She has been rendered as "take', as a mere statistic of the Australian
kangaroo meat and leather industry that reduces millions of kangaroos annually from the status
of unique and protected native animals to commercial products, and cruelly dismisses their
young to worthless by-products.

Through butchering animals become absent referents...without animals
there would be no meat eating yet they are absent from the act of eating
meat because they have been transformed into food

Through the device of 'the absent referent', even the environmentally-aware have been coerced
into accepting the "clean, green meat" label by which kangaroo products are successfully
marketed. It is a distancing device by which the public are immured from the unpleasant and, as
with any form of advertising, encouraged to accept, even relish, the emotionally unacceptable.
Adam's argues that our culture teaches children to consume meat by introducing

discontinuity between the component parts of the process from living animal to 'lamb chop', 'drumstick', 'steak' and so on.

In examining the reactions of children to the literal truth about meat eating, we can see how our language is a distancing device from these literal truths. Children, fresh observers of the dominant culture, raise issues about meat eating using a literal viewpoint.

By examining the "bare bones", as it were, of outback kangaroo killing we find nothing in the nature of the emergent commercial kangaroo industry that is either 'clean or green' or 'sustainable'. However, through the device of 'the absent referent', even the environmentally - aware have been coerced into accepting the "clean, green meat" label by which kangaroo products are successfully marketed. Let's examine the myth of 'sustainable harvesting' against...

Some facts about the commercial killing of kangaroos

- The commercial slaughter of kangaroos for meat and skins that takes place in the four largest states (Queensland, NSW, South Australia and Western Australia) represents the largest massacre of land-based animals on the planet.
- In 2004 five new commercial killing zones were opened up in New South Wales and a kill quota of 4.4 million animals was set nationally despite severely depleted kangaroo populations due to extended drought conditions, diminished habitat and previous over-harvesting.
- The quota represents only the numbers allotted to permit holders. There is no account of the toll from illegal shooting nor do we know how many animals are wounded but not killed and bound away to die slowly from their wounds.
- Kangaroo population numbers, from which the annual commercial kill quota is set, are "guesstimates". Aerial counting of kangaroos is the most reliable method but effort varies between states with no national standard.
- A voluntary Code of Practice purportedly safeguards the welfare of kangaroos by identifying humane killing practices. However it is not mandatory, and even if it were, the nature of kangaroo shooting is such that-as a usually solitary, nightly outback activity - is virtually impossible to regulate.
- The Code of Practice does not acknowledge the fate of juvenile kangaroos: young-at-foot. Shooting of their mothers creates thousands of orphaned young annually. Incapable of independent survival they will invariably perish from starvation, exposure and predation. Their inevitable deaths are not recorded in the kill quotas.
- The Code of Practice enshrines an even more callous death for in-pouch joeys, allowing for their removal from the shot mother's pouch to be dispatched by skull crushing. How this is to be achieved is left to the shooter's discretion. Methods include crushing under foot, bludgeoning or dashing against a tree-trunk.

Neither Clean & Green...

The outback conditions under which kangaroos are shot are hardly testimony to physical cleanliness: their bodies being dragged through the bush to be hung from hooks on the backs of trucks, there to remain exposed for hours until the shooter fulfils his nightly quota before they are delivered for refrigeration. The endemic cruelty to the joeys negates any claim to moral cleanliness. Nor do adult kangaroos escape incidental cruelty: not always killed by the "clean head shot" prescribed in the Code of Practice, they die slowly and, as with the example of the mother kangaroo considered above, are possibly carved up and hung, in the shooter's haste to move on, while still alive.

...nor Sustainable

Clearly in the case of commercial kangaroo killing 'clean & green' is a brand, not a product description. As with "Bush Food" it appeals by linking to the sustainability myth: an emotional appeal that especially targets those with an ethical and environmental consciousness who, in choosing to remain carnivorous, do not wish to support the worst aspects of meat production. In order exploit a public awareness of intensive animal breeding in 'factory farms' as rife with animal suffering and productive of environmentally-polluting effluents, the "greening" of kangaroo killing emphasises the "game meat" element. Thus the environmentally-sensitive are seduced with the implicit promise of guilt–free meat consumption. Kangaroos, it is argued, are unlike the hard-hoofed, erosion-causing sheep and cattle whose insatiable appetites are replacing our forested ecosystems with overgrazed pastures at an alarming rate.
However, the kangaroo meat and leather industry also thrives on depletion. Laying claim to 'conservation of the species' as the lofty ideal in the name of which it undertakes its annual

Plates of meat to be consumed by a few or personalities to be enjoyed by many? (Photo: Ulrike Kloeker)

slaughter, the profit-driven industry takes the biggest and strongest of the mob, depleting those individuals most likely to ensure survival of the species (and) calls this a sustainable harvest .

It has already been noted that commercial kangaroo killing has its own idiosyncratic forms of cruelty - different from factory farming but capable of causing undeniable animal suffering nonetheless. Further, it is naïve to believe that the developing market in kangaroo meat and leather will replace or even diminish the sheep and cattle industries. It will more likely add to, rather than replace, these entrenched systems.

Besides, despite the frequently alarmist descriptions of kangaroos as "marauding mobs" breeding "in plague proportions" in fact wildlife populations are finite and under considerable stress. When wild kangaroo numbers are exhausted, when habitat shrinks further precipitating starvation and population crashes, how will a greedy industry supply its global market? Ultimately market demand will dictate the captive breeding and intensive farming of kangaroos. In which event the 'clean, green and sustainable' brand will be seen to have represented false advertising.

Death by definition...

The idea of a 'sustainable harvest' of kangaroos could not have taken hold except that it's path has been paved by the relentless degradation of the status of the kangaroo from popular national icon, fully protected under wildlife legislation, to that of 'just a bloody pest', it's populations purportedly 'exploding' in plague proportions.

Michael Archer, former director of The Australian Museum asserts that 'there's a lot of wisdom now about how you could actually start to turn to utilizing native resources in a sustainable way'

Whiptail wallabies were until recently killed in Queensland and their skins used to make toy koalas - a rather perverse use of a natural resource.

Within such discourse that aims to foster the acceptability of commercial exploitation, reference to kangaroos as native animals has been replaced by 'resources'. For Archer the kangaroo is no more than millions 'of years of evolutionary experience in maximising meat yields without causing damage to the surface of Australia'.

This extraordinary statement, that appears to

attribute agency to the kangaroo for its own conversion from animal to meat, as though 'maximising meat yields' were its evolutionary purpose, articulates the trajectory of death by definition identified by Carol Adams.

Through the cycle of objectification, fragmentation and consumption that links sexual violence and the butchering of animals in our culture 'a subject is viewed or objectified through metaphor. Through fragmentation the object is severed from its ontological meaning. Finally consumed, it exists only through what it represents.' When we turn an animal into meat 'someone who has had a very particular, situated life, a unique being, is converted into something that has no distinctiveness, no uniqueness, no individuality'. Those of us involved in direct action at the point of sale of kangaroo meat, in major supermarkets, recognise the trajectory of degradation from animal to meat pitifully represented by the bloodied slabs of plastic-encased flesh marketed by Macro Meats, refrigerated and promoted as Gourmet game meat.

The intrinsic characteristics of kangaroos, such as their unique genetic contribution to the Australian natural environment, their adaptability to the range of ecosystems supporting their survival, the complex and intricate social structure of the mobs, the sensitive and extended relationship between kangaroo mothers and their joeys, are not valued or acknowledged by the discourse of exploitation. Rather their worth is defined by market terminology: quotas and carcasses, butchered slabs of flesh 'boned into saddles, striploins, shanks, butts and legs'.

Developing a commercial model for the non-destructive utilisation of native wildlife

It is thus necessary to critically examine and debunk the myth of a 'sustainable harvest' of kangaroos, politically and ecologically, in order to guarantee future species viability. However debunking a myth entails replacing the scientific paradigm that informs it.

An alternative model exists, aligned to the terminology of conservation rather than destruction. It speaks of habitat restoration, the establishment of interconnecting wildlife corridors that link wildlife habitat fragmented by human encroachment, and the development of a sensitive tourism industry based on the popularity of our national icon that will bring money, visitors and jobs to regional Australia. It is the only model whereby the kangaroo can be enabled to "pay its way" without sacrificing its status as a unique, intrinsically valuable and irreplaceable part of the Australian environmental landscape.

Conclusion: Where have all the conservation scientists gone?

This paper has sought to challenge the notion of 'sustainable harvest' that currently informs discourse, scientific and lay, justifying and perpetuating the commercial killing of kangaroos.

The Kangaroo's salvation from the greed of a profit driven industry lies in the articulation of an alternative scientific paradigm: one that does not fail to notice the lessons of history-namely that no wild species has survived the onslaught of a commercial harvest bent on short term profits at the expense of wildlife survival. The Kangaroo is no exception. Evidence that population numbers and body size of a favoured industry target - the Big Reds - are fast diminishing warns that the writing is on the wall for our national icon.

There has never been a more urgent need for scientific voices willing to follow in the path of Peter Rawlinson with the courage to refute the prevailing myth of a 'sustainable harvest' and replace the discourse on kangaroos with the language of conservation.

The 'Tibooburra red', is considered the largest race of red kangaroos. Few large males are now seen off protected areas like Sturt National Park. (Photo: David B Croft)

'BUSH-TUCKER' OR 'RUSSIAN ROULETTE'?

THE IMPACT OF 1080 ON NON-TARGET SPECIES.

WILL BOTH OUR WILDLIFE AND OUR INDIGENOUS PEOPLE JUST SIMPLY REMAIN

"THE DEAD, THE MISSING, THE LOST, AND THE VOICELESS"?

By Mary Lander

Sodium fluoroacetate (1080), (also known as sodium monofluoroacetate), is a fluorinated carboxylic acid ester with high to very high toxicity to birds and mammals. It is widely used in Australia as a poison for the control of vertebrate pests. In 1987, Dr Peter Rawlinson, zoologist La Trobe University and ACF Councillor, 1987 wrote "When ingested, wallabies, possums, wedge-tailed eagles that feed on smaller prey, are progressively debilitated and die a slow, agonising death as functions fail. Death may ultimately result from a variety of causes ranging from heart failure to suffocation. For these reasons, human exposure to 1080 is very severely restricted by law. The same does not apply to animals in baited areas."

"The major animal welfare concern over the use of 1080 relates to its extreme cruelty and its lack of an antidote. The major environmental concern relates to its indiscriminate nature and its effects on non-target animals, either through ingestion of baits or by secondary poisoning." ('A Public appeal for the immediate Prohibition of Broadscale Baiting with 1080' Peter Rawlinson 7 August 1987 ACF Public Rally to ban Broadscale baiting with 1080)

The red-necked wallaby *(Macropus rufogriseus)* also known as 'Bennett's Wallaby' is subject to 1080 poisoning in Tasmania. (Photo: David B Croft)

Once ingested 1080 is metabolised to fluorocitrate, which interferes with energy production in the Krebs cycle, a metabolic pathway that breaks down carbohydrates to provide energy for normal cell functions. The malfunctioning Krebs cycle results in an accumulation of citrate in the tissue and blood, energy deprivation and death. 1080 is a highly toxic poison and no antidote to 1080 exists.

While there are strict guidelines, set by government, to ensure that animals intended for slaughter undergo testing for chemical residues and that such meat is 'safe' for human consumption, does the same apply to kangaroo meat? It appears that an assumption is made that as kangaroos are free-roaming they are therefore toxin free, and so they do not need to be subject to the same testing under the guidelines set for farmed animals.

This is particularly concerning given that 1080, a highly toxic chemical and other toxins have been used extensively across Australia, for many years for the purpose of 'pest' or 'rodent' control on target species such as rabbits, mice, foxes, wild dogs and dingoes. Baits such as carrots and oats laced with 1080 are used to poison rabbits and mice and baits such as fresh or dried meat laced with 1080 are used to poison foxes, wild dogs and dingoes.
These baits are either set by hand or where wider applications are deemed necessary, aerial baiting methods are used.

1080 is classed as a highly toxic poison, however different species do have a different level of 'resistance' against the toxicity of this poison. Toxicity is one thing (ie. poisoning resulting in death) but what of the longer-term effects of sub-lethal doses of 1080 on various species? Nothing is 'known' about this poisons' carcinogenic, mutagenic or teratogenic effects. It is known that it does have an effect on the reproductive system and can cause reproductive and developmental harm, eg. birth defects, infertility, sterility and impairment of normal growth and development. It is also known that it has an effect on the endocrine system, the hypothalamus, testes and the thymus.
It is unknown whether it is a ground water contaminant. There are no maximum residue levels set for 1080 as it is not used on farmed animals intended for human consumption.

-   How much 1080 gets into the food chain and what are the impacts of non-lethal quantities of 1080 on both wildlife and any other animals or humans that may, in turn, consume them?
-   What is the impact of 1080 on non-target species of Australian wildlife such as wallabies and possums deliberately poisoned with 1080 baits in Tasmania?
-   What is the possibility that kangaroos commercially harvested for human consumption and pet food may contain sub-lethal doses of 1080? There is 'no risk' according to the authorities. Remember, the official line is that kangaroos are free-roaming and are therefore toxin free.
-   What is the impact of 1080 on other wildlife including reptiles such as goannas and other non-target species that may ingest dried meat baits laced with 1080 intended for foxes or dingoes? Very little is known, but from information I've sourced, if it is not highly toxic to them, the only apparent physical symptom is that it may slow them down a little. It is unknown how long the toxin may remain in the system of all species. That makes them both 'fair game' and 'easy game' for those who may enjoy 'bush tucker'.

Realistically, the chances of human beings ingesting 1080 in sufficient quantity via game meats or 'bush-tucker' to be immediately lethal to them is not a risk. However, what are the longer-term effects of ingesting very small quantities of the poison particularly given that nothing is 'known' about its carcinogenic, mutagenic or teratogenic effects?

What is known about the effects of 1080 on human beings?

A case study of a health woman in the US who deliberately ingested an unspecified dose of sodium florocetate reveals: "The woman experienced nausea, vomiting, and abdominal pain 30 minutes after ingestion, with subsequent seizures occurring 60 minutes after the initial onset of symptoms. Neurological examination after 2 weeks revealed severe cerebellar dysfunction. By 18 months, memory disturbances and depressive behaviour persisted".

What is known about the effects of 1080 on mammals, based on scientific studies to date:

Eastern Grey kangaroo in silhouette: What pesticide residuals does it carry in it's meat?
(Photo: Bill Corn)

"The highest concentrations occur in the blood, with moderate levels in the muscle and kidneys, and the lowest concentration in the liver. All traces of the toxin are, therefore, likely to be eliminated within one week. Very recent studies indicate that elimination of 1080 from the milk of sub-lethally exposed livestock will occur in a similar time period. 1080 is highly toxic to infants"

While it has not been scientifically proven that there is any link between chronic illness such as diabetes as a result of 1080 in the food chain nor, to my knowledge, has there been any exploration of the possibility that 1080 may be excreted through breast milk if an infant's mother consumes bush-tucker containing sub-lethal doses of 1080. None of this has been the subject of any detailed scientific analysis.

Bush-tucker is deemed to be highly nutritious yet, with regard to our own indigenous people, most of their health problems are apparently related to their diet. The range of health issues our aboriginal people have had to deal with include:

- An infant mortality rate which is three times higher than the national average.
- Diabetes - and other diseases of the endocrine system. The rate of diabetes is six times higher among aboriginal people. It is estimated that diabetes affects between 10 to 30 per cent of the Aboriginal population.
- Cancer - particularly lung, cervical and liver cancer. According to the South Australian Cancer Registry, the death rate among the aboriginal population is higher because the cancers are typically diagnosed at a later stage.
- Mental Health – they say is also increasingly becoming an issue.

What are the possible effects of sub-lethal doses of 1080 on the endocrine system and could it cause conditions such as diabetes?

Studies into diabetes reveal that: "A large shift in the insulin secretory phenotype (75% loss in G3 cells) is observed, this is accompanied by coordinated changes in glucose oxidation and in citrate-derived lipid metabolism, which in turn can be explained by an orchestrated change in gene transcription. The current analysis of the glucose-responsive phenotype of rat [beta]-cells strongly indicates that cataplerosis via citrate and ATP-citrate lyase (ACL) is a major metabolic pathway of [beta]-cell activation, both acutely and as chronic adaptation to changes in extracellular glucose."

Government however, remains baffled as to the cause of aboriginal health problems.

Would there be a natural tendency for government to find causes that are more likely be limited to a range of 'things the aboriginal people themselves may be doing wrong and their lifestyle'? Realistically there is a fairly good chance it would be their preference to consider only those possible causes that the government itself is not responsible for.

Perhaps it is time that the government asks itself whether, in fact, we have not only taken the best of the land but also poisoned their food supply and left them with a range of resulting chronic illnesses in lieu? Perhaps this should be the subject of a detailed scientific assessment before the Prime Minister succeeds in his objectives to "put an end to their welfare mentality"? Then again, perhaps he feels we have done enough for them already? Is there a chance that government and industry have been "throwing both our wildlife and our aboriginal children and people overboard for the sake of a strong economy and export dollars". Will both our wildlife and our indigenous people just simply remain "the dead, the missing, the lost, and the voiceless"?

While in no way related to my own comments on the broader range of possible implications resulting from 1080 in the environment and the food chain, a particular paper is beautifully written which "draws on Australian Aboriginal concepts of interspecies connection and responsibility, and seeks to engage with questions of how extinctions are understood. What happens when people's animal or plant kin disappear from their world? What is the manner of the loss, the quality and dimensions of this absence?" (www.abdn.ac.uk/chags9/1-rose.htm page accessed 10/6/05).

Perhaps we have something to learn from our aboriginal people and should learn to respect all forms of life in our environment. Remember, it's not the powerful governments and commercial interests that make Australia unique, it's our beautiful unique wildlife and heritage that makes it so.

THE KANGAROO BETRAYED

By Kakkib li'Dthia Warrawee'a

Kakkib li'Dthia Warrawee'a is an Aboriginal Spiritual Teacher/Philosopher, Doctor of Ya-idt'midtung Medicine and senior elder of the Ya-idt'midtung language group of south-eastern Australia. He is the author of There Once Was a Tree Called Deru published by Thorsons and PerfectBound (imprints of HarperCollinsPublishers) and of numerous papers. He lectures in Medical Philosophy and TraditionalMedicines to the medical faculties of several universities in Australia and overseas.

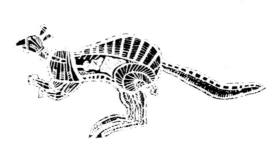

(Artwork: Mark Evans)

After I had given a recent lecture I was handed a copy of *The Kangaroo Betrayed* and was asked if I would please pen an article for a future publication. A week later, the book worked its way out of my bag and onto my cluttered desk; I'd been busy - on the road lecturing, preparing for an overseas trip, moving house - I threw the book onto a pile of bits and pieces beside my new jury - rigged desk.

And it was then that the title hit me: *The Kangaroo Betrayed.* I was enraged:

THE BLOODY KANGAROO BETRAYED! I howled, *WHAT ABOUT ALL OF THE OTHER ANIMALS AND BIRDS AND FISH AND PLANTS THAT ARE NOW EXTINCT SINCE EUROPEAN PEOPLE INVADED THESE SHORES. WHAT ABOUT MY MOB! WHAT ABOUT EVERYTHING - ALL BIRDS, ANIMALS, REPTILES, PLANTS, INSECTS… WHAT ABOUT… WELL, WHAT YOU EXPECT FROM THESE FELLAS, EH? IF IT MOVES, SHOOT IT; IF IT DOESN'T, CUT IT DOWN.*

A couple of hundred years ago some fellas rowed ashore on this continent and preceded to shoot everything that moved or flew, and chop down or dig up everything that didn't: how the Aboriginal people standing and watching this event survived that day is a miracle. These whitefellas were collecting specimens to take back to their Motherland: a scientific expedition. They looked at the mob of Aboriginal people and said to each other that these people were primitive children: *Look, see, they don't have any clothes on, and they talk like little birds.* In time - long after these whitefellas had gone back home to their families, attitudes to the "primitive children" changed to one of *pest or monkey* and so the extermination began.

Brave conservationists and "anti-slavers" protested at the slaughter of the natives, and so the "primitive children" were summoned to learn about the compassion of Jesus and the beliefs of whitefella: assimilation.

Now, the Aboriginal people standing on that beach the day that the longboat rowed ashore saw a completely different picture: *Look at these ghost-like fellas in this big canoe; they are wearing their blankets too tight–get sick that way. … Why they wearing any blankets at all? … Look at all the things they killing–they'll never eat that much. Don't they know that they are killing themselves? Why are they so destructive? … Maybe they're children.… Sure acting like it. Look at those fellas there–they just chopped down that tree, stripped off its bark and cut off its branches and threw all that away and then they've tied a blanket to one end of the tree and replanted the tree … as if the poor thing would ever grow again … and stood there shading their eyes in front of this tree … of course they need to shade their eyes–it hasn't got any branches left to give them shade: they cut them off. Yep! These whitefellas are children: selfish and destructive and silly. … Maybe we should tell them some stories to help them learn: Come here white fella, we tell you about the big frog who lives…*

Two hundred years later and these whitefellas as just as greedy and destructive. Most of my mob have since learned the whitefella ways – speak their language, studied their Jesus and mathematics and money – then have turned back to what we know is right and true: to a oneness with *all* of this universe. Whitefellas don't know anything about the country they invaded: not a thing – can't speak the language, and have no real knowledge of the plants and birds and animals and fish and insects and earth. But they think they know everything, and since they have power, they experiment with that knowledge: children.

Kangaroos Betrayed?
All of us are betrayed!!

When you write something, would you tell about your relationship with the kangaroos: what they mean to you. What the kangaroos mean to me seems pretty irrelevant: I've lived a long time – time enough to have a lot of white hair and wrinkles like rain-eroded gullies – and I've long since learned that to greedy whitefellas, what an Aboriginal person thinks is secondary to what the greedy and arrogant white thinks.

Sound angry? I'm not. Just realistic. I've worked with plenty of environmentalist organizations and groups, and well know that they'll gladly use Aboriginal people for

(Artwork: Mark Evans)

numbers or leverage; but what they fight for will be for what the white environmentalist wants. Do you know why this book hasn't got more Aboriginal voices in it? Do you know why Aboriginal people are reluctant to write something for the book? You can be used and abused just so many times before you simply give up on the self-centred childishness of Australians.

If you don't like what I've written here, sad–but I hardly care. Children eventually grow up: you will too.

It isn't important to save the kangaroo, for Aboriginal people, for future generations; for the right of kangaroos to exist; because the current culls disturb the balance of genetic quality; because it is morally right; or any of that stuff. They are a part of *your* value systems. We have different value systems that are born of a different culture. And though you know almost nothing about our cultural value systems after knowing us for a couple of centuries, I'll briefly try to outline it all again.

The sundry macropods are not just a fine animal that looks cool on a coat of arms, they are a part of this land. **Dtjowdtjba**, the Eastern Grey Kangaroo, **Macropus giganteus**, is not my brother or sister: **Dtjowdtjba** and I are one. Hurt Dtjowdtjba–and you hurt me. I, just because I'm human, am not superior to Dtjowdtjba; neither is Dtjowdtjba superior to me: we are simply one. Sure, I will eat Dtjowdtjba if I am hungry–but only after asking Dtjowdtjba if I may. Sometimes we die, and we provide food for the grasses that will feed Dtjowdtjba. This is life. Dtjowdtjba and I are a part of the universe: a part of the web of life. Vital and important to that web as the other.

Bungchja'ee the Red-necked Wallaby, **Macropus rufogriseus**, isn't more important because there are fewer of Bungchja'ee. Everything is one. **Inna** the Wallaroo, **Macropus robustus**, and Bungchja'ee are not more important because they are a part of **BaQwa**–a part of our totemic system in my mob. Though, if Inna becomes extinct, so will the people of that totem.

I guess that my original reaction to the title KANGAROO BETRAYED (as expressed in the first paragraph of this paper) is the point: what about the whole lot. To separate the kangaroo from the picture is like separating Aboriginal people from the rest of humanity–children, in their ignorance, and racists in their arrogance and idiocy, may think they can do that, but we are grown and intelligent aren't we? It is not that the kangaroo is betrayed: we, all of us, are betrayed by our own arrogance and idiocy.

(Artwork: Mark Evans)

THE KANGAROO TOTEMIC CONNECTION

A PSYCHOLOGICAL, CULTURAL AND SYMBOLIC PERSPECTIVE

By Fiona Corke

Actor, transpersonal counsellor and homoeopathic practitioner, speaker and campaigner for environmental and wildlife issues.

(Artwork: Mark Evans)

"The Australian aborigines describe the time of creation as the dreamtime. The first beings dreamed the animals and the plants; they painted the dream images on the rocks, filled them with a soul force, and from the rock-paintings the souls of the beings represented spread over the world in a physical shape." (Andreas Lommel quote taken from *The Strong Eye of Shamanism* by Robert E Ryan. Pge 118).

Psychology and psychiatry generally end at the edge of suburbia. The main concerns are diagnoses of the human mind and behaviour and our interaction with other humans, our urban problems and issues, our dramas and city neurosis. It doesn't venture into the realms of our relationship with the earth, trees, plants or animals. A large proportion of this country's population live in rural areas where they are in direct contact daily with the natural world. Studies on happiness report people who live in the country are generally happier than our city fellows. So what lies beyond our interaction with people?

New streams of psychology such as eco psychology, green psychology and Deep Ecology put forward the concept that through connection with the earth, and forming a relationship with and within it, can provide a very powerful healing effect mentally and emotionally. In fact if we restore the earth we will restore our mental and physical health. Eco and green psychology is concerned with how we can integrate this missing link previously ignored by modern mainstream psychology. As mentioned by both Jung and later in his life Freud, there is a completeness in the spirit and psyche when one is connected to the natural world and its non-human inhabitants but there have been no mainstream psychological studies on the connection or relationship between humans and nature.

Our connection or relationship with the earth allows us to contact our primordial self or original self, the unconscious and creative aspect, the wilderness and unknown of our being. In indigenous communities the totem or animal familial represents an individual's pre existent state as a primordial being.

The word totem originally comes from Indigenous North American peoples. It actually refers to animal or plant species that are held in high esteem by groups of individuals. Totem is not a God or deity as some perceive: nor is it idol worship. (Cowan 1989)

According to aboriginal belief, humankind appears on earth as a reincarnation of a primordial being from the Dreaming. He comes into existence as the manifestation of a more rudimentary form of life to which he never the less owes his allegiance while he lives on earth. Man is, in a sense incomplete, living the life of a shade in the stygian realm of the dreaming. (Cowan 1989)

In our western culture we are not given or shown tools to explore or decipher this aspect of ourselves in relation to nature, we do not have a dreamtime to connect us, we are removed from the natural world spending most time indoors thinking and talking about everything but the present because we can't see it. Eco psychology, green psychology and Deep Ecology inquire into the ecocentric viewpoint that the connection and integration of nature and spirituality provides the individual with many reasons for living outside of the material and economic sphere. Whereas in western culture anthropocentric superiority and domination of nature is rife, we find few reasons for living outside of the urban, material or economic world.

We in the western world mostly live with want not need, we have immediate and potential material freedom, even spirituality has become somewhat corporative and yet we are the sickest we have ever been.
We are experiencing more chronic disease, depression and mental health than ever before in our history. What are our reasons for living? Where do we fit in the scheme of things? Where do we find our sense of meaning and belonging? What provides us with a sense of meaning besides the almighty dollar?

As a mythological creature the Kangaroo has intrinsic cultural value as a totem (in totemic ancestry). In non-indigenous society whether it be on our Coat of Arms or an inflatable icon at an overseas sports arenas, the kangaroo has become Australia's mascot and national emblem.

(Artwork: Mark Evans)

There is worldwide identification of the kangaroo with Australia.

Why? Because we have created our own modern day stories and myths. This gentle, cheeky and lovable creature features in many popular children's books, movies, songs and a very famous television show. A whole generation of Australians were brought up on the adventures of a caring and smart bush kangaroo, Skippy, and her adventures in the Waratah National Park and beyond. The Kangaroo appears constantly in our modern cultural landscape, for example; Qantas, the world's safest airline, a kangaroo painted on every plane. Appearing or symbolized in numerous advertising campaigns and tourism advertisements, football teams and mascots, business logos, Skippy cornflakes and the boxing kangaroo. The Australian one-dollar coin depicts a small mob of kangaroos, and at the Australian Tennis Open in the winner's cup there was a kangaroo soft toy as a symbol and gesture of our country.

But how do we really value it?

The kangaroo has always been portrayed as being wild and free, even Skippy could come and go as she pleased. Only when she was kidnapped by the baddies do we see her threatened or caged, but we always knew Skippy would win in the end, now we are not so sure.

The Australian Government has other plans for Skippy, after they have sold her skin in their trade agreements they want us to eat her – rare, and what's left over sell for a $1.50 a kilo for pet food! A complete contradiction of what we are culturally 'served' up.

Meanwhile the connection between human and kangaroo lives on. In Tanjil, South Gippsland in 2003, in true Skippy style, a kangaroo named Lulu saved farmer Len Richards' life by alerting the family of his accident, and on following her, they found the unconscious Len and he was subsequently saved (Lulu, received the first time ever for a marsupial, RSPCA Bravery Award) It would seem that kangaroos have a strong sense of family, loyalty, are aware and concerned about what is happening in their immediate community, are helpful and kind, all the good qualities society have us strive for.

Many people in this country and overseas are consciously and unconsciously affected by environmental destruction, it's no wonder we have such a huge problem with depression in our society. The killing of millions of kangaroos annually leave many people feeling confused, outraged and helpless. To these individuals and communities it is as if something within them has been desecrated, been lost.

As with indigenous belief, if what is sacred to them is severed or destroyed, they experience loss on a very deep level. Losing their totemic lifeline, which connects them to the dreamtime, can cause a deterioration of health and loss of life as their reasons for living have gone, there is nothing to grasp, nothing to nurture them spiritually. There are a growing number of non-indigenous individuals who choose to live with respect for the environment and the other creatures upon it; these people are also deeply affected by such destruction.

'BAND-AID' CODE

WILL NOT STOP JOEY CRUELTY

ONLY AN END TO THE PRACTICES CAN DO THAT

By Glenys Oogjes

Executive Director - Animals Australia. www.animalsaustralia.org

Any reasonable person would think that animal welfare Codes of Practice exist across Australia to influence and improve the way in which animals are treated. This is a reasonable assumption, but the reality is very different.

The national 'Code of Practice for the Humane Shooting of Kangaroos' was introduced in 1985. Like other Codes of Practice, it has been accepted as a good 'minimum' standard of treatment, and used as the standard defence when an industry or a specific practice is questioned by animal welfare advocates. Because Codes exist, and due to their name, the automatic assumption is that animal treatment has improved. There is no evidence that this is true.

Problems with the Codes

Codes of Practice have largely been drawn up with primary input from the industries involved and thus most merely describe the most common methods used in that industry. The existing 'Code of Practice for the Humane Shooting of Kangaroos' describes the use of high powered spotlights and rifles at night using head shots because that is how most shooting occurs on the mainland and a head shot is seen as humane. However, because particularly in Tasmania, smaller wallabies are shot in bush or farmland areas during daylight hours, and when the wallabies are mobile, the Code provides a description of that activity – and allows the fleeing animals to be shot in the head, neck or chest with a shotgun (shotgun pellets spray an arc, often wounding). Such concessions to current practice indicate that the code is merely a descriptive, rather than a prescriptive or proscriptive document and that the Code title of 'humane' is a variable measure.

The Code of Practice is silent on the treatment of young-at-foot like this eastern grey kangaroo. (Photo: Bill Corn)

Of great concern is that compliance with even the described (often deficient) practices provides an automatic defence to the general provisions of animal welfare legislation in most Australian jurisdictions. Would shotguns still blast away at wallabies in Tasmania if other legislation and the Code (a Standard in Tasmania) did not stand in the way of that State's Animal Welfare Act?

Another concern is that, no matter how deficient a Code may be, many people in some industries are even unaware of the existence of the relevant Code.

Enforceability and compliance:

Unfortunately the ability to enforce even minimal Code standards is compromised in most industries. Non-compliance with a Code is not an offence per se (exceptions include the scientific Code and agricultural codes in South Australia).

In the case of the current kangaroo Code, shooters in the commercial industry are required to comply with the Code as a condition of their licenses (issued by State authorities) under State Kangaroo Management Programs (KMPs) in Western Australia, South Australia, New South Wales and Queensland. However, compliance is virtually impossible to measure and enforce, as there is no monitoring or policing at the point of kill where most cruelty breaches occur.

Compliance officers see carcasses of shot kangaroos and cannot readily police the shooting. (Photo: Ulrike Kloecker)

The problems of measuring or ensuring compliance were outlined in the 2002 Report of RSPCA Australia 'Kangaroo Shooting Code Compliance – A survey of the extent of compliance with the requirements of the Code of Practice for the Humane Shooting of Kangaroos'. The stated and significant qualifications on the outcome of that survey of compliance (which showed an increase in the percentage of head shot kangaroos at processors - the RSPCA assessment point - since 1985) included that:

- only those dead kangaroos taken to processors could be assessed (others may have been left in the field, e.g. chest or body shot),
- other kangaroos shot and injured and not retrieved were not in the sample, and there could be no assessment of the treatment of joeys, nor any measure of the welfare effect on dependent offspring of shot female kangaroos.

A key problem in any direct assessment of Code compliance is that commercial kangaroo shooting is usually conducted at night in remote areas and monitoring is difficult to impossible. Assessment is in any event unlikely given the low numbers of inspectors; for example just 12 rangers for all of the Queensland commercial industry, never at the point of kill (due to OH&S concerns), and inspection of buying points just twice a year.

Past reviews of Code compliance

RSPCA Australia accepted a consultancy in 1984 from the (then) Australian National Parks and Wildlife Service to 'enquire into the incidence of cruelty to kangaroos during culling operations'. The RSPCA's May 1985 report had similar difficulties (to the 2002 report) in regard to veracity of processor-point surveys, but found that 'about 15% of all kangaroos culled for the industry have been taken inhumanely', and that there was an even higher incidence of cruelty in the non-commercial killing and more so in the illegal killing.

The RSPCA 2002 report, on this occasion commissioned by Environment Australia, using a similar survey method, with its acknowledged limitations, found that some 4% of kangaroos ending up at processing points had not been shot humanely. (Many kangaroos inhumanely shot do not make it to the processors, and are not part of the flawed cruelty statistics AQIS Inspector). However, Dr Hugh Wirth (RSPCA President) commented that "...we cannot ignore the 4% of kangaroos still being shot inhumanely – this represents around 100,000 kangaroos every year." [Media release 7/9/02]. Wirth was scathing about the lack of controls for landholders and non-commercial hunters, referred to recreational shooting of kangaroos as 'barbaric', and even suggested that no female kangaroo carrying pouch young be shot to prevent the inevitable suffering of her young.

Specific Problems with the current kangaroo Code

The current 'Code of Practice for the Humane Shooting of Kangaroos', like most Codes, merely describes practices, and fails to address the question of justification for the animals to be shot. As stated, the Code allows the use of shotguns for smaller macropods, and allows the point of aim to include the neck and chest – thus a lesser standard than a head shot. This is significant with 7,000 permits issued for recreational shooters to shoot for 'crop protection' in Tasmania in 2002.
The Australian Wildlife Protection Council submitted to the WA Review "Presumably it is OK to use shotguns in the 4 states, if shotguns are used for non-commercial purposes, such as killing kangaroos to feed farmers' dogs, or recreational shooting of smaller macropod species or 'hoon/yabo' shooting or as 'pest/vermin' control."

The Code also fails to require the shooter to be trained and competent – leaving this to the discretion of State authorities. Even now, Western Australia is just introducing proficiency tests for shooters, and a shooter in the commercial shooting States need pass only once and is not re-tested – this is despite many shooters being part time and unlikely to hone their marksmanship using inanimate objects prior to shooting trips. Non-commercial shooters (farmers, hunters) do not require any such tests.

The Code also allows joeys to be decapitated or be killed by a heavy blow to the skull, but does not indicate how young-at-foot should be killed if a female kangaroo is killed. The issue of dependent joeys that escape the killing area is virtually impossible for the Code to address. Ingrid Witte discusses this issue in this volume and estimates that more than a million young-at-foot have been left to die with the killing in the commercial industry of the last decade. The suffering of dependent young includes inhumane attempts to bludgeon, decapitate or shoot, distress, dehydration, exposure, predation etc.

A kangaroo code review underway

The existing Code is the 2nd edition, reviewed in 1990. After the 2002 report by RSPCA Australia, the Natural Resources Management Ministerial Council decided that a formal review of the Code was required. After some delay a working group was appointed and met in 2003. A Discussion paper was released for public comment in June 2004 and these were used to produce a 'draft' Code which is due for release for further consultation through 2005.

It is no surprise that the issues up for debate include the welfare of joeys, wallaby shooting, and non-commercial shooting, a name change to drop the word 'humane', and appropriate ballistics to assist recommendations to ensure the capabilities of firearms and ammunition.

Can and will the problems be fixed?

Unfortunately the review is unlikely to alter the primary animal welfare problems – particularly the number of kangaroos injured during the commercial and non-commercial kill, and the dependent joeys who are killed after their mother has been targeted, or who escape and perish.

In this commercial industry which uses brutal and deadly methods to collect its 'products' or quarry, the prospects of shooters getting an instant kill every time, let alone ensuring the welfare of all joeys, is nil. Even a brilliant Code cannot eliminate unnecessary suffering - and one that is not mandatory and that purports to regulate activities which take place at night in remote areas has no chance of doing so. Only an end to the practices can do that.

The Kangaroo in Court

Summary of the Evidence and Submissions by Counsel,

Barrister Cliff Papayanni, for the Applicant in Proceedings Before the

Administrative Appeals Tribunal

Applications were made by the Wildlife Protection Association of Australia Inc. against the Minister for Environment and Heritage CW (Commonwealth) in the Administrative Appeals Tribunal for reviews of the declarations of the Minister of his approvals of wildlife trade management plans ("management plans") under section 33FO(3) of the EPBC acts in December 2002 for the states of Queensland South Australia and Western Australia for 2003 – 7 in respect of Kangaroos.

The applications came on for hearing on 17th March 2004 just prior to the Australian Wildlife Protection Council Inc being joined as a co-applicant. The hearing continued on 18th and 22nd March and 2nd – 5th August 2004. Judgments were reserved in each case.

The application's emphasis was mainly directed towards the killing by shooters of in-pouch joeys and the indirect death of the ex-pouch joeys from predation, starvation and other causes after their mothers were killed or died from wounding by shooters.

The Management Plans are concerned only with the killing of kangaroos for commercial purposes and do not deal with those killed for damage mitigation by farmers. The act requires in respect of the Management Plans that

a) Management controls be specified to ensure that the impact on the Kangaroo taxon is ecologically sustainable s 303FOC(3)
b) Measures be included to monitor and mitigate and slash or minimize the environmental impact of the activities of the Plan and to respond to changes of such impact s 303FO3(e)
c) The plans be consistent with the objects of the Act under s 303BA, one such object under ss (1) (e)

Juvenile male common wallaroo - future target of the kangaroo industry. (Photo: Ulrike Kloecker)

being to promote the humane treatment of wildlife

d)   In respect of the killing of Kangaroos the regulations applicable to the welfare of the specimens be complied with s 303FO3(f).

The regulations in s 9A.05(4) state in ss(b):- (b) if the animal is killed, it is done in a way that is generally accepted to minimise pain and suffering. The Code of Practice for the humane shooting of Kangaroos applies to the shooting of Kangaroos. The Code attempts to set out an achievable standard of humane conduct as a minimum for persons shooting Kangaroos and includes the method of shooting, dispatch of injuries Kangaroo and pouch young and specifies firearms, ammunition and points of aim. It does not specifically deal with in-pouch young. A number of submissions were made in respect of the fact that there was no monitoring at the scene of the killing to ensure compliance with the code.

Each of the persons responsible for the preparation and management of the Management Plans in the respective states admitted that there was no such check on shooters and could only rely on random checks at chillers and processing plants and the adequate records kept and supplied by shooters and processors.

Evidence was given for the applicant in respect of welfare considerations, to which the main submissions were directed, Pat O'Brien, Maryland Wilson, Dr D B Croft the foremost expert on macropods, John Auty and carers, G. Friebe and D. Barnden. Exhibited were the films 'Faces in the Mob', 'The Kangaroo Betrayed', a Survey of the Kangaroo Shooting Code Compliance of July 2002 by RSPCA Australia and other records.

The submissions made by Counsel for the applicant were directed towards the illegality of the killing and indirect deaths of in-pouch joeys and out of pouch joeys and animal welfare considerations generally.

In respect of the illegal killing and indirect deaths of joeys and consequent cruelty and barbarity and inhumane treatment, it was pointed out that all kangaroos under the respective legislation in the three states were protected and the killing of Kangaroos and cruelty towards them were offences in each state unless authorised under the respective Management plans, which set the respective quotas. The Management Plans and their quotas of the numbers to be killed did not include the joeys of females shot. The licenses of the shooters to kill the Kangaroos were for the purposes of sale, which did not include joeys who were not killed for the purposes of sale and consequently such killing was unlawful. Where the mother was killed and the joeys out of pouch were either killed or left to be killed by predators or die from starvation or other causes, whilst still dependent was also unlawful and offences. The Code of Practice, which allowed the killing of in-pouch joeys, whose mothers had been killed did not apply except to killings under the Management Plans. There was no provision in the Code for out of pouch joeys. No argument was advanced by the Respondent to answer this submission in any specific way. It was submitted the Management Plans should not have been approved as being inhumane.

The figures for Queensland for 2003 showed 39% of female Red Kangaroos were shot representing about 184 700 and Grey Kangaroos 26% being about 283 050 females shot making a total of 467 750 females shot. Due to size selection it would be expected that the females shot were over 18 months of age and likely to have an in pouch joey and possibly an out of pouch joey. This could represent between 468 000 joeys to 936 000 joeys being also killed or left to die.

In South Australia in 2003 similarly 92 000 female Kangaroos were killed with the possibility of 92 000 to 184 000 joeys also being killed or left to die. In Western Australia in 2003 125 000 – 250 000 joeys being killed or left to die.

The submissions as above were put as a matter of grave concern in respect of animal welfare considerations which were not taken into account in the Management Plans.

Submissions in respect of animal welfare generally were made as follows: -

    a)   Only South Australia included an animal welfare component in their aims.
    b)   No animal welfare representatives on any Advisory Council or Committee in any State
    c)   Compliance with Code of Practice not monitored or checked at the scene of shooting.
    d)   Random checks of shooters, chillers and processors not adequate
    e)   Record books and returns do not reveal injured Kangaroos shot and who escape.
    f)   Articles in the book 'The Kangaroo Betrayed' and evidence of Maryland Wilson
    g)   Evidence given by witnesses
    h)   The deficiencies in the provisions of the Code of Practice, particularly as to joeys.
    i)   Criticism if the provisions in the Code of in-pouch joeys being decapitated by a sharp instrument or properly executed heavy blow by a blunt instrument to kill larger joeys.

Eastern grey kangaroos are the main targets of the Queensland commercial industry because they live closest to more settled areas with better roads and access. (Photo: Bill Corn)

Particular mention was made of recommendations made by the RSPCA in their survey and also the fact that the Code of Practice was not compliant with respect to head shots in an overall 4.1% of Kangaroos shot and an estimated 1% of Kangaroos shot and injured and escaping. This means of the kangaroos killed the year 2000, 112 578 were not head shot and it was reported that this was a matter of considerable concern.

The above is an outline of the submissions made on behalf of the applicants at the hearing and opinions were given as to whether the killing of female Kangaroos being prohibited would be a solution to the cruelty and inhumane treatment of the in pouch and out of pouch joeys without any consensus being reached.

The decision of the Tribunal was given on 14 October 2004. The Tribunal stated it was satisfied that the pre-requisites to approval had been met and that approval was warranted to each management plan under the Act.

However, disappointingly the main submission that the killing of joeys in pouch and at foot was illegal and an offence was not addressed directly by the Tribunal.

The submission that joeys are individual kangaroos and are protected under the EPBC Act (Cw) which Act allows quotas under management plans for the killing of kangaroos for sale and the evidence given was that joeys are not part of the quota as they are not intended to by killed for sale was not accepted by the Tribunal.

The Tribunal held that the state legislation in effect over-ruled the EPBC Act (Cw) (which is not the law) by making licenses subject to compliance with the Code of Practice and thus the joeys became part of the licensed arrangement. Even if this were so legally the Code makes no provision for out of pouch joeys and in WA particularly and similarly in the other two states the licenses are issued to kill kangaroos for sale. Joeys in pouch or out of pouch are not part of the quota or the management plans authorised by the EPBC Act, as they could not possibly be for sale.

Somewhat amazingly the actual quota in one case in WA was exceeded by 15 000 being killed and with the fact that about 90% of females killed had joeys at foot and in pouch (on the evidence makes it more than probable that if the quotas are met the quotas will be greatly exceeded if the joeys are included. The question of the Code of Practice not providing in the judgment for out of pouch joeys was not given any importance and no attempt was put forward by the Tribunal to provide any solution. The Code recognises only that it is cruel to kill a female with an in pouch joey.

Each state relied upon the integrity of the shooters complying with the Code of Practice at the scene of the shooting and offered no provision for any monitoring. The same shooters were prosecuted for a number of breaches of the Code at the scene of the shootings.

The Tribunal considers that the process of development of Plans would be enhanced if sustained efforts were made to improve the public image of the kangaroo industry, and if public consultation regarding the management and welfare of kangaroos as well as considerations in relation to quota setting were more enthusiastically embraced by the States and the Respondent.

This final paragraph of the Tribunal's decision exemplifies the Tribunal's apparent attitude to the Kangaroo industry, that is, its' primary function and concern appears to be, to assist the industry to continue its undeniably cruel undertakings for commercial gain.

Governments are indifferent to cruelty inherent in commercial kangaroo industry. (Photo: Ulrike Kloecker)

LINCHPIN OF EXTINCTION

By Halina Thompson

Who together with Dr. Teresa Buss-Carden established Australians for Wildlife,
a sub committee of World League for Protection of Animals

The Australian Government and the profit making proponents of the commercial kangaroo industry claim that the kangaroo breeds prolifically and will reproduce infinitely to supply bottomless commercial demands for its flesh and skin - just like the magic pudding. As a result of that fantasy the commercial kill quotas have been rising steadily as the commercial kangaroo killing industry has inexorably expanded.
Our skewed electoral system ensures that a handful of rural voters determine which party gains power. politicians stay alert to self serving messages and demands from the rural sector, for taxpayers subsidies when unsustainable farming practices regularly rebound on them.
The agricultural industry demands the total destruction of the kangaroo, the Government facilitates it and the commercial kangaroo killing industry is happy to oblige. This three cornered collusion is the linchpin of extinction.

Farmers, graziers and pastoralists have demonized the kangaroo as a 'pest eating them out of house and home'; a 'pest' slur which was taken up by scientists and bureaucrats and became codified as the loophole in our Native Wildlife Protection laws which permits the killing of our protected native macropod species as 'damage mitigation' for the benefit of the agri-business sector. Any species of animal unfortunate enough to carry the 'pest' label, is dealt a certain death warrant .

The kangaroo supposedly a protected species, inhabitant of its native land, is condemned by word association with introduced species like rabbits and foxes or the biblical locusts, the killing of which is considered to be almost a patriotic duty by those with a vested interest.

The mythical claim by farmers is, that kangaroos compete with sheep and cattle and provide a substantial and unacceptable grazing pressure on the pastoral and grazing industry, a myth recently dispelled by Professor Gordon Grigg co-author of the 'Commercial Harvesting of Kangaroos in Australia' made an extra ordinary about-face in 2001. At the AGM of the

Australasian Wildlife Management Society held in December that year he admitted that the damage caused by kangaroos on grazing lands has been overestimated by up to 500% and stating the obvious he said:

"This would mean that kangaroos are a much smaller component of the total grazing pressure than is generally accepted" (Grigg) also... "The hope of getting a significant improvement in wool production by pest control of kangaroos is probably doomed to failure" (Grigg)
Professor Grigg's research which exonerated the kangaroo is not widely disseminated and is ignored by the government, media and scientific community. The demonisation of the kangaroo as a pest is part of the arsenal used by the rural sector to manipulate public opinion and sway sympathy (and gain subsidies) in favour of farmers.

Another point is that the question of kangaroos competing for feed even during drought ought to be a non sequitur.   At the onset of drought the farmer knows that his stock will starve and he had better "sell them before he can smell them". Farmers who do not de stock pre drought, are gambling on the duration of the drought and usually lose - then turn to the taxpayer for drought relief subsidies. European style pastoralists and farmers who capitalize their profits and socialize their losses are gamblers who continue to blame their economic woes on kangaroos when history tells us that drought is a regular season. This driest of Continents is not suitable to be used as a feedlot for the supply of sheep and cattle to the meat markets of the world.

Before passing the 'pest' death sentence on the kangaroo, no scientific research was carried out to substantiate or quantify the extent of damage caused to farming production by kangaroos, yet in the 1970's this myth led to the opening up of a commercial killing industry in kangaroo skins

for luxury goods and for the pet trade and later for human meat consumption.
The contemptuous sentencing of the kangaroo as a pest by scientists and government without taking into account truth and facts, is a clear illustration of the phrase 'kangaroo court', one devoid of truth or justice for our native wildlife.

The farmers folklore 'myths' of the kangaroo as a pest was propagated by a media, controlled by rural vested interests, to a mainly city based and uninformed population. This spurious knowledge about the supposed damage caused by kangaroos to farmers' livelihood, was quoted by scientists as accepted fact and incorporated into 'scientific theory'. The Commercial Harvesting of Kangaroo in Australia, (Pople & Grigg 1999) is the basis of kangaroo management for the commercial industry. This government publication refers to the kangaroo species as a 'pest' 40 times. The dictionary meaning of a pest is something extremely destructive, hurtful or annoying, a pest is plague, pestilence.

There is an urgent need to address the pathological impulses at work here, in as much as:
- The kangaroo is a protected wildlife species. It is the icon of Australia and features on limitless government crests, regalia, on almost every letterhead state and federal, businesses etc ….
- Worldwide the unique kangaroo is marketed as the symbol of Australia and is the tourism draw card which sustains a tourism industry worth $$$billions
- Red and grey kangaroos are treated as a pest, despite scientific research proving otherwise. Millions are shot each year and their skins and flesh exported. Recently they were re-classified as a 'sustainably harvestable resource'.
- For political expediency the Australian Government continues to facilitate and support a commercial kangaroo killing industry which bases its 'sustainable credentials' on a population counting methodology which has been criticized for decades and has been changed so often that it no longer has any value or credibility.
- The Precautionary Principle at the heart of wildlife management is not implemented. Kangaroos are shot by the millions, even through the recent worst two droughts in recorded history, to fulfill export markets for skin and flesh.

The nightmare of "utilizing wildlife resources" supposedly in order to save it, was exposed as such in 1994 by John A. Hoyt, former President of Humane Society International in his book *Animals in Peril – How sustainable use is wiping out the world's wildlife.* He warns that "unless enough people speak out and take action to stop the sustainable use behemoth that is bulldozing its way through the world's conservation community, wild animals will soon become just another commodity to be bought, sold, traded, and finally used up, when, inevitably, the demand exceeds the supply."

Ronald Wright in "A Short History of Progress" sets out a well known litany of species lost for eternity and concludes that "a bad smell of extinction follows man."

In April 2003 an alert was sounded in a Federal Government biodiversity audit, leaked to the ABC. It reports that thousands of Australia's birds, mammals and reptiles face extinction this century. The report blames vegetation land clearing for the extinction crisis. Previously, in the 1996 and 2001 State of the Environment report there were also clear calls to arms about our environmental problems.

Taxpayers unwittingly subsidise the sourcing of new kangaroo meat and skin exports, with Korea being the latest market to be opened up, as reported by Michael Mulligan of the Kangaroo Industry Association of Australia in the Presidents Report 2004 in which he commiserated that "the supply of 'raw materials', carcasses – skins-meat, was not easy for anyone in 2004". Yet the industry continues to aggressively chase new markets for kangaroo flesh export.

Eastern grey kangaroo male and female - raw materials for the KIAA. (Photo: Bill Corn)

The Herald Sun newspaper, 5th March 2005 with the headline "Roo leaps ahead in Asia," trumpets that the launch of kangaroo meat in South Korea has been a big success and the export prospects are jumping. It quotes Queensland Government spokesman Matthew Kang as saying that in South Korea "..people will soon be able to taste it at ordinary restaurants on the streets". The market in Japan is also expected to grow. As predicted by Wildlife Conservationists, now that the historically slow Asian market has been penetrated, future export quotas will, no doubt, rise exponentially to supply the demand.

The population of South Korea is around 42 million and of Japan around 128 million. Even if kangaroo consumption remains a niche market in those two countries, supplying the Asian market alone will ensure that demand will exceed supply, and for the kangaroo this guarantees a path on the road to extinction.

John Hoyt's (1994) warning, that wildlife exploitation leads to extinction, will come to pass "...many of the schemes (ie commercial sustainable use of wildlife) can be made to appear quite feasible on paper. A few may even work over the short term, particularly if they are highly localized and heavily subsidized. But the vast majority simply cannot, and do not produce the intended results under real world conditions, particularly if they involve the international sale of wild animals or their products."

The government signs off on annual kill quotas based on annual survey figures, which are then estimated and manipulated to produce population figures of mythical proportions. Yet the fact is that scientists are unable to provide precise numbers of red and grey kangaroo populations, which have in recent years been substantially decimated by the worst ongoing droughts in recorded history. Non commercial shooting, huge die off in drought, bush fires and road kill are unmonitored and not taken into account when quotas are set. No account is kept of the cruel death of millions of in pouch and at foot joeys which are bludgeoned to death, have their throat cut or are abandoned to a slow death after their mothers are shot. This barbarism is kept out of the public record, as those gruesome numbers are the by catch of the 'sustainable use' of wildlife and are considered invalid in the scheme of kangaroo commercialization and export.

During two recent Administrative Appeals Tribunal (AAT) hearings (AAT 2003, 2004), initiated by wildlife protection groups, which challenged the NSW, Queensland, WA and SA Kangaroo Management Programs, it became clear that State NPWS evidence to defend their management of commercial kangaroo killing and protect kangaroos and joeys from extreme cruelty, failed to present recent up to date research and scholarship. The conclusion is that the science on which the Government has based the killing of Australia's national symbol could be seen as deficient.

The Kangaroo Industry Association of Australia states in their Newsletter Sept. 2004 "Annual aerial surveys may not be the most efficient survey frequency", a fact self evident to wildlife protection groups, but one which seems only to have become apparent to the commercial industry since our recent challenges to their State Kangaroo Management Programs, through the AAT. Wildlife groups insist that population surveys ought to be carried out twice a year in view of the decimation of kangaroo populations due to drought and global warming. In 1983 kangaroo populations dived, in 2002-3 Red Kangaroo numbers crashed by 50-75% in NSW and populations have continued to be drought affected in 2004-5. The fact is that the kangaroo industry will not stop killing kangaroos even during the worst drought on record because they need to supply their markets. They will not heed or comply with the Precautionary Principle, a vital scientific component for the ongoing survival of the species.

By its own admission the kangaroo killing industry is worth only around $230 million annually, today's equivalent of the biblical 30 pieces of silver for the Kangaroo Betrayed. The mantra of sustainable commercialism continues to be supported by its proponents.

Professor Michael Archer, the then newly appointed director of the Australian Museum speaking of his FATE project in a radio interview with Michael Condon on the ABC 24.2.1999 said "What we are trying to do is say that there's a lot of wisdom now about how you could actually start to turn to utilizing native resources in a sustainable way. To value them first and then understand that they are an economic resource ...and in the process secure our biota into the future and make everybody filthy stinking rich along the way". The FATE project proposes 'farming' Australia's iconic kangaroos instead of sheep and cattle and breeding up native animals like crocodiles or koalas for export. Prof. Michael Archer is a leading light of 'sustainable use' of Australia's wildlife even whilst holding the appointment of Dean of Science at the University of New South Wales.

The commercial kangaroo killing industry as well as the Australian Government claim vociferously that the killing of millions of kangaroos each year for export is based on good science and sustainability. The public and wildlife protection groups view that statement through the perception that science in recent years has become the minion of raw commercialism and economic rationalism whilst insisting that its independence and autonomy is not compromised in such a symbiotic relationship.

The critical point is that the survival of any of our wildlife species depends on a multitude of interrelated complex factors. If we exert continual pressure through the shooting of the biggest and best animals, the carriers of strongest genes, this could very well precipitate the rapid extinction of the commercially shot kangaroo species.

The current emergency in Tasmania regarding the possible extinction of the Tasmanian devil, is a case in point. A species once considered to be common and plentiful only 5 years ago, has been decimated by up to 70%. NPWS state that the cancer is linked to a virus.
However, when one examines the epidemic of cancer rates in humans it is hard to ignore the fact that numerous pesticides, are implicated as a causal factor in cancer. It was predicted decades ago that cancer rates would increase once synthetic chemicals became commonplace in our lives. After World War 2 billions of tons of chemicals were released into our environment.
The use of chemicals and pesticides by the timber plantation industry is well known in Tasmania and 1080 a poison banned in the USA and other countries is used extensively in order to kill native wildlife which may graze on plantation seedlings and Tasmania devils being scavengers feed on the poisoned native animals. Wildlife conservationists are wondering, what is the part played by the diverse and deadly chemicals used in Tasmania on the epidemic killing the Tassie Devil from facial cancer?

If second hand chemical poisoning is leading to the shutdown of the animals immune response to a virus, and chemicals are the causal factor of the cancer, conservationists warn that it is unlikely anyone will be able to halt the Tasmanian devils slide towards quasi extinction in the next few years. There is a call for the species to be placed on the endangered list, but that in itself will not halt the disease and the species' slide to extinction. The facial cancer killing the Tasmanian devil has caught the Government agencies unprepared, under-funded and scrambling to contain the destructive impact such a wildlife disease has on the tourism market and on the supposedly clean, green image of Tasmania and its valuable food exports.

One can only imagine what effect a similar disease wipe-out of kangaroos would have on the image of Australia abroad, not to speak of the psychologically destructive effect it would have on how Australians view themselves through our unique icon.

The kangaroo is not a species magically immune from commercial exploitation. In addition to that onslaught, Tim Flannery in his book 'Country' provides an urgent warning regarding the negative impact of global warming on red kangaroo fertility. He reports that a study in 1980 by Alan Newsome shows that low male fertility results from heat stress on the testicles of reds which have moved to treeless and shade-less plains.

"Newsome's study provided a valuable insight on how delicately balanced life is on this continent, and how easy it is to damage its creatures. It also filled me with fear for the future of the large kangaroos in the face of global warming." (Flannery 2004)

THE ECONOMIC AND ECOLOGICAL INFEASIBILITY

OF LARGE VOLUME KANGAROO FARMING

By Geoff Russell

B.A Hons, B.Sc (Maths), Animal Liberation SA

Page 292 of Jared Diamond's (2005) massive new book *Collapse* is the most remarkable page of any book I've read for a very long time.
It describes how the people of the tiny pacific island of Tikopia decided 400 years ago that eating pigs was unsustainable. They made a judgement that pigs cost more to raise than they contributed by way of being eaten. Keep in mind that this was a society that liked eating pigs. The decision wasn't taken because they loved their little *babe* mates, --- on the contrary, they killed them all --- it was a totally rational decision taken by an entire people who were acutely aware of the finite nature of their resources and the need for efficient management if they were to avoid catastrophe.

Many Australians are waking up to the massive costs of raising traditional western livestock. Our cattle produce even more greenhouse gases than our infatuation with motor cars (Australian Greenhouse Office 2002). The meat and dairy industries are also prodigious users and polluters of water. Some of this water is to grow grass and is thought to be 'free' but as more intensive livestock systems are used --- our cattle feedlot capacity is now some 10% of the herd size (Australian Bureau of Statistics 2002) --- the water they use comes from rivers and dams. Meat industry pollution sources include abattoirs, feedlots, and, in particular, the pig industry. The usual measure of the quality of water is the BOD (Biochemical Oxygen Demand --- the amount of oxygen required by bacteria for the decomposition of organic matter in 5 days at a standard temperature). The BOD of human sewage is 300 to 500 mg per liter, piggery effluent has a BOD of more than 5,000 mg per litre (FSA - Environmental Queensland 2000).

But, unlike the Tikopians, most Australians just can't seem to put 2 and 2 together. The love of BBQs is obviously as ingrained and counterproductive as the love of motor cars and alcohol (all too frequently together). So they seize on any alternative that saves them from biting the bullet and giving up eating meat. Kangaroo farming is just one of many 'wild food' fads that has gained attention. No-one can argue against the possibility that shooting, skinning, and butchering some kangaroos might be a profitable niche industry with suitable marketing and a global economy that can put rich, self-centred 'gourmet' consumers with jaded taste buds in touch with suppliers.

But it is easy to show that a niche market is all that it is or can ever be. The kangaroo industry won't replace either the sheep or cattle industry, it won't solve the problems we have created by mining our countryside with cruel and inefficient animal based industries. All you need to see this is a little common sense, a bit of basic data, and a little numeracy.

Kangaroo killing is performed at night with a spot light and is not a task favoured by graziers who generally work during the day. (Photo: Bill Corn)

First some common sense. Kangaroos don't herd. You can't pack them into trucks and deliver them fresh to abattoirs for processing. Kangaroo shooters work at night and it is unpleasant, lonely, difficult and back breaking work.

Despite kill quotas of over 6 million in some years, actual numbers killed are more likely 2 to 3 million. Hardman (1996) states that the average age of graziers is 57. Do you really think they want to give up their nights in front of 'Big Brother' to spend all night shooting kangaroos?

Now for a few sums. We currently kill about 15% of our kangaroo population annually and get a mere 600 tonnes of meat for human consumption (Hardman 1996). That's about 240g per animal. Even if we add in the meat sold as pet food, each kangaroo yields just 6.8 kg per animal. Even if we stop leaving kangaroos shot for the skin trade to rot in paddocks, we still have to realise that they are small animals. The biggest of our kangaroos, the male reds, have an average live weight of only 65kg, with the females a mere 25kg (Strahan 1983). Take out the bones, skin and the other inedibles, and there just isn't much left. Grey kangaroos are even smaller at about 2/3 of this weight. A Queensland Department of Primary Industries study \cite{hardman} into the harvest of kangaroos used in its calculations a figure of about 10kg of saleable meat per kangaroo --- with just 3kg as prime meat and the rest as only suitable for "manufactured meat". Note that this figure of 3kg is quite different from the average of 240g per animal --- which shows just how many animals are not even butchered but left to rot.

The time between kills for a kangaroo shooter range from 4 minutes to around 20 minutes (Hacker *et al.* 2004) and are surprisingly not very dependent on kangaroo density. At say 10 minutes per animal, a Kangaroo shooter takes 6 per hour which is a grand total of 60Kg of saleable meat for an hours' hard work - and the butchering still has to be done. Compare that with a 300kg dressed cattle carcase.

In fact, the Queensland DPI puts the maximum potential supply of Kangaroo meat at just 57,000 tonnes per year (Hardman 1996). In comparison, cattle supply over 1,700,000 tonnes of beef each year (Australian Bureau of Statistics 1999: 424). To get 1,700,000 tonnes of kangaroo meat for human consumption, we would need, at present efficiency rates, to be killing the entire kangaroo population hundreds of times over each year.

Nor is finger-lick'n possum a real option as a mass production meat industry. We currently put 370 million chickens in sheds each year (Australian Bureau of Statistics 1999: 424) and raise a 2 kg bird in 7 weeks using 3.2kg of feed (plus a stack of antibiotics - of course)(SARDI 1999). Try that trick with brush tailed possums. Firstly, they are solitary animals which fight when housed in groups. Second, they take about 8-12 months to get to a 2kg liveweight, and lastly they eat a big heap of food getting there.

If significant numbers of Australians were to regularly eat kangaroos, or possums, or ducks, or any other of our native species you care to mention, then those animals would be wiped out in no time.

Many people forget that we have had widespread 'wildlife utilisation' for most of our history and that many of our wildlife protection laws arose because of the damage that was done to our wildlife during that period. For example, the 1885 Game Act in South Australia outlawed the use of the punt gun, a device mounted on a boat which could reputedly kill 150 pelicans with one shot. The sale of wild ducks was banned in 1928 in South Australia to protect the population, and even earlier in Victoria (Stokes 1990).

Our current choices of domestic crops and animals aren't an accident. They have been purpose bred and selected for thousands of years. The modern corncob is much larger than its 1/2 inch ancestor and the animals are bigger, and easier to herd and manage. Jared Diamond's (1997) book *Guns, Germs and Steel* gives a solid history of food and the imperatives behind the change to farming and away from wildlife utilisation --- which is really just a fancy word for hunter-gathering. With 20 million people in Australia, there is no going back. Wildlife can never provide serious food for such a population.

What's the most efficient way of feeding people? Thats easy. A quick glance at the Australian Year Book tells us that about 65% of Australia is listed as agricultural and 95% of this is used for grazing --- and we export about half of the animal products produced. The other 5% (of the 65%) is cropped. It is therefore obvious that if you want to maximise the number of people fed while also minimising the land used to do it, then you won't eat animals --- wild or domestic.

The Tikopian's worked this out 400 years ago --- but we as a society are just a little too thick and a lot too greedy.

THE LAST BIG RED?

By Katherine Rogers

Vice president of World League for the Protection of Animals

You'll see him on our coat of arms and on T-shirts. He's prominent at sporting events. We see him in story books for children. We see him almost anywhere we want to express our national pride as Australians. He's Big Red – the largest, the fastest and the strongest of our kangaroos. And he may be on the way out. The escalating shooting of Australia's symbol, for his skin and his flesh may mean the only Big Red we'll be seeing will be on the tail of a Qantas jet.

An exaggeration? Sadly, no.

Tonight, and every night of the year, four-wheel drives will crisscross the fragile soil of rangelands seeking their kill. Tonight and every night, thousands of kangaroos will be shot. Not all will die quickly. Many will be wounded, to linger on over days or weeks till death ends their suffering. Joeys will be torn from the pouch and clubbed to death, or flee into the bush to die of starvation. As the killing continues unabated, inevitably the time will come when the last Big Red, pinioned by a spotlight in the night, joins in death the millions of his fellows who have been killed to supply the world with soccer boots, or the thrill of eating the flesh of a wild and unique animal. Or perhaps, Big Red will be wiped out by a disease sweeping through the populations as the diversity of their gene pool is eroded through the killing of the largest and strongest – the Alpha males who lead the mobs and, together with the older females pass on the ancient wisdom that has enabled them to survive in this dry land.

Young male red kangaroo destined to box his way up the hierarchy to mating success or be shot?
(Photo: Ulrike Kloecker)

Perhaps the last Big Red will die as the last Tasmanian Tiger did – in a lonely enclosure behind the wire in a zoo. When this happens, an animal perfectly attuned to the Australian environment through thousands of generations of evolution will be lost to us forever.

How have we come to this point?

Whether for food, fun or profit, Australia's wildlife has been in shooters' sights since before the First Fleet. Captain Cook fed his starving crew on kangaroo meat. "The Kanguru are in the greatest number," he writes in his journal on 4th August 1770, "for we seldom went into the country without seeing some."

But today's massive commercial kill of kangaroos cannot be justified on the grounds of starvation, or even cost-effectiveness. Unlike sheep and cattle, kangaroos have not been bred for thousands of years to be food animals. They are slow to grow and have little flesh on their bones. If the eating of kangaroo flesh took off in a big way then the kangaroo industry would soon shoot itself out of existence.

What then is the justification for the kill?

Throughout much of the 19th century, all that was local, all that was Australian, was little valued. Many people – whether new settlers or Australian born - could see no beauty in Australia's olive green forests, could hear no music in the song of her birds. There was even a proposal to bring in monkeys to provide interest to an unexciting landscape. Possum hunts were common, as was the hunting of kangaroos and other wildlife, though not in the huge numbers we see today.

But over time, attitudes changed, both in Australia and overseas. With wilderness areas and wildlife increasingly disappearing over the last 150 years, has come a realization that wildlife, and the wild places of the world, are precious. Together with this, has come an increasing perception that killing or capturing wildlife is cruel and cannot be justified. It was in this context, that in the 1990s, the Federal Government put forward the concept of the of the commercial use of wildlife

What does this phrase mean? Basically, it means turning wildlife into a marketplace commodity on the principle that if we can make money out of wildlife, we have a strong motive to preserve it. In a submission to the Government on this issue, the Hon. Richard Jones, MLC wrote:

"The sustainable use strategy designed to protect wildlife by giving it a commercial value has been an abysmal failure globally. It was intended primarily to ensure the survival of dwindling species in third world countries as the habitat of endangered species was slashed and burnt and cleared for other human activities. . .(However) it has increased pressure on wildlife populations and done nothing to conserve species." (Commercial Utilisation of Native Wildlife. Public Hearing Parliament House Macquarie St Sydney 9 September 1997 Submission No. 197)

There are many myths about the kangaroo - the ancient myths of the aboriginal people linking them to their land. And more recent myths with a different purpose - myths designed to hide the facts and obscure the truth. For example the myth that killing kangaroos is sustainable.

The so-called "sustainable use" strategy appears to justify the kill. It says: By putting a dollar value on our wildlife we will save it for future generations. Or so the rhetoric goes. So kangaroos and other fauna are no longer living, feeling creatures. They are "resources" to be 'utilized'. That is, hunted, captured, killed, sold, made into handbags or sausages or scrotum purses - whatever the market desires.

In 1996 John A. Hoyt President of the Humane Society International wrote in *Animals In Peril: How 'Sustainable Use' is Wiping Out the World's Wildlife:* "The biggest problem with sustainable use is that it is not sustainable. After a while, you begin to run out of animals to 'use'. In short, sustainable use is defensible only in theory; it is unworkable in application and tragic in effect. It usually results in overexploitation and decimation of the species involved. Profit incentives have never protected wildlife.

Male red kangaroos fight in a method akin to boxers sparring. The goal is to assess the skills of the opponent and gain training for later fights over mating rights.
(Photo: Ulrike Kloecker)

There is something fundamentally wrong with the concept of exploiting and utilising wildlife for profit, not the least of which is that it benefits only a handful of individuals and companies."

In reducing the kangaroo to an animal which provides us with its flesh to eat in a restaurant or its skin to put on our floor or turn into soccer boots, we are doing neither the kangaroo nor ourselves any favor. For many people, the kangaroo is a magical creature - an animal that can speed over the ground almost in flight on its gigantic hind legs, an animal that is born as a tiny little grub-like creature, that can find its own way to the mother's pouch, and lie there secure for many months, attached to her nipple - an animal unlike any other in the world, an animal unique and wonderful.

If we wish to make money out of these magical creatures, we could do so by emphasizing their uniqueness, by instilling a sense of wonder at their capacity to survive in this harsh land and encouraging people from round the world to come to Australia to see them alive in the wild.

Our community is undergoing significant social changes, with substantially increased awareness of the institutionalized cruelties and suffering inflicted on animals together with a conviction that these cruelties should not be allowed to continue. These changes are not reflected in the current push to commercialize our wildlife. Moreover, we have still a great deal to learn about the complex inter-relationships existing within the wide range of Australian ecosystems. It has been estimated that only 15% of Australian species have yet been identified. We are, it is said, blundering about the natural environment "like an elephant in a pansy patch". Because our understanding of ecosystems is so limited, we can only guess at the possible impact of commercial utilisation activities. But there can be no doubt that such activities as the massive killing of kangaroos could have a substantial impact on the functioning of entire ecosystems. As the wild places of the world continue to disappear at an alarming rate, Australia could move to a policy of genuine conservation and preservation of its remaining wilderness areas and accept the fact that current land uses in marginal areas are disastrous for the environment on which our economy and wildlife depend.

The way to protect biodiversity is to strongly promote and encourage a view that the natural world is valuable for its own sake and essential - because our survival depends on it. The commercial use of wildlife may change irreparably such functioning.

Sadly, we haven't learnt much in the last 50,000 years. Like the first humans who came to this continent we are treading a path which may lead to massive extinctions. Or we may with our awareness of the dangers ahead, act with caution and compassion, so that the kangaroo and other wildlife will survive and flourish.

The kangaroo is part of the Australian landscape. In its droppings it carries the seeds of native grasses with which it replenishes the land. It is an enduring symbol of us, as a nation. It is up to us, today's generation, to determine whether it will continue to be so.

The choice is ours.

Large red male kangaroo in the vast expanse of a Mitchell grasslands faces an uncertain future.
(Photo: David B Croft)

POLITICS VERSUS ECOLOGY

By Lindy Stacker

Former Greenpeace Campaigner, 15 year member of
the NSW Kangaroo Management Advisory Committee,
and Spokeperson for the Australians Against
Commercialisation of Wildlife.

A 'trial' commercial harvest of eastern grey kangaroos was
approved by the Commonwealth Minister for Environment and
Heritage in December 2003 and commenced in March 2004.
The Commercial Kangaroo Killing Zone was extended into South
Eastern NSW (Goulburn, Braidwood, Gundagai, Yass, Queanbeyan
and Cooma) Rural Land Protection areas – a first, as for decades
previously the Commercial Zone only existed west of the Dividing
Range. The 'trial' will run until 2007.

The Yass, Queanbeyan and Cooma Rural Land Protection Areas are the last undisturbed areas
where kangaroos still retain their rich, complex, family-structured mobs intact. Alpha males are
still fighting for the right to pass on their strongest genes and are the much-needed role model for
younger males, while females teach their offspring how to survive. The areas are also home to a
number of endangered and threatened birds, reptiles and vertebrates.

Due to escalating industry and farming pressure, it is unrealistic to
expect a cessation to shooting in the south east extensions in 2007.
National Parks and Wildlife Service assure us that the industry "will be
closely monitored to ensure conservation status of the eastern grey
kangaroos". In reality, this means when the species is so over
'harvested' and stressed, reducing economic incentives, where it is
uneconomical for shooters to go out at night and shoot, the industry may
get a reduction in quotas. When kangaroo species were reduced to 50%
to 80% across their entire range over NSW in 2003, the killing did not
stop.

During 2003, the Premier Bob Carr was stating that this was the worst drought in one hundred
years. Still no reduction in the quota was forthcoming. The commercial NSW quota for 2004 is
1,388,411. With an additional special quota available on top of this quota, just in case the
industry needs it. How scientific! With export markets for leather and kangaroo meat now driving

Maligned eastern grey kangaroo faces threat at Googong Dam. (Photo: Bill Corn)

to shoot the eight hundred kangaroos. Wildlife groups stopped the kill after an unknown number of kangaroos were shot, and Animal Liberation ACT sought information via a Freedom of Information request. The FOI documents include internal e-mails, draft briefing statements, annotated reports and details of arrangements made with neighbouring farmers during the Googong kill. The documents also revealed that the kangaroo kill had indeed worried some scientists.

The FOI documents show that after shooting started, Environment ACT kangaroo expert Dr Murray Evans wrote to senior staff, " ... as expressed previously. I still have reservations over the decision to go ahead with reducing roo numbers."

Senior ecologist Don Fletcher, who is studying kangaroo populations at Googong for his doctoral thesis, repeatedly complained his advice was ignored and requests to be involved in decision-making regarding the cull were rejected.

"At the moment," he wrote, (post 18 January 2003) "the Googong roos might be a water supply insurance asset for Canberra and Queanbeyan". He argued ground-cover was "consistently lower where roos were shot" on neighbouring properties, and low ground-cover at Googong was partly due to the impact of a severe storm in March 2003. He also suggested the cull could potentially increase bushfire risk.

FOI documents show Mr Fletcher persistently called for Government officials to "re-think" the decision to kill the grey kangaroos at Googong, arguing it was not science-based, poorly thought out and did not meet Government policy standards. In an email to senior staff, he wrote, "In the twenty eight year history of (Parks and Conservation) wildlife monitoring programs, there has rarely been such a dramatic change as the recent decline in kangaroo density at Googong.
An environment agency needs a culture that respects knowledge and learning, rather than a culture of expediency. One of the senior proponents of the roo shoot said to me that the shooting was needed for political reasons, and he did not care if it was ineffective".

Clearly the ACT Government's own scientists had strong reservations about the Googong kangaroo kill. The Freedom of Information file also show that the operation was by initiated by ACT Parks ranger Peter Mills. He wrote that farmers shooting kangaroos on properties adjacent to the reserve had complained Googong was harbouring kangaroos. As preparations for the cull proceeded, he again wrote to Environment ACT that six local farmers were "tickled pink that we are heading down this road".

As part of their strategy to gather public support for a kill, the ACT Government claimed that kangaroo populations at Googong had exploded. However, the FOI documents confirm Government data showed kangaroo numbers had crashed by 65% in recent months. After these facts were made public, a Government spokesman said the Chief Minister was "well aware" the population had dropped by 65%.

Political expediency defeats scientific facts for eastern grey kangaroos in the ACT. (Photo: Bill Corn)

But Environment ACT executive director Dr Maxine Cooper has dismissed all the scientific dissent as "robust debate", claiming the documents represent only "part of a conversation" about the cull. She said the scientists concerned had assisted with compiling reports to support the cull as part of "a team effort". A spokesman for ACT Chief Minister Jon Stanhope said the minister had authorised the cull based on advice received from Environment ACT. "Robust debate is vital in any organisation and Environment ACT is no different," he said in a statement. "Information provided in FOI material, particularly e-mail correspondence, is very easily taken out of context and can be interpreted many ways depending on who is reading it."

Animal Liberation spokeswoman Simone Gray has called for Mr Stanhope to make a public apology for the Googong cull. "There should be an independent inquiry into why the advice of two experts was completely ignored and an overhaul of the whole Environment ACT process on how decisions are made to kill animals," she said.

This carnage was a first in Australian history, not just because it happened in a fauna reserve, as this has happened before, but because never before had the industry been allowed to commercialise the animals shot within a fauna reserve. How incredibly convenient that this region had only been opened up to the commercial industry some six months previously. Coincidences like this don't happen every day. Our kangaroos were used as the voiceless scapegoat, yet again in our nation's obscene race for profit, where our irreplaceable wildlife is only viewed as a consumer commodity by powerful institutions and vested interests.

This is exactly what environmentalists and animal welfare organizations predicted would happen, once industries and Governments joined forces to promote wildlife as a mere "Renewable Resource".

The Chief Minister for the ACT Jon Stanhope has yet to answer my many letters and faxes in relation to the FOI documents, or prior to receiving them. However, he has responded to letters from concerned citizens, relative to the Googong kill, by stating they are uninformed and the killing of the kangaroos was necessary based on Government advice which instructed him to take this action. This is certainly not what the FOI documents revealed, many of which were inter-departmental documents. The fact remains that the above-mentioned documents (and more) revealed an insidious plan to shoot 800 kangaroos as an expedient political measure no matter what the advice was to the contrary and no matter what the cost. The entire brutal exercise was a fait accompli.

A NPWS Queanbeyan Office also was of no assistance, refusing to answer correspondence and simply passing on our enquiries to Head Office in Dubbo. They too did not bother to answer our enquiries until weeks later. In other words, a wall of silence became the game plan until all publicity faded away.

The ACT government failed to undertake any meaningful public consultation before deciding to shoot hundreds of kangaroos in a fauna reserve. They made no attempt to negotiate a solution with environmentalists, ecologists, the general public, scientists, or animal welfare organisations.

Government representatives had decided to again take sides with the farming community, who had instigated the commercial killing of kangaroos in the south eastern region in the first place. At every given opportunity the same officials talk up the values of "balance", sustainability, objectivity and science based outcomes and decisions. All of which is a total nonsense, because when push comes to shove, our Government representatives choose "subjectively" as to whom they selectively decide to listen to. When scientific advice is given by experts in the region, appeasing rural interests definitely outweighs all other interests combined. To the detriment of us all, profit (and votes) supercede ecological decisions, animal welfare considerations and last but not least, common sense.

In simple terms, we all stand to benefit from eco tourism, whilst only a few benefit from short term commercial killing. Wildlife industries are not sustainable; no-one needs products derived from the suffering of wild animals who have needs independent of our own. Until politics is removed from ecological decision making, incidents such as the infamous Googong Dam slaughter will continue. We will see more and more of our wildlife decimated and senselessly exterminated.
We humans are not the centre of the universe, and our needs are not paramount over other species. Another way must be possible otherwise we are all doomed to the same sad fate as our diminishing wildlife.

Boxing male eastern grey kangaroos: malign, kill and use once or use their fascinating behaviour many times in wildlife tourism? (Photo: Jan Aldenhoven)

Eastern grey kangaroo at Googong Dam. (Photo: Bill Corn)

SLAUGHTER AT GOOGONG DAM

By Mary Lander

Kangaroos - an integral part of the Australian environment, it's heritage and it's landscape but the culling and the indifference to the plight of Australia's maligned and misunderstood Majestic Marsupials continues… Googong Dam – 2004

I'd like to commence with a few of my favourite quotes….

"If you have men who will exclude any of God's creatures from the shelter of compassion and pity, you will have men who deal likewise with their fellow men. Not to hurt our humble brethren is our first duty to them, but to stop there is not enough. We have a higher mission - to be of service to them wherever they require it."

~ St Francis of Assisi

"The love for all living creatures is the most noble attribute of man."

~ Charles Darwin

"The world is a dangerous place, not because of those who do evil, but because of those who look on and do nothing."

~ Albert Einstein

….and add, by way of contrast, a not-so-favourite quote….

"We're going to keep killing the kangaroos, and if the commercial shooters are not allowed to do it and sell the bodies, we will dig a big hole in the ground and dump all in the dead kangaroos in it!"

~ Jon Stanhope, ACT Chief Minister and Minister for the Environment

Jon Stanhope authorised the culling of kangaroos on the Googong Dam Foreshores, land managed jointly by ACT and NSW Government. He claimed that the kangaroo cull was essential in order to protect the quality of drinking water from Canberra's water supply. At face value this sounded like a responsible gesture, but was it?

Water from Googong Dam is fully treated and this involves conventional treatment such as coagulation by liquid alum and a polymer coagulant aid, flocculation, clarification and filtration, disinfection by chlorination, pH adjustment and stabilisation with lime, fluoridation by sodium silico fluoride.

In addition to this, his claims that overgrazing by kangaroos had reduced ground-cover at Googong to a level that presented a threat to water quality from run-off, were somewhat dubious as well, given drought conditions at the time.

Juvenile eastern grey kangaroos of no commercial value at Googong Dam. (Photo: Bill Corn)

Kangaroos are soft-footed and not hoofed animals and do no damage to the environment. They are in fact, an integral part of the Australian environment and it just wouldn't be Australia without them. The soft padded feet and long tail of the kangaroo are essential for the ecological health of the land as regenerators of native grasses.

In keeping with the Spirit of Australia, a protest was arranged by Animal Liberation who then sought the assistance of Pat O'Brien, the co-ordinator of the National Kangaroo Protection Coalition, an alliance of 29 Australian animal welfare and wildlife protection groups. Representatives demanded that Jon Stanhope produce the scientific evidence to support his claims of water contamination. Challenged by citizens who sought to hold him accountable for claims made publicly and without the scientific evidence to support those claims, Jon Stanhope, ACT Chief Minister and Minister for the Environment became most indignant and called in the NSW Police to stop the protest.

"This was not the first time that NSW National Parks has issued kangaroo kill permits in a Protected Area, but it was the first time they have used commercial kangaroo shooters in this manner. After some investigation we discovered that NSW National Parks were developing management Plans for new National Parks, which included a clause to allow them to commercially shoot kangaroos in those National Parks as well!

In other words, a strategy was being developed within the two government departments, without due consultation process, to provide commercial kangaroo shooters with access to Protected Areas, including National Parks! Nowhere in NSW or ACT would be safe for kangaroos, there would be no refuge anywhere for our unique and special kangaroos!"

~ Pat O'Brien, National Kangaroo Protection Coalition

The move to extend commercial harvesting into the 5 new zones around Canberra outraged animal welfare groups, who expressed their disgust with methods used to kill the kangaroos and their joeys. Animal rights advocates delivered a dead joey to the ACT Government, claiming it had been bashed to death after its mother was shot.

"After their mothers are shot, joeys are bashed to death. Female kangaroos are targeted which means for every female killed, there is one joey killed. Joeys are killed either by decapitation or by a blow to the head - this normally means their heads are bashed against the side of the shooter's truck or they are hit on the head with an iron bar or water pipe.

These methods are approved under the Code of Practice for the Humane Shooting of Kangaroos. Unfortunately, Australians get very upset about Koreans eating dogs or cats and baby seals being clubbed, but they really now need to look at how we're treating animals in our own back yard. "

~ Animal Liberation ACT Spokesperson Simone Gray

But Jon Stanhope would not give in, stating that they are killed using approved and humane methods.

In addition to this, water test results obtained from ACTEW showed no sign of contamination to the water in the dam at the time of the cull. The only incidence of contamination was a few months prior and contamination consisted of a blue green algae bloom.

As Googong Dam is in a rural catchment area, the most likely cause of blue green algae would be the presence of chemicals and pesticides used in rural catchment areas and which find their way into the dam through run-off during periods of rain. As some forms of blue green algae may be toxic to fish, birds and wildlife, it is quite irresponsible for government not to address this issue with farmers in the rural catchment area. This was particularly so, as the Googong Dam

Foreshores are a wildlife refuge and recreational area attracting those who like picnicking, bird watching and viewing wildlife, bushwalking, mountain bike riding, sailing or fishing.

Hoping to redeem himself and present himself publicly as a compassionate man, Jon Stanhope then claimed the reason for the cull was because the kangaroos were starving.

"The kangaroos at Googong are definitely not starving."

~ Simone Gray, Animal Liberation

"A NSW RSPCA inspector was then taken into the Dam site by Environment ACT to justify these statements, and he claimed the kangaroos were starving because they were eating in the middle of the day, and were not afraid of people.

However kangaroo expert Dr David Croft publicly refuted the claim, saying that kangaroos often fed in the middle of the day in winter, and the kangaroos at Googong were used to people and unafraid of them. We then realised that made it much easier for the shooters to kill them too, as they could get quite close, almost put the gun up against the head of the near-tame kangaroos and shoot them."

~ Pat O'Brien, National Kangaroo Protection Coalition

Of course, commercial shooters are after their 'pound of flesh' and if the kangaroos were emaciated then there would be no 'pound of flesh' to get.

Habituated eastern grey kangaroo in repose. (Photo: Bill Corn)

"Unfortunately the weather at the time around the Googong Dam site was as cold as the heart of the ACT government, so continual on-site protests were not easy. I must say that I have spent more than 30 years trying to find better options than killing wildlife, and trying to instil better attitudes towards wildlife management decisions within government. I have attended hundreds of meetings with politicians and bureaucrats, some easy going, some a bit tense, but mostly all productive. Unfortunately I must also say that in this case that I have never been treated so badly by any government department, or any politician."

~ Pat O'Brien, National Kangaroo Protection Coalition

Although the protestors did their best, gun-shattered silence did the rest at the direction of Jon Stanhope and somewhere between 800-1000 kangaroos were killed and their joeys bludgeoned to death. Only a dozen or so were salvaged and taken to local wildlife carers for rehabilitation and release.

And while government continues to have no regard for creation and the environment, while our common natural heritage suffers devastation due to financial greed and our kangaroos are killed capriciously and are egoistically destroyed, their dying eyes will keep asking us "Why?".

Orphaned eastern grey joey. (Photo: Bill Corn)

"Hopefully, through this campaign we have got our message across to the community at large, that the commercial kangaroo Industry is not based on sustainability, or any credible environmental criteria. It is based on political expediency, and the need for politicians to pacify noisy, vested interest rural groups.

Most of all, the commercial kangaroo Industry is based on greed, deliberate scientific misinformation, and the cruel and unsustainable financial exploitation of our unique and gentle kangaroos."

~ Pat O'Brien,
National Kangaroo Protection Coalition

PARADIGM SHIFTS

IN PUBLIC PERCEPTION AND CONSERVATION MANAGEMENT OF MACROPODS

By Mark G. Cairns

BSc (Biol), Post.Grad.Dip (Zoology)
Currently Zoologist for Endangered Species Recovery, and formerly Director of Research and Monitoring, Australian Landscape Trust, Calperum and Taylorville Stations, Riverland (Bookmark) Biosphere, South Australia.

Unlike typical science, it is hard to discuss social change to biological problems without the support of rigorous scientific data. Yet, it is compelling to see and report what can be possible when immersed in a proactive community with a need and want for professional input and continued education to wildlife issues in their own backyard.

The environment and perceptions

It would be both naïve and foolish to think that we can continue to live life as we currently do, and expect that somewhere along the line somebody or something will solve all our environmental problems for us. It is almost a given fact that nearly everybody is going to have to play some part (be it only very minor) in making real progress in reversing deleterious processes. We cannot ignore the issues and debates over global warming, with plenty of evidence to suggest we should be expecting a dryer climate for a number of years to come. We cannot ignore the fact that we have had roughly 25 non-drought years in the last 100.
With fragmented habitats and altered ecosystems never has there been such stress placed on native fauna populations and the remaining habitats that they rely upon. Despite the perceptions, large kangaroo species throughout Australia are under considerable stress.

We should also accept that there is no such thing left as true wilderness. Unfortunately the fact remains that we have to impose some degree of management on protected areas.
We simply can no longer lock up conservation estates and expect them to look after themselves. With 12% of the earth's terrestrial ecosystems protected (doubling since 1993) extinction rates continue to escalate (Terborgh 2004). Recently the chief executive officer of the Nature Conservancy, arguably having the largest private network of conservation reserves on the planet with a philosophy focussing on saving the last great places, has acknowledged that work and conservation must be served beyond their park boundaries. Keeping islands of wilderness fenced and made off–limits to the ravages of human development will only become vestiges

for further animal extinctions (McCormick 2003). It is agreed that Australia is still a biome of infinite diversity and uniqueness with finite resources. Yet, there are still those with a hypothetical dysfunctional intelligence gene that renders them with the fantasy that there are infinite resources to be exploited in Australia's extremely precarious and delicate ecosystems sensitive to human vibrations. The last 200 years has proven otherwise.

As a nation we are lucky to have real backyard wildlife. There are now very few places left on earth in the developed world that can make this claim and it makes outsiders envious. This is ironic when it is under considerable threat.

To argue over the levels of endangerment for species, and consequently their importance, is irrelevant because if current trends persist everything will be under threat (Phipps, G.R. pers. commun.). Much of the ignorance is born by the fact that most people are not in connection with the outside world. Our children are sold by the commercial electronic entertainment industry, which continually fosters a separation from the real world and its issues. Ultimately biological heritage, empathy and its understanding are lost.

In many semi-arid/arid rangeland regions many land managers can work their whole professional career (~40 years) and still never witness all the ecological processes. Many rural dwellers have now been around long enough to see the changes in the environment for themselves, with what they see not matching the stories told by relatives past. These are changes that have, and have not, been predicted by science.

The conservation and management of macropods, is placed in its own arena by suffering pressure from economics and sustainability. Kangaroos, and their management, are at the forefront to changes in public perception. Conservation culling occurs purely and solely as a result of altered landscapes and unsustainable practices.

Rock wallabies, like the black-footed rock-wallaby, are marooned in isolated reserves under threat from goats and foxes.
(Photo: Pat O'Brien)

Temperate woodlands and semi-arid shrub/ grasslands are the greatest refuge for large kangaroo species. These habitats are probably at greatest risk to the influence of climate change. With already altered ecosystems further changes could see significant transformations in kangaroo population densities. Historic productive areas that represented refugia for kangaroos no longer exist and are forced into marginal rangelands.

Management responsibility

An easy way out has been the use of the commercial kangaroo shooter.

If commercial harvesting were a sustainable and profitable industry it would already be a significant contributor to Australia's gross national product. It is not.

Current kangaroo control measures are counterproductive to their conservation management, as they do not mimic the natural ecological integrity of undisturbed wild populations. It has behavioural consequences. Ignoring the genetic based ramifications, culling (if it has to be implemented it should be for conservation outcomes only – not sustainability) should be demographic not physiographic.

Large battle-scarred male common wallaroo in a population protected from shooting. (Photo: Ulrike Kloecker)

Once the large males have been removed displacing natural sex ratios, disrupting behavioural population controls through group dynamics, the effective population is diminished. But with the onset of maturation of previously 'undersized' males, coupled the increased availability of females per individual male, within three years the total population is almost at twice the previous density.

-    This puts a greater strain on already meagre environmental resources for fauna.
-    Has a negative impact on the preservation and restoration on conservation estates.
-    Reduces the overall population health and stability of macropod species.

To artificially spike kangaroo numbers due to irresponsible management via an unsustainable and unregulated industry is both unethical and completely counterproductive to all natural values.

Unlike the inherit nature of a bureaucratic system that unwillingly rewards the status quo, with new scientific literature taking a long time to infiltrate the management policies and procedures, those who are currently perceived as 'amateurs' (or those charged as volunteer leaders) have the interest to keep up-to-date with scientific literature and see no reason to delay and implement logical solutions that provide measurable conservation outcomes. They (the community) are becoming well informed, as it is not just ethical and emotional conservation issues driving them. They are becoming empowered.

New drivers of change

Local communities are concerned and seek retribution for environmental losses. They are no longer satisfied with the continual downward slide of the environment for the sake of urban lifestyle ignorance, and the ever-increasing desktop management epidemic. They want more input into management and action, and up until recently they have not had the means to do this other than through the normal political avenues.

Trials have been initiated on developing the commercial value of wildlife for sustainable wildlife enterprises, which is squarely focussed on developing incentives for organizations and individuals to restore on-farm habitat for wildlife, particularly in rangelands, driven by financial outcomes (AFFA 2004).

Perhaps the greatest change to come has been through the development of community groups in the Riverland region of South Australia. Formation of an incorporated body, Community Land Management Inc., which is involved directly in conservation land management and sits at the forefront of paradigm shifts. Both with and without professional support these full time employed community members in their spare time coordinate kangaroo surveys and perform transects, control feral pest species, monitor, evaluate and report population health status, as well as remain actively involved in other aspect of biodiversity conservation throughout the Riverland (formally Bookmark) Biosphere region and elsewhere.

Some examples of knowledge base concepts adopted as a result of on-ground community action include:

- Observation of local behaviour patterns showing that kangaroos, given the opportunity or when key factors have been removed, will move and become nomadic therefore making it unnecessary to regard large densities in one spot a long-term problem.
- Recognising key regions where kangaroos a most likely to survive on a local level and managing them accordingly, and enhancing core habitat areas based on highly variable semi-arid/arid zone ecological principles.
- Recognising the importance and differences on impacts of kangaroos compared to introduced grazers, particularly goats, and actively implementing control measures for these introduced pest species.

The community has grown impatient and tired of waiting. Realistically their only choice has been to become empowered with knowledge and experience, and learning through adaptive management. These are some of the more pertinent decisions made as a result of on-ground involvement in management:

- To not use commercial shooters.
- To develop strategies to reduce factors relating to heightened population numbers e.g. watering points.

- Management by destruction is only through strict policy and procedures in a controlled, ethical and an ecological acceptable manner.
- Social capital is now recognised as the linchpin to the success of long-term conservation goals.
- We are at the end of the day in the kangaroos domain and should behave, manage and respect it accordingly.

One interesting observation, as a result of community empowerment, has been the community's interpretation of local and regional sustainability. Some say previous definitions of sustainability are flawed, and to an extent unworkable, such as the destruction caused by feral goats, which many landowners secretly 'foster' in numbers to supplement their income. It's easy for the community to see that current practices are not sustainable. This ironically comes from many whom themselves make a living off completely unsustainable industries, who are fully aware of it and not proud of it. People deeply want their children to see what they have seen, and with luck, experience the natural world in a way they have not. This is socially unique and significantly advanced for the western industrialised world.

This rural affirmation is totally beyond the expected outcome for which the future of kangaroos will most likely rely upon.

Hill-dwelling species, like this common wallaroo, and rock wallabies are threatened by feral goats which are kept and culled only when the price is right in spite of being more direct competitors to livestock. (Photo: Ulrike Kloecker)

Change agents and future outcomes

Many scientists are coming to the conclusion that modern humans are inherently unable to plan and implement sustainable and altruistic outcomes beyond their own lifetime and generation. With this in mind it should perhaps be considered advanced, that any one of us commits to a conservation cause. Therefore many local community advocates can be considered very progressive thinkers.

Both the community and field workers identify that continual culling is not the answer to management. Rather than direct attack on a species in question, a much more practical, long term, and probably less expensive solution is a focus on the drivers that cause numbers of kangaroos to be perceived as a problem. More importantly is to determine what are normal and elevated numbers on local and regional habitats. The typical 'knee-jerk' reaction to obliterate the problem, and then justifying it by covert 'utililisation of a sustainable product that would otherwise go to waste' can no longer be justified in the eyes of the community.

A change agent for existing governing bodies will have to be proactive rather than reactive, otherwise there will be an inevitable shift to other/new sources of management.
The community want tractable dynamic solutions with outcomes. It is, in fact, forcing those responsible to unlearn and re-educate. There are all the warning signs from the environment and enough political pressure from the public. Like many things that are pushed to change it often requires an extreme to get things moving.

The community, bottom-up hands-on responsive and adaptive ethos to environmental concerns, is challenging the archaic top-down dictatorship approaches embedded in history.

This is truly democracy at work. The custodians of our precious wildlife perhaps soon will lie with those whose intentions are pure in the eye of real experience and appreciation of their environment.

Yellow-footed rock-wallaby was shot out of the ranges around Tibooburra and is threatened in the one remnant population in NSW and elsewhere. (Photo: Mark Cairns)

KANGAROO – THE WORLD'S TREASURE

(KANGAROO - MALTREATED BY AUSTRALIA, CHERISHED BY THE WORLD)

By Dr. Teresa Buss-Carden

The kangaroo – oh gentle, majestic, unique marsupial! You are the target of the biggest land wildlife slaughter on this planet! Why? Revered and admired all over the world - you have your fate sealed in Australia by human stupidity, ignorance and indifference. This has been propped up by irresponsible legislation created by heartless politicians, spread by media propaganda, supported by some self-serving scientists and of course - the money and greed that drives the kangaroo killing industry.

When many years ago I came to Australia from Europe - I fell in love with Australia's natural world and its wildlife. What a heartache it has become for me now when observing what is being done to the beautiful creatures inhabiting this land. I remember my first bush walk. It was love at first sight! I was totally knocked from my feet by the sounds, and smells and sightings in the bush. Colorful rosellas in tree canopies, lavishly plumed parrots rising into a clear sky- like ascending angels, gentle kangaroos observing us from a distance, lizards basking in the sun…I thought – it is a paradise.

What I learned was beyond my worst nightmare. A major disaster called 'commercialisation' faces Australian wildlife. A Senate report on the Commercial Use of Wildlife (June 1998) recommended using wildlife as a commodity, to be traded like grain or minerals, with no respect for its intrinsic value. These tonnes of 'products' were once living creatures who feel pain, cold, loneliness and fear - exactly the same as we humans do. I wondered how many kangaroos, possums, go into one tonne of product? And how many lives of wallabies need to be shattered to create one fur-lined jacket?

I learned that every night, shooters' vehicles criss-cross the fragile soil of rangelands seeking the kill. The killing must be carried out according to the Code of Practice, creating an impression of regulated high standards of animal welfare. However, this is nonsense as 'the code' is not legally enforceable, is impossible to police, and kangaroo killing takes place at night in remote areas. Unless every kangaroo shooting trip is accompanied by an animal welfare officer and compliance of the code is monitored in the field when shooters are not aware that they are being 'observed' by law enforcement agencies, this Code of Practice is not worth the paper it is written on.
The written word however 'principled' means nothing if it can not be checked for its compliance. Just a few extracts from the code indicate its obscenity:

"..In circumstances where, for dispatch of a wounded kangaroo, a shot to either the brain or heart is impractical or unsafe, a very heavy blow to the rear of the skull to destroy the brain is permissible. To ensure a humane kill, a suitably hard and heavy blunt instrument must be used (e.g., metal pipe, billet of wood etc., carried for this purpose)." One must ask questions such as: how many blows to the skull does the shooter have to apply in order to kill the fully grown animal? or if bashing the animal could be really considered as 'the most appropriate and humane means' of 'dispatch' in any civilised society?

"…Shot females must be examined for pouch young and if one is present it must also be killed. Decapitation with a sharp instrument in very small hairless young or a properly executed heavy blow to destroy the brain in larger young are effective means of causing sudden and painless death." The method of killing joeys described above is one of most barbaric ways to kill any animal by any standard in any civilised society. If the above method is not acceptable to kill other animals, for example our pets, why is it approved for killing kangaroos?

In order to learn more about Australia's wildlife the next step was to travel around the continent. One of the trips was to Central Queensland. And what heartache it became! To my dismay, I drove past endless bare fields with stumps of lonely dead trees reaching to the skies, some dried up creeks, banks devoid of native vegetation for long stretches. At dusk, I searched in vain to find mobs of kangaroos, but only saw dead wallabies on the roads. I heard some gun shots and was told that people were shooting kangaroos.

The very sad thing was the realisation that not so long ago this was a land of paradise and its degradation did not occur as a result of natural disasters - it is man-made. In the past, farmers were encouraged through government subsidies to clear vegetation and to carry out unsuitable and unsustainable European farming practices in this semi arid and arid continent. This led to massive environmental destruction. The Australian Conservation Foundation (ACF) states that it will cost approx. $10 billion a year to repair this degradation and the CSIRO states the cost is approx. $37 billion a year (the difference in estimates relates to the scope of repair).
The destruction of habitat means the death and destruction of our wildlife.
Australia produces enough food to feed 80 million people but our population is only 20 million. Therefore we are producing agricultural goods simply for the export dollar - to make some farmers and multinational companies vast profits. All this is at the expense of our kangaroos and other wildlife and at the expense of our land.

Wildlife can be used to make money but this can only be achieved through their non-consumptive use as a tourist draw-card. Kangaroos are famous and recognised all over the world.

Australia's appeal as a tourist destination is promoted by an aggressive $500 million Federal Government sales pitch to key international markets. Last year 'Tourism Australia' announced its $360million Brand

Australia campaign for several key markets to add iconic images such as Kangaroos to make it more recognizable for international tourists.

A record 5.2 million visitors were set to visit Australia in 2004. And yet we are jeopardizing billions of dollars of tourism money by supporting the $200 million worth (if that) killing industry. The $70 billion Australian tourism industry, which employs 500,000 people, could be damaged by the massacre of kangaroos and their joeys.

I believe that the concentration of tourists in the main cities fails to address the need to diversify the tourism industry. Recently "The Australian" stated "the onus is on the (tourism) industry to create a new kind of experience". Today one quarter of travellers to Australia spend four times as much as traditional tourists, but are not interested in guided tours or iconic trips to Sydney. They want to 'go where the locals go, not where the tourist go'. Within 10 years this type of tourist will constitute 50% of all travellers. Observing wild kangaroos would be undoubtedly the highlight of their holidays and a fantastic draw-card.

No wonder that there are so many concerns about tourists staying away. Publisher Lonely Planet blames the Federal Government's immigration policies for Australia missing out on a revival in international tourism. It accounts for almost 11.2% of total export earnings for Australia).
With more international awareness about the fate of Australia's animals surely there will be even more reluctance for visiting our continent. During my past travels overseas and my association with many international organisations and individuals I have never heard them expressing a wish

Princess Mary and Prince Frederick of Denmark at Yarralumna with the Governer General Michael Jeffrey and Mrs Jeffery and their head gardner. (Photo courtesy Penny Bradfield / FairfaxPhoto)

to visit a zoo or wildlife park or dine on kangaroo flesh. They always said: 'I would love to come to your country to see wild animals in the wild – not on a plate, not in a cage or on display'.

It would be much more desirable and beneficial for all Australians, to create an attractive tourism base in the outback, with opportunities to see wild animals in their natural environment. That way many jobs can be created in rural areas, which presently suffer high unemployment. It would benefit greatly for example the Northern Territory which is on transit from Malaysia & Singapore. According to a tourism discussion paper almost half the tourists coming to Australia by 2012 will be from Asian countries excluding Japan .

One needs only to ask a group of Japanese youngsters what they like best about Australia and the answer comes back quickly - the animals: wombats, koalas & kangaroos!.

The beautiful wild birds and animals grace our natural environment. Apart from those misguided people who kill or wound them for money or fun, most of tourists derive a feeling of joy from hearing the dawn chorus of feathered singers offering a free public concert every morning or scenes of kangaroo mobs under the red skies at dusk. However such scenes of rural splendour are tarnished by the awareness that our bush countryside is turned into an open-air abattoir and shooting gallery.

Last year (2004) the federal Minister for Tourism said that Australia needs to work harder to alert tourists to its virtues at the launch of the Australia's biggest ever push for visitors - in the hope that they would become "life-time ambassadors" for Australia. While in Queensland, I had an opportunity to observe how the foreign tourists interacted with kangaroos (they were tame). People of all sorts of gender and age were melting over kangaroos. They were mesmerized! When tourists learned about the killing industry, the expressions on their faces turned into sadness, shock and horror. Would they really go back home as our ambassadors?

Why do we maltreat our best ambassador – the kangaroo?

The TV show 'Skippy the Bush Kangaroo' was first shown in Australia in 1968 and by the end of 1969 was broadcast in 80 countries, and dubbed into French, German, Spanish and Portuguese. Skippy is still going strong 38 years after he first hopped into our lounge rooms. Skippy continues his world domination with the sale in 2001 of Skippy the Bush Kangaroo to broadcasters in Norway and France. Skippy's international distributor, Southern Star, has sold all 91 episodes of the 1960's children's series, digitally re-mastered from the original 16mm negative kept safe at the national Film and Sound Archive. Skippy the Bush Kangaroo brings goodwill towards Australia and Australians. Peter Moore, the Australian travel writer, escaped injury or possibly even death during a riot in Addis Ababa. When enraged rioters were told that Moore was from 'the land of Skippy', only then their anger turned into amusement. Another film 'Kangaroo Jack' has surprised audiences by reaching the top of the US box office in 2003 – it achieved this success only when more of the 'kangaroo scenes' were added to the film.

Putting economical factors aside, doesn't our wildlife deserve protection on ethical grounds? The current plight of kangaroos may be described as legalised hell with the stamp of approval from the highest authorities and indifferent masses. I see it as a failure of mankind's responsibility for this gentle animal – the kangaroo. Can we really call ourselves a civilized society when the lowest, repugnant acts of cruelty against the most vulnerable members of our society - the animals, are not condemned vigorously? Would we be so selectively demented, if similar torment was inflicted upon one of our own? Matthew Scully, author of 'Dominion' said:

'Skippy the Bush Kangaroo (Photo: AWPC library)

"Animals are more than ever a test of our character, of mankind's capacity for empathy and for decent, honourable conduct and faithful stewardship. We are called to treat them with kindness, not because they have rights, power or a claim to equality, but in a sense, because they don't. They all stand unequal and powerless before us."

The fight for the betrayed kangaroos must go on. It will only finish when the kangaroos are granted the status they deserve: of our national icon, one of the most important components of our wildlife heritage, the treasure of the world - roaming free on this continent which is rightly their's.
The genocide of kangaroos and cruel abuse of wildlife must be outlawed. These peaceful creatures should live out their short humble lives in our bush with no fear of the ever-pursuing blazing gun, or the hands that poison. And the rest of us - Australians and tourists alike - should be able continue to take a walk in the bush… without being subjected to the sights and sounds of cruelty.

Australia sees the kangaroo as a pest or commodity. The rest of the world sees our kangaroo as a unique treasure. I can't help pondering on the words of poet Robert Burns: "Oh, what a wondrous gift it would be to see ourselves as others do".

A NEW FRONTIER:

THE ROAD ENVIRONMENT AND ITS IMPACT ON KANGAROOS

By Daniel Ramp

BSc. Hons. PhD (Melbourne)
School of Biological, Earth and Environmental Sciences, UNSW Sydney.

Take a trip along any country road throughout Australia. You might see patches of remnant vegetation in linear corridors along the roadside and the occasional koala, wallaby or kookaburra, but perhaps more often you will see evidence of exotic weeds and the carcasses of wildlife killed from collisions with vehicles. It would be fair to say that most of our experience of the environment and wildlife is facilitated by roads and yet what sticks in the mind are vast stretches of agricultural land and roadkill.

Our thirst for land and the creation of a means to move around that land has marked our planet unlike any other species driven change. Our roads are getting larger and denser and our cars are getting faster. Over the last 50 years the road environment in developed countries has expanded at phenomenal rates as governments attempt to provide access and amenities for current and future populations. It is a world-wide phenomenon that in many locations the only vegetation left for wildlife to occupy, and hence habitat, is that which surrounds roads (Bennett 1991). Wildlife are often drawn to the verges alongside roads as they provide refuge and other resources like food and water. As a consequence, the clash between wildlife and the road environment has opened up a new frontier.

Road corridors are not only a haven for wildlife – they are their ultimate downfall.

We are only just beginning to understand the repercussions of the road environment on our efforts to conserve Australia's biodiversity. Despite a pervasive awareness of this issue in the community, consideration of roads as driving forces in ecology has only recently gained international awareness (e.g. Forman *et al*. 2003; Sherwood *et al*. 2002). To date, little is currently being done to alleviate the carnage. At best, most dollars are spent mimicking strategies and technologies developed and employed in the USA, Canada and in Europe, with varying degrees of success. What we need are strategies that are tailored to Australian wildlife and our environment. This chapter will first examine the extent of the road environment and identify the key impacts of roads on wildlife. It will then explore how the road environment impacts on kangaroos and other macropod populations and will address the range of issues that surround attempts to reduce road impacts on these species.

Counting the cost of roads on the environment

Our need for transportation has a major impact on the environment. The use of fossil fuels as a

tend to attract kangaroos, and it is not because they want to play 'chicken' (although they do invariably end up playing, whether this is a conscious decision or not). The reason for this attraction is that roadside verges can be a source of habitat, they can provide high quality food in the form of grass (frequently mown grass is well known to be of higher quality than grass left to senesce), and they can provide access to water from run-off and condensation from dewfall (Fig. 1). This attraction is common in rural areas where often the only remaining habitat is situated along the road corridor. It is this attraction to roads and their verges that is causing so many kangaroos to be hit by vehicles.

Fatalities of kangaroos on roads

So this helps to explain why kangaroos are frequently killed, but the next important question is just how many kangaroos and wallabies are being killed on Australian roads? Over the last few years there have been a few small-scale studies that have estimated the frequency of collisions, typically over a relatively short period of time. Studies by Coulson (1982) and Osawa (1989) pioneered research to address this issue. Since then, a number of studies have been conducted in order to broaden the information base on fatalities (Cooper 1998; Coulson 1997a; Klöcker et al. In Press; Lee et al. 2004; Ramp et al. In Press; Ramp et al. In Review; Taylor & Goldingay 2004). Each of these studies was conducted in different environments, on different types of roads with different traffic volumes, and with different wildlife populations with inherently different sizes.

It seems that despite the variation between study sites and species, a fatality rate for kangaroos and wallabies of around 0.04 per km per day appears to be a reasonably good estimate of collision frequency. For example, in a study conducted along the Snowy Mountain Highway in southern New South Wales, between the townships of Tumut and Talbingo, there were 646 eastern grey kangaroos *(Macropus giganteus)*, 51 swamp and red-necked wallabies *(W. bicolor* and *M. rufogriseus)*, 54 common wombats *(Vombatus ursinus)*, 103 feral animals and 80 birds recorded as killed along a 40 km stretch of road in 2003 (Ramp et al. In Press).

It is tempting to use this general figure of 0.04 per km per day to extrapolate to areas where fatalities have not been recorded. For example, given that New South Wales has 182,006 km of road, divided almost equally between bitumen and gravel roads, we could use this estimate to suggest that somewhere in the order of 7,280 kangaroos and wallabies were being killed on New South Wales roads every day (or 2,657,287 per year). But this would not take into account different rates between bitumen and gravel roads and does not account for urban roads where although possums are frequently killed along with some wallabies, kangaroos are not (Canberra in the ACT being an exception). Given the large degree of spatial and temporal error that must be associated with estimating state-wide or even nation-wide totals from these small amounts of data it is clear we must obtain more high quality spatial and temporal data of collisions before we can be confident of our predictions.

As a first step towards achieving state-wide estimates of collisions, David Croft and I have conducted a research project since 2001 that seeks to obtain estimates of fatalities across the state of New South Wales. This project, entitled "Saving Wildlife: Saving People on our Roads" was funded by the Australian Research Council in conjunction with the International Fund for Animal Welfare, the NSW National Parks and Wildlife Service, the NSW Wildlife Information and Rescue Service and Roe Koh & Associates Pty Ltd, while funding assistance was also provided by the Roads and Traffic Authority of NSW, the Wildlife Preservation Society of Australia and the Sherman Foundation.

As it would be impractical and expensive to have someone constantly driving around recording roadkill, we developed a system that uses expert volunteers to assist with data collection. Volunteers were either National Park staff involved in kangaroo management, or member of WIRES. At the time of writing this chapter the data obtained by these volunteers between 2002 and 2005 is in the process of being analysed, so results are not able to be reported here. However smaller scale studies of fatalities resulting from this project have been published (or in the process of being published), the findings of which have been reported elsewhere in this chapter (Klöcker *et al.* In Press; Lee *et al.* 2004; Ramp *et al.* In Press; Ramp *et al.* In Review).

The barrier effect and kangaroos

There is great variation in the Macropodidae, not only in body size and morphology, but also in behaviour and sociality. All of these differences have implications on how the road environment impacts on macropodid species. As mentioned earlier, the larger species of kangaroos tend to be attracted to rural roads. In rural Australia it is unlikely that roads are having a deleterious and fragmenting impact on kangaroo populations, although they do influence movement and space use. In addition, dispersal and movement by individuals should protect kangaroo populations from genetic drift resulting from any fragmentation effects that might occur as suggested in the context of reserves by Tenhumberg *et al.* (2004).

For smaller species of wallaby, the road environment may indeed pose significant restrictions on movement and space use. Most research on the barrier effect has focussed on small mammals, where road crossings are prevented when the road reaches a certain width (Goosem 2001). That wallabies are frequently killed on roads suggests that while crossing may be difficult, and sometimes unsuccessful, crossing nevertheless does occur. To date there has been no published research that examines how wallaby species use roadside habitat and whether or not this differs to the use of habitat away from the road edge.

To address this paucity of information we have conducted a project over the last year that examines how swamp wallabies use roadside habitat adjacent to the F3 Freeway, just north of Sydney. We have radio-collared individuals at two locations, one where road crossing is possible and fatalities have been observed, and one where a large underpass has been constructed to facilitate movement of wallabies and other wildlife. This data is in the process of being analysed, but initial exploration suggests that the wallabies living adjacent to the F3 Freeway have different space-use patterns to those living within core areas of the neighbouring Muogamarra Nature Reserve (MNR). Swamp wallabies are typically solitary species. In the relatively undisturbed core of MNR, overlap in the home range of different individuals (where the home range is the area within which an individual spends most of its time) is typically around 40 % (Ben-Ami 2005). In contrast to this, the swamp wallabies we have tracked next to the F3 Freeway typically have up to 90 % overlap in their home ranges. In addition, despite frequent tracking, none of the individuals we tracked crossed the road, even at the site with the underpass. More research is being conducted to explore the exact mechanisms behind this shift in space use.

Effects on kangaroos at a population level

Even if we knew how many kangaroos and wallabies, along with other wildlife, were being killed, this would not tell us exactly how the road environment is affecting populations of these species. Surveys of kangaroo populations are typically conducted using aerial survey techniques, as they are large and forage in open country (e.g. Caughley & Grigg 1981; Pople *et al.* 2000; Priddel 1988). Estimates of populations of these species suggest that the total numbers of kangaroos in Australia are several million. Yet this total population is comprised of many local populations that are variously connected by dispersing individuals. It is at this local scale that we will see impacts on kangaroo populations.

We have already observed that roads must presumably be influencing the use of the landscape by kangaroos, but Graeme Coulson from the University of Melbourne raised the additional possibility that road-based fatalities may be influencing the demographic structure of populations. In a study he conducted in South Australia, Coulson (1997a) observed male bias in five species of kangaroo and wallaby. He speculated about whether males of some species come into contact with roads more often than females as it is typically males who disperse. There does not appear to be any biological reason why males would be more susceptible to fatalities than females, other than a difference in the likelihood of them being within the vicinity of a road.

In a study by Lee *et al.* (2004) along the Silver City Highway adjacent to Fowlers Gap Arid Zone Research Station, just north of Broken Hill, New South Wales, fatalities of euros *(M. robustus erubescens)* were also found to be heavily male biased. However, when the source population was examined it was found that male euros frequented the road environment far more than females. Spatial segregation in the source population, in this case female euros hanging out in the hills and males along the flats (where the road is), will obviously influence the propensity of different sexes to be involved in collisions.

In addition to bias in sex ratios, Lee *et al.* (2004) observed that far more juvenile and sub-adult kangaroos were killed than adults. While young individuals would certainly take more risks and be naïve of the perils of the road environment, the age distribution of fatalities reflects the typical pyramidal age distribution of kangaroo populations (Norbury *et al.* 1994). Morrissey (2003) also found that more sub-adult swamp wallabies were killed in a study of roads within the Royal National Park, just south of Sydney. Without accurate assessments of the age structure in the populations there is no way of knowing if juveniles are more susceptible to being involved in collisions. If biases are occurring in either sex or age classes this may have ramifications for the long-term survival of local populations, yet we currently do not have a great deal of data to assess this.

While we do not have any data on how kangaroo populations might be affected by fatalities at a local scale, the study of a population of swamp wallabies living within the Royal National Park suggests that although this species is common throughout its range, this particular population is likely to become functionally extinct within the next 50 to 100 years if fatalities on roads within the park are not curbed (Ramp & Ben-Ami In Press). Therefore, while roads may not necessarily lead to the extinction of species, they are undoubtedly causing localised extinctions of populations of wildlife, including members of the Macropodidae, living adjacent to roads. Information of this type of threat is just starting to become available. It is clear that when road-based fatalities combine with other forms of disturbance and threats to populations, the consequences have the potential to be severe.

How can we reduce the impacts of roads on kangaroos?

Much effort has been spent examining the effectiveness of various mitigation strategies worldwide for reducing fatalities of animals on roads or improving the permeability of roads (Groot Bruinderink & Hazebroek 1996; Romin & Bissonette 1996; Waring et al. 1991). Given that the impact of the road environment on wildlife is considerable, research that identifies how to create preventative measures and better design roads is a high priority for conservation managers. While concerted efforts have been made to do this overseas (e.g. Clevenger et al. 2001a; Clevenger et al. 2001b; Dodd et al. 2004; Jaeger & Fahrig 2004), little rigorous research has been conducted to explore the applicability of overseas techniques under Australian conditions. Strategies implemented overseas have been adopted in Australia without a thorough examination of their effectiveness before being implemented, often at great cost.

One reason why they have had little success is that Australia's larger marsupial herbivores differ from their overseas placental counterparts, and as such need tailored preventative measures to suit them. For the most part they are non-migratory; typically have high site fidelity and occupy relatively small home ranges (Strahan 2002). Thus, mitigation strategies employed for migratory deer in Europe, the USA and Canada may not be effective for preventing wildlife fatalities under Australian conditions. The following is a discussion of some of the major strategies currently being implemented in Australia to help reduce fatalities of kangaroos and other wildlife.

Wildlife warning reflectors

Some strategies have been developed to target those animals within the vicinity of roads, such as the use of reflectors designed to reflect oncoming vehicle headlights into the eyes of animals on the roadside to frighten them before the vehicle arrives (e.g. wildlife warning reflectors - Strieter Corporation 2001). These devices have been developed for reducing collisions with deer, elk and moose in Europe and the USA. There are two different manufacturers of the reflectors, one European and one American, and they come in a variety of colours. Despite their popularity, scientific evidence for their effectiveness in reducing collisions with deer suggests they have little or no effect (Ujvari et al. 1998; Waring et al. 1991).

Testing of the applicability of wildlife reflectors to kangaroos and other macropodids in Australia has received some attention, although little success has been had and most trials have been poorly designed (Lintermans 1997). To address the concerns expressed by Lintermans (1997), and in an effort to clarify whether or not there was any biological basis to suggest that the reflectors may reduce collisions with kangaroos, David Croft and I decided to undertake a comprehensive study of the responses of kangaroos to the reflectors under controlled conditions. To do so we built an artificial road in a paddock and made observations of the behavioural reactions of captive red kangaroos, eastern grey kangaroos and red-necked wallabies to the reflectors (Fig. 2). We set up pairs of headlights every ten metres and wrote a computer program to switch the headlights on to mimic the passing of a car (Fig. 3). The system was designed so that the reaction of kangaroos to the reflectors could be monitored in the absence of moving vehicle and the sounds they produce. It was felt that this system was the only way to properly evaluate how kangaroos respond to light and whether coloured light perpendicular to the road would increase the likelihood of kangaroos fleeing the road.

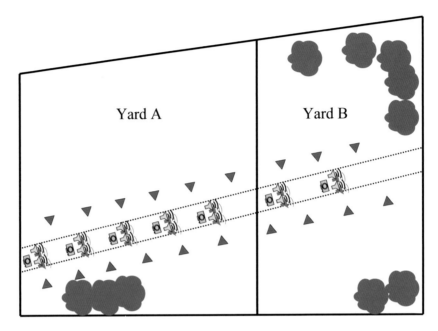

Figure 2. Experimental setup of captive trials of wildlife reflectors at Cowan Field Station. Two separate yards were used to segregate different species. Seven sets of headlights with infra-red cameras were installed along the artificial road. Reflectors were situated along the road using the recommended design by the manufacturers.

The response of the different species was assessed by examining the behaviour of individuals located on the road when only the headlights were used (the reflectors were covered up) and when the headlights were used with the reflectors. Both types of reflectors were used in a variety of colours. For the species tested, 60% of individuals on average exhibited a vigilant response to the headlights (i.e. raised head, upright posture). Flight in response to the light occurred very infrequently as would be expected by captive animals (around 1% of the time). The addition of reflectors did not significantly increase the vigilance or flight response of individuals, regardless of the colour or manufacturer. Indeed, the spectrometric characteristics of the reflectors suggest that the light emitted by the reflectors is in fact extremely low (around 1 lux) and the angle of reflection is very important (Sivic & Sielecki 2001). We were unable, given the experimental conditions, to find any behavioural mechanism promoted by the reflectors that might encourage kangaroos to flee the road over and above their natural inclination to flee fast moving objects.

Sound deterrents

Another possible basis for preventing collisions is through the scaring of animals from roads or oncoming vehicles using sound as a deterrent. The use of sound as a warning cue is widespread

Figure 3. A paired set of headlights were placed every 10 m at the height of a standard 4x4 vehicle. An infra-red sensitive video camera was placed at each headlight station and used to record behaviour of kangaroos along the artificial road. The road itself was mown to attract kangaroos to it.

in the animal kingdom, and sounds are used by kangaroos and other macropodids in this fashion (Coulson 1997b; Jarman 1991). As such, there is a strong behavioural basis to encourage the development of an auditory repellent device in relation to roads, although it should be noted that vehicles produce a significant amount of noise on their own at a range of frequencies.

Devices purported to deter kangaroos away from roads are already on the market. These include devices that are fixed to the front of vehicles such as the Shu Roo wildlife dispersal systems (Shu Roo Australia Pty Ltd) and ultrasonic whistles. Both of these devices claim to use ultrasonic, or high frequency sound (>20 kHz), to scare animals away from the oncoming vehicle. While this concept is very attractive, the scientific evidence suggests that these devices are ineffective at reducing collisions (Bender 2001; Bender 2003). Perhaps a more fertile area of research would be to explore the response of kangaroos to natural sounds derived from themselves (like foot thumps) or predators. This is the field of bioacoustics and its application to non-lethally deter wildlife from areas we wish to protect.

Odour deterrents

The use of odour as a deterrent has recently gained attention in Australia, not just as a means to repelling animals from roadsides but also as a non-lethal mechanism for preventing browsing on agricultural lands. The odours that appear most fruitful are ones that utilise the innate aversion of predators by prey species, as this is the most ethically acceptable means of warding animals away from a specified area and has a solid behavioural basis. Recent trials of the response of different wallaby species to a synthetic predator odour, mimicking dog urine (Plant Plus, Roe

Koh & Associates Pty Ltd), suggests that the development of odour deterrents may indeed prove possible, although responses may be species specific (Ramp *et al.* 2005). In this study, parma wallabies *(M. parma)* had aversive reactions to Plant Plus, while red-necked pademelons *(Thylogale thetis)* appeared to be attracted to it.

At first glance the attraction by red-necked pademelons seems contrary to how we might expect a wallaby to behave, yet there are many benefits to going to the source of a scent and then scanning the horizon in an attempt to locate the predator (Fishman 1999). The environment is often littered with the scents of both predator and prey species (Banks *et al.* 2000), so it pays to figure out exactly what the threat is before fleeing. As such, the use of odour deterrents has potential but will require a great deal of research to determine how best to use odour as a repellent.

Physical structures – fences, underpasses and overpasses

One area that requires considerable attention is that of those physical structures designed to assist with, or prevent, animal movement across roads. There is a lack of data on the effectiveness and suitability of wildlife crossings for different species in different environments. Some research in Australia has examined common strategies such as the installation of fences to prevent movement of wildlife and the installation of underpasses to facilitate the safe passage of wildlife (e.g. Abson & Lawrence 2003; AMBS 1997; Jones 2000; Mansergh & Scotts 1989; Taylor & Goldingay 2003). These studies report various levels of success, but often the definition of success is problematical.

The implementation of physical structures often comes at enormous cost. Yet once built, research to examine their effectiveness is often cursory. For example, the success of underpasses is typically gauged by recording animal presence within them by using infra-red cameras or sand plots (AMBS 1997). In reality, all this tells us is that animals use the underpass – it does not tell us how many animals use it and whether or not it is reducing the frequency of collisions on the surrounding road.

One pivotal question that remains unclear is whether wildlife crossings are meant to prevent collisions or to facilitate road permeability for wildlife, or both? If the aim is roadkill prevention, surveys of the change in fatalities adjacent to the crossing must be gauged prior to, and post construction, or else measured at control locations. If the aim is the facilitation of animal movement, surveys of the change in animal crossings adjacent to the crossing structure must also be gauged prior to, and post construction. For both of these issues it is vital that the population structure of animals surrounding the crossing is examined to evaluate what changes occur as a result of the crossing being constructed, both in terms of spatial aggregation and in demography. Before we can take these structures as serious mitigation technologies, hard data of this sort must be obtained.
Community perceptions

Amelioration of the impact of roads on the environment is a responsibility that lies squarely on our shoulders. We choose how fast we drive, when we drive and where our roads go. We also choose how we design our roads. Kangaroos and other wildlife cannot avoid getting in the way.

It is pertinent that as our knowledge of the environment and our impact upon it increases, our concern and control appears to have somewhat diminished (Fig. 4). Recent writings by leading conservationist David Suzuki and evolutionary biologist Jared Diamond implore us to take action, yet rather than making a concerted effort to reduce global warming, poverty and famine, we are transfixed by consumerism and celebrities.

Figure. 4. Who is responsible? This euro died in the centre of a long straight road with no concealing vegetation on either side. Bad driving is the only explanation.

In this regard, it is important to examine how the community perceives the problem of fatalities of kangaroos on roads and why so little has been done to alleviate the problem. There is undoubtedly a broad spectrum of views in the community regarding this issue. In order to obtain some insight into how the community responds to collisions we engaged in a survey of driver attitudes within the Royal National Park, including both visitors to the park and residents of the two townships located within it (Morrissey 2003). Of the one hundred and fifty-six people surveyed almost 50% had been involved in collisions with wildlife. Over 80% of respondents indicated that they minimised the amount of time that they drove at night and that they drove slower in areas where they knew wildlife were about. To verify this, we used traffic counters to measure the volume and speeds of vehicles at known areas of collisions. We observed average speeds consistently over the speed limit, including some excessively high, while speeds tended to peak in the evening or in the early morning, precisely when animals were most likely to be on the road (Fig. 5 over page).

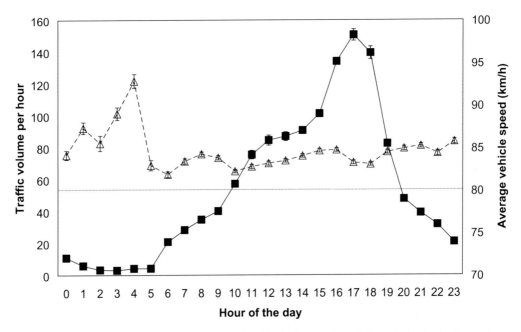

Figure 5. Traffic volume (vehicles per hour, squares) and vehicle speed (km/h, triangles) entering the park east-bound along Farnell Avenue. Means and standard errors are represented for both, while the legal speed limit is depicted with a hashed line.

As another example, not all vehicles pose an identical threat to wildlife. In Australia, our decision to transport goods via our road network is having a dramatic influence on collision frequency. Road trains, an Australian phenomenon, are prime movers with massive trailers joined together that travel along rural roads to and from townships. Most road users are aware of the dangers of driving on rural roads at night and typically avoid driving at these times, as the crepuscular or nocturnal nature of Australia's wildlife means that this is when they are likely to be present on roads. In contrast, road trains must get from A to B at the speed limit regardless of the time of day, and as such are often unable to avoid collisions with wildlife. It is likely that road trains and other freight trucks are responsible for the majority of wildlife fatalities on rural highways (although there is currently no hard data on this). This is a sad state of affairs for both the drivers of these vehicles and the animals in their way.

Most people do not intend to collide with wildlife, but animals do get hit and driver speed is highly correlated with collisions. The answer to this problem is quite straightforward: drive slower and less often and fewer animals will be hit. We need more sociological research to examine why this does not occur. We have the ability to build sustainable transportation systems but it will take more than good science to affect change. *Actions speak louder than words.*

Bad road design for wildlife and driver safety. This road passes a large earthen tank to the left that waters livestock and wildlife. As the road meets the dam it turns sharply obscuring the driver's view of animals that cross the road to drink at the tank.

REQUIEM FOR KANGAROOS?

By Sue Arnold

A former Fairfax journalist who founded Australians for Animals Inc. (AFA) in 1981.

The kangaroo was moving in the strangest way, trying to hop, falling down, staggering up again to a half standing position, desperately trying to regain its balance. Then collapsing in the middle of the road, trembling.

It didn't take long for me to realize a vehicle had hit the kangaroo. Some heartless bastard had left the dreadfully injured animal to die a slow painful death. My mind fixated on how different things would be if this were a human who lay bleeding and broken in the middle of the road. People would stop. Help would come; people would bend over backwards to give comfort and succor to fellow humans.

But not so with wildlife. Save for the rarest humans, the creatures' plight is seen as collateral damage. Animals are things with no capacity to feel pain. Their agonizing deaths do not rate much of a reaction on the human emotional Richter scale.

Eastern grey kangaroo on a collision course with a heavy 4WD vehicle. (Photo: Bill Corn)

I swiftly parked my car off road, got out and walked slowly towards the wounded, frightened animal now lying paralyzed on its side, the fear in her eyes palpable.

My heart sank as I saw the extent of the injuries. The blood stained kangaroo fixed me with her gaze, our eyes locked as souls met, we became one. I felt every millisecond of her terror, her agony. Oh God, I prayed for guidance. She was too heavy for me to pull off the road, too badly injured to move, her breathing heavy, uneven, great shudders wracking her body. All the time staring at me, dark eyes fringed with great black eyelashes - begging for mercy.

There was nothing in my car that I could use to put the kangaroo out of her misery. With devastating clarity I remembered how an American friend of mine had suffocated a wounded deer with her windcheater when confronted with a similar situation. I remembered the horror I felt listening to her story, hoping I would never experience such an awful choice.

I couldn't do what she did. I don't know how to kill an animal, even a badly wounded one. I felt helpless, powerless, and completely useless. A silent witness incapable of lifting a finger. Paralyzed by the choices, the thought of having to kill an animal or watch it die horribly made me feel ill. So I stood in front of the kangaroo and stopped every car, every truck, and every vehicle which came by. Begging for help – for someone to put the animal out of her misery. Wanting to cradle the kangaroo in my arms but afraid that someone would run over us both. Or that my physical closeness would only increase her trauma. Minutes ticked by becoming like hours, the suffering unbearable to witness.

Car after car passed. So did a few trucks and a bus. A woman stopped. "I haven't got anything in my car that would work," she said. "Sorry." Driving away.

Finally an older man stopped. He got out of his car, coming over swiftly to inspect the situation.

"I'll put the roo down," he said. "You go. I'll do it with my tyre lever. Then I'll pull the corpse off the road. Just go". The coward in me left; relieved I didn't have the responsibility of bashing the kangaroo to death. I wept all the way into the nearest town. Queanbeyan. I had found the kangaroo just a few kilometers from what was to become the infamous killing fields at Gulgong Dam, where hundreds of kangaroos were shot down with consent of the ACT and NSW governments in the winter of 2004.

I wept for the pain and suffering of this creature, whose agony I could not ease. I prayed that death came quickly and agonized again and again over the brutality which is the fate of so many wild creatures. The singularity of her death - a window into the magnitude of the collective suffering which is the hallmark of Australia's national slaughter of kangaroos.

Who will mourn the passing of these magnificent animals? Who will remember how the bush once danced in rhythm with the thumping, jumping kangaroos who flew over fences – their great tails drumming on the earth? Who will remember the big red male kangaroo lying in the desert sun, his coat almost indistinguishable from the red earth from which he came?

What will happen to the spirit of this ancient dreaming land without the great mobs of kangaroos bounding across the song lines, energizing the land? Will the sunset and dawn mourn the passing of the creatures who danced in their light?

Mob of eastern grey kangaroos - a feature of the Australian landscape and not an aberration generated by pastoralism. (Photo: Bill Corn)

My farmer brother in law will not mourn their passing. His ute has been wrecked many times by collisions with kangaroos. Sometimes he puts his foot down when he sees one – driving straight into the hapless animal. Smashing the roo and his roo bar at the same time. Worth every cent in terms of the satisfaction he gets he says.

"Rotten bloody bastards. I say shoot the fuckers, the sooner we get rid of the bloody roos the better. They drink the water, take the feed, and wreck our vehicles. You greenies need to get a grip. Best kangaroo is a dead one."

A nation grown weary of environmental campaigns and never-ending issues can barely raise its head to agree or disagree with his sentiments. Living has become a smorgasbord of environmental campaigns – take your choice – save the whales, dolphins, Tasmanian old growth forests - stop the live animal trade, close down battery farms, ban aquaculture. The list is growing like some monstrous out of control giant, too much for most people to handle.

Anyway, who has time to go into the complexity and confusion surrounding these environmental campaigns? Easier to believe the spin doctors, far too hard to argue with your mates over kangaroos.

Politicians don't care – they know the kangaroo slaughter will never be given the exposure it deserves in the national media. All the associated corruption and murders in the kangaroo industry (which have been well documented) now in the same basket as all the other corruption, lies and evil perpetrated in the name of "protecting the environment." Without a court that deals with crimes against nature, wildlife remains valueless, its survival entirely in the hands of humanity.

The media remains mute – big business long ago worked out if the public didn't know what was going on in terms of the kangaroo slaughter, greenies would never turn the tide. The media is big business, pre-occupied with protecting itself. Better to keep a lid on the cruelty, suffering, loss. Better to keep the public in ignorance – whipping out the old chestnut – 'there's millions of kangaroos out there – millions and millions – they breed like rabbits' whenever anyone happens to raise a criticism of kangaroo management.

If you believe the media, Australia is indeed a remarkable ecological miracle. The only country in the world with an inexhaustible supply of kangaroos; where millions of kangaroos can be killed decade after decade, the remaining populations somehow withstanding drought, bushfire and flood– and still number in their millions.

According to the politicians, bureaucrats, wildlife agencies and the kangaroo industry, this inexhaustible supply of kangaroos can be killed on a steady state yearly basis in huge numbers even when their populations are going down because of natural disasters.

The same kangaroo populations according to the dark forces which prey on them, can somehow withstand a loss of more than half their numbers during drought and still recover sufficiently to have the remaining 50 per cent shot out.

No one pays attention to the fact that nature goes in cycles; that kangaroos would exquisitely designed to survive drought by withholding its young until better times. That any responsible industry which predates on wildlife must adopt management policies which reflect these cycles.

A heuristic model of the California Gray Whale ,which Australians for Animals had developed by a leading Australian research scientist , demonstrated with exquisite clarity how the cycles of climate affected the status of the whales' population. If the whales were killed when their numbers were going down as a result of El Nino incidents or regime shifts, then the whales would be driven to extinction.

The only time to carry out a kill in a responsible way was to wait until the populations were on an upward curve of recovery. Exactly the same lesson applies to kangaroos and all wildlife.

Their lives are governed by nature's cycles; their survival is continually affected by climatic changes which dictate life and death.

To continue to kill kangaroos when their populations are being so desperately affected by drought, excessive out of control commercial exploitation is an act of madness. But then ecological madness is not well documented or published within the scientific community.

Commonsense and our increasingly sophisticated level of ecological knowledge would tell the government financed scientists who support the kangaroo slaughter that killing big numbers of indigenous wild animals is an act of folly, of supreme environmental irresponsibility. The evidence is irrefutable. Only the most blinkered scientists could support this slaughter and claim it is scientifically managed or adds anything to the future health of kangaroo populations or the environment.

Legal challenges are expensive and most lawyers, like the public, don't want to be bothered with complex, controversial, costly environmental issues. Not unless they get well paid.

Ministers of religion, academics, business leaders and some environmental groups manage to ignore the slaughter as well. Their mantra goes something like this…

Eastern grey kangaroos in the rifle sights of myopic politicians and their narrow-minded constituency. Do they live in Australia or are they still yearning for Olde England? (Photo: Bill Corn)

Better to farm kangaroos than cattle.

We provided them with water so it's an artificially large population. Solution? Take away their water, let them die of thirst.

There's more important issues.

Aah. Australia is such an amazing country. Its beauty shielding the rivers of human and animal blood which stain our history. The mindless slaughter of our unique wildlife is one of the great tragedies of the 20th and 21st centuries. Millions of koalas and kangaroos have perished, killed for profit, without conscience to line the pockets of a few.

Carers and activists who continue the long fight to stop the slaughter of kangaroos are to be blessed for their actions. However, many of these actions have alienated sections of the broader community who need to be convinced that kangaroos must be spared further destruction. To do this requires many more activists and concerned people.

The kangaroo slaughter could have been stopped years ago with some imaginative and obvious legal actions. AFA still believes that a few good legal challenges would turn the industry upside down and make approval of the monstrous annual quotas difficult to obtain.

As well, there are many actions that could be undertaken internationally. But to do justice to the possibilities would require funds, dedicated public interest lawyers as well as international lawyers.

Faced with these kinds of odds, it's fair to say there's a sense of desperation in the community of people who care for our wildlife.

Australian animals are unique, intelligent, amazing creatures. The kangaroo is a magnificent, incredible animal. The remaining populations have a right to exist and to live in peace. To do what they do, that is - revegetate native grasses. To raise their young and to live in social harmony in their mobs, moving from rainstorm to rain storm, cycling their reproduction in harmony with nature.

As global warming underlines the fate of this desert continent, turning the land to dust, Australians would do well to pause and consider their own future.

It cannot be divorced from the fate of our wildlife. Look no further than the kangaroos.

KANGAROO CONUNDRUMS:

KANGAROO MANAGEMENT IN THE PERI-URBAN ENVIRONMENT

By Dror Ben-Ami

School of Biological, Earth and Environmental Sciences, UNSW Sydney.

The conundrums

Aldo Leopold played a pivotal role in formulating the wilderness concept in the United States (Miller & Hobbs 2002). Yet during the last decades of his life he focused on small farmsteads in human-dominated landscapes and "… the oldest task in human history; to live on a piece of land without spoiling it" (Leopold 1991). He recognised that large protected areas were not sufficient for conservation. The realisation that there are too few extensive wild lands for the preservation of biodiversity (Grumbine 1990; McNeely et al. 1994; Newmark 1995) has given rise to a broader focus in conservation planning that encompasses protected areas, smaller reserves and unprotected lands (Miller & Hobbs 2002).

Biodiversity hotspots typically coincide with higher-than-average human population densities and growth rates (Myers 1988; Myers 1990; Mittermeier et al. 2000). In the USA, urbanization has been identified as a primary cause, singly or in association with other factors, for declines in more than half the species listed as threatened or endangered under the U.S. Endangered Species Act (Czech et al. 2000; Miller & Hobbs 2002). Similarly, Australia is one of the most urbanized nations in the Asia-Pacific region with a population that is 85% urban (UNPD 2001). The 'State of the Environment' report (Williams et al. 2001) concludes that the condition of Australia's ecosytems has worsened over recent years. It reports that to maintain biodiversity measures must be taken to conserve diversity in disturbed environments.

Signs of future trends are not encouraging for urban wildlife. A study of wildlife sightings around Melbourne indicates that the mammal community at the time of European settlement in 1856 was diverse, with 50 species recorded. However, a broad measure of distribution in the last 20 years recorded only sixteen species (of the 50) in fewer local government areas than previously (van der Ree 2004). This is disturbing because urbanisation is still increasing at dramatic rates. Projections are that over 50% of the world's population will reside in urban areas in the near future (UNPD 2002).

Today, we can find some of the last medium to large size kangaroo species in urban and peri-urban national parks and reserves. How long will we be able to walk in their company?

A number of Australia's macropodoid species such as rock-wallabies *(Petrogale spp.)* (Flannery 2004) and the parma wallaby *(Macropus parma)* (Maxwell *et al.* 1996) occurred in the urban environment and are now endangered or vulnerable. Other more common species such as the swamp wallaby *(Wallabia bicolor)*, the red-necked wallaby *(M. rufogriseus)*, common wallaroo *(M. robustus)*, eastern grey kangaroo *(M. giganteus)* and western grey kangaroo *(M. fuliginosus)* also inhabited what are now urban centres and are now relegated to peri-urban environments where they are also showing signs of decline (CSIRO 1996). In Adelaide, the western grey kangaroo can still be found in the periphery but the wallaroo is locally extinct (BioCity 2005), and Darwin, our smallest capital city, has an unfenced population of agile wallabies *(M. agilis)* within the city boundaries (Stirrat 2002). In Sydney, the swamp wallaby, the red necked wallaby and the eastern grey kangaroo can be found in peri-urban reserves (Fig. 1) within and just outside the city centre, such as Lane Cove National Park, Manly Dam Reserve, the Royal National Park (the nation's oldest national park), and the Blue Mountains National Park (a world heritage site) and Ku-ring gai National Park.

Agile wallabies *(Macropus agilis)* are still found within the boundaries (East Point Reserve) of our smallest capital city, Darwin.

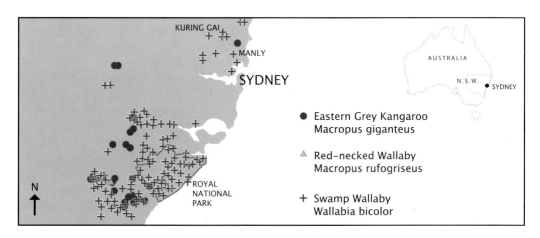

Figure 1. The red necked wallaby, swamp wallaby and the eastern grey kangaroo in Sydney, Australia as of 5/5/2005,   NSW Dept of Environment and Conservation (NSW NPWS 2005).

Human - kangaroo conflict: myths versus facts

Unfortunately, as urban centres infringe on kangaroo habitat, human-kangaroo conflicts ensue. While some human-kangaroo conflict issues are more myth than fact, others constitute real problems that have to be resolved if urban conservation is to be achieved. Road fatalities affect both humans and wildlife profoundly (Table 1). The Roads and Traffic Authority (2001) records indicate that in NSW of the 388 accidents reported that involved an animal-vehicle collision, 283 were with either wallabies or kangaroos. Two resulted in human fatality and 82 in human injury. On a national level, the National Road and Motorists' Association (NRMA) estimated that the cost of animal/vehicle collisions, including injuries to humans and property damage, was $10 million in 1998 (Cooper 1998). This figure does not include scenarios where harm was rendered as a result of drivers trying to avoid hitting wildlife.

Table 1. Reported animal-vehicle collisions in New South Wales in 2001 (RTA 2001).

Object Hit in First Impact	Fatal Accident	Injury Accident	Non-Casualty Accident	Total Accidents
Kangaroo/Wallaby	2	82	199	283
Other Animal	0	46	59	105
Total	2	128	258	388

Although harm to humans from kangaroos in urban areas is rare, it does occur. In some northern NSW towns 100 percent of people saw kangaroos everyday. In 15 instances (out of an unknown number of reports) kangaroos had either growled at people or chased them away (National Geographic 2005). However, a media release by NSW NPWS (2002) states:

> "Conflicts with kangaroos can occur if they perceive a person as a threat to themselves, their mates or young. With males this can also be perceived as a threat to a sparing partner or as a challenge to their group dominance."

The cases that are usually heard of involve just the males of one species, the eastern grey kangaroo, which may be found in golf courses and open areas in the urban and peri-urban environment. It is suggested that domestic dogs may also be the victims of kangaroo aggression as seen in the following media release (PlanetArk 2004):

> "Australians living in the nation's drought-ravaged capital were warned yesterday to keep their distance from aggressive kangaroos after the iconic marsupials attacked one woman and killed a pet dog. Eastern Grey kangaroos, which can grow 1.7 metres (5.6 feet) tall and weigh 70 kg (154 lb), have started moving out of the parched bush into inner Canberra suburbs during the day to look for grass and water, increasing their contact with people."

In fact, the perception that a kangaroo will initiate an attack on a dog is a fallacy, as kangaroos are the natural prey of dingo (Robertshaw & Harden 1986), feral (Meek & Triggs 1998) and domestic dogs (Meek 1999). It is not in their behavioural repertoire to actively seek to harm pets. Rather a male kangaroo will seek refuge from dogs in water where the dog is disadvantaged and may then proceed to kick and hit the attacking dog, and may submerge it under water in the process. It is up to responsible dog owners to ensure that kangaroos are not hounded and for humans to behave responsibly towards native mammals. For example, the Cobar office of the NSW National Parks and Wildlife Service made the following media release in the 2002 drought (NSW NPWS 2002):

> *"People are advised not to approach the animals, to keep dogs leashed and where possible keep yards and garden gates closed, according to NPWS Acting Cobar Area Manager, Hugh McNee. Drought conditions have left emus and kangaroos short of food and water in their usual habitat and brought them into town bringing them into contact with traffic and domestic dogs, Mr. McNee said.*
>
> *The NPWS would remind the public that all native animals are protected and wherever possible we are encouraging people to give animals a wide berth, not to approach them, keep dogs well away and for motorists to be extra vigilant.*
>
> *Residents should also restrict access to gardens, keep dogs secured and only contact NPWS in the case of an emergency, where the animal is hurt or is at risk of being injured."*

Kangaroos can exacerbate the problem of zoonotic diseases; i.e. those that are carried by wildlife and passed to humans. For example, the hydatid tapeworm *(Echinococcus granulosis)* is one of seven tapeworms known to infect dogs in Australia. The lifecycle of this parasite can involve a number of animals, including humans, but the most important species involved are sheep, kangaroos and dogs. Hydatid disease is diagnosed in tens of humans every year (Queensland Government Department of Primary Industry and Fisheries 2005). The tape worm is carried by native wildlife, including kangaroos and wallabies. Although harmless to the kangaroo, the tape worm will pass from its gut to pasture only to be taken by grazing cattle. Dogs that have scavenged carcases or eaten kangaroo faecal pellets may pass the tapeworm on to humans by licking them or defecating in their vegetable gardens. To humans, in particular children, tape worms represent a significant health risk. However, in dogs they are easily eradicated by anti worming tablets.

Kangaroos can be a hindrance to hobby farmers and avid gardeners by browsing on their produce. The swamp wallaby in particular is known to frequent gardens, consuming both ornamental plants and garden vegetables (Watson 1993). However, easy solutions, such as mesh rather than the typical single wire fencing of sufficient height will deter kangaroos from either going through or hopping over a fence.

Human impact on kangaroos in the urban fringe

Although the impact of peri-urban kangaroo species on humans is real it is dwarfed by the impact of humans on the kangaroo species that have persisted in the urban or peri-urban environment.

Often wildlife populations in the peri-urban environment inhabit patchy habitats in which they are isolated. Human-related impacts therefore have compounding effects on the persisting species. For instance, predation by foxes and roaming domestic dogs can severely impact a peri-urban kangaroo population without immigration of new individuals to replace those that have been killed. This following advice from the Anglesea Shire (Anglsea Online 2005) is telling:

> "As residents or visitors to Anglesea, we are very fortunate to be surrounded by beautiful bushland with abundant native wildlife. Anglesea is famous for its kangaroos which can be observed grazing peacefully on the Anglesea Golf Course.
>
> Unfortunately however, our kangaroos and joeys are being maimed and killed at an alarming rate due to careless drivers and dog owners particularly in the vicinity of the Golf Course and Great Ocean Road."

In Jervis Bay, NSW, domestic dogs were found to roam up to 30 km into forested areas adjacent to an urban community in search of prey, in particular the eastern grey kangaroo and the swamp wallaby (Meek 1999). Dogs are also known to impact populations of the yellow-footed rock-wallaby, *Petrogale xanthopus*, in the far west and the brush-tailed rock-wallaby, *Petrogale penicillata*, in the east of New South Wales (Dovey *et al.* 1997), and Lumholtz's tree-kangaroo, *Dendrolagus lumholtzi*, in fragmented habitat in north Queensland (Newell 1999).

Swamp wallaby *(Wallabia bicolor)* is a victim of roaming domestic dogs in reserves surrounding Sydney.

In Muogamarra Nature Reserve on the northern outskirts of Sydney, domestic dogs roamed into the reserve from peripheral towns and hobby farms and preyed primarily on the swamp wallaby (Table 2). The dog densities were higher near the urban dwellings and lower in the core of the reserve (Fig. 2). Secondary effects of the predation pressure exerted by the dogs, and to some extent foxes, on the wallabies was that the fitness levels of wallabies nearer the reserve edge were significantly lower than in the reserve interior (Ben-Ami 2005).

Table 2. The percentage of prey items found in scats of domestic dogs and foxes within Muogamarra Nature Reserve (Ben-Ami 2005).

Prey	Common name	Dog faeces (%)	Fox faeces (%)
Wallabia bicolor	Swamp wallaby	28	17
Perameles nasuta	Long-nosed bandicoot	4	0
Isoodon macrourus	Northern brown bandicoot	5	0
Bandicoot spp		2	6
Canis lupus familiaris	Dog	31	0
Homo sapiens	Human	2	0
Trichosurus vulpecula	Common brush tail possum	11	17
Rattus fuscipes	Bush rat	2	24
Rattus rattus	Black rat	4	6
Thylogale thetis	Pademelon	2	0
Pseudocheirus peregrinus	Common ring-tailed possum	7	12
Hydromys chrysogaster	Water rat	0	6
Oryctolagus cuniculus	Rabbit	2	12
Total faeces		54	17

Figure 2. Mean (± SEM) predator visits (paw prints) at 200-m intervals from disturbance sources (towns and farms) at trail heads into Muogamarra Nature Reserve (Ben-Ami 2005).

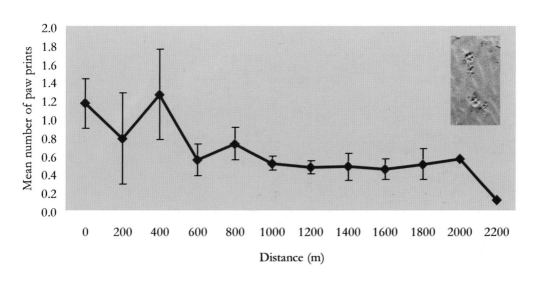

Loss of habitat due to human settlement is recognised as a leading cause of decline in biodiversity (United Nations Centre for Human Settlement 1996). In urban centres, wildlife will most often loose their habitat as a result of housing or business development. Their habitat is usually developed without any regard for the welfare of the affected animals. In an extreme example at the St Mary's Australian Defence Industries (ADI) site in Western Sydney, more than a third of the 1545-ha site that includes endangered flora and fauna species, ecological communities and populations of emus and an estimated 3000 eastern grey kangaroos is slated for residential development (talkStMarys 2005). The site developers are claimed to have submitted a proposal to cull 2500 of the kangaroos to facilitate the construction of 5,000 dwellings. Fortunately, the cull was opposed by the NSW Attorney General and Environment Minister Bob Debus, concerned residents and animal welfare groups (World League for the Protection of Animals 2003).

Loss of level terrain may have a negative impact on kangaroo species that have such habitat requirements. In the parks around Sydney such as the Blue Mountains and Ku-ring-gai National Parks and Muogamarra Nature Reserve development has occurred along the ridge tops and plateaus leaving mainly the slopes and hilly terrain for conservation. The percentage of level terrain (slopes of 0° – 2.5°) in Muogamarra Nature Reserve (41.7%) is less than half the amount available in the adjacent towns of Cowan (91.2%) and Berrowra (90.7%) (Fig. 3). A number of species that may have been impacted as a result of habitat loss and fragmentation in and around Sydney include eastern grey kangaroos, common wallaroos, red-necked wallabies, brush-tailed rock-wallabies and red-necked pademelons *(Thylogale thetis)*.

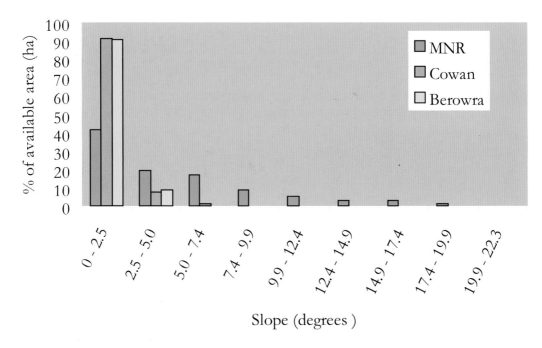

Figure 3. The relative proportions of flat (0-2.5°) through to steep (19.9 – 22.3°) slopes in the terrain of Muogamarra Nature Reserve (MNR) and the contiguous urban areas of Cowan and Berowra (Ben-Ami 2005).

Road fatalities have been mentioned previously in respect to human fatality and property loss but the estimated impact in terms of wildlife fatality is of horrific proportions (see chapter by Ramp on impact of roads on kangaroos). The peri urban environment often contains a network of roads that crisscross semi-rural and remnant habitats. The macropod road fatalities on these roads can have adverse impacts on isolated populations within these habitats. A Population Viability Assessment or PVA enables us to model various scenarios to look at the impact of a range of factors on a population. I incorporated both ongoing and stochastic (random or unpredictable in timing and magnitude) factors to construct a PVA for an isolated swamp wallaby population in Muogamarra Nature Reserve using Vortex(Lacy 1995). These factors represented both environmental and anthropogenic factors such as fire, disease, predation by both foxes and dogs, and road fatalities. Five hundred permutations of the various factors were modelled a thousand times each. The standard deviation around the mean indicated the upper and lower limits of prediction values. When the best estimate (BE) values of the effect of the various factors on the swamp wallabies' mortality and reproduction were incorporated into the model the swamp wallaby population was found to be in decline and at risk of quasi-extinction (females extinct) within 30 years (Fig. 4). A logarithmic regression indicated that adult and young female fatalities have a significant influence on the model (Table 3) (Ben-Ami 2005). Modelling based on values acquired from other studies (Cooper 1998; Morrissey 2003) indicated that the prevention of road fatalities would dramatically decrease the absolute risk of local extinction to 1% in 50 years and 13% in 100 years (Table 4). Thus, when viewed in the context of a multitude of anthropogenic disturbances, the elimination of road fatalities would decrease the human pressure on the local swamp wallaby population. If management practices paired the prevention or reduction of road fatalities with some other measure, such as the reduction of wallaby predation, then it is likely that the risk of quasi-extinction would be eliminated (Ben-Ami 2005).

The Royal National Park also contains an isolated population of swamp wallabies. In this park, major disturbances include wildfires, disturbance and predation by foxes, competition with deer for resources and road fatalities. There are an estimated 130 wallabies killed annually on roads within the park (Morrissey 2003), with a population suspected to be between 600 and 1,600 individuals (Moriarty 2004). Presumably mitigation of road fatalities will have significant impact on the viability of the swamp wallaby population in the Royal National Park.

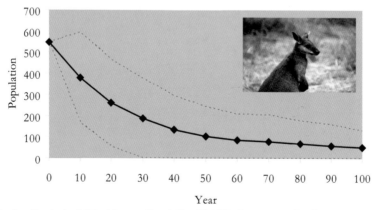

Figure 4. The best estimate (solid line) from a Population Viability Assessment for the mean population of swamp wallabies in Muogamarra Nature Reserve under current impacts of mostly anthropogenic origin. The dashed lines indicate the upper and lower limits of the standard deviation around the mean (Ben-Ami 2005).

Not all human impact is detrimental to the persistence of kangaroos in the urban and peri-urban environment. As mentioned earlier the urban fringe is often a resource of food. In fact in the Muogamarra Nature Reserve swamp wallabies frequent towns and farms that are the source of exotic vegetation on the reserve edge (Fig. 5). There is also some evidence to suggest that the fire management that is often implemented in the vicinity of urban centres is beneficial for wildlife including kangaroos (Lunney & O'Connell 1988; Ben-Ami 2005).

Relationships between neighbours are often complex. Humans and kangaroos are neighbours in urban areas and our relationship is no different. We are impacted by them and impact upon them. Unfortunately our negative impact upon them in the urban and peri-urban environment outweighs any positive effects. Without a change to our practices we stand to lose some of the last medium to large sized wildlife, the kangaroo species, in our midst.

In addition to our ethical responsibility to conserve species and prevent extinction, scientific literature also suggests that they are of value to us in the urban and the peri-urban environment, as explained in the next section, and should therefore be conserved.

Conservation benefits and future directions

There are some compelling scientific reasons to conserve kangaroo species in the urban and peri-urban environments. The effects of urbanisation provide a context for answering ecological questions of general importance and applicability, as well as questions that are specific and unique to urbanisation (McDonnell & Pickett 1990). For example, urbanisation can provide large-scale experiments to test the effects of habitat fragmentation on ecological communities (McDonnell 1997). The disturbed landscape also presents a pre-manipulated environment in which to study the evolutionary forces acting on persisting species.

The enhanced value of the urban ecological resource is not just due to its inherent scientific interest per se, but also to its accessibility to local people (Rotherham 1994, 1999). The exposure of people to wildlife and natural systems can lead to action to safeguard the environment as public awareness leads to grassroots action. Awareness and action are recognised as effective precursors to environmental management. Urban areas are accessible to an increasing portion of the population, in particular decision makers who influence economics and politics at regional and national levels (Jones & Rotherham 1998; Rotherham 1999). Furthermore, enhancing the quality of life in urban areas (Worster 1973) and decreasing the immigration of urban residents to the countryside surrounding cities may stem development in rural areas (Shutkin 2000; Miller & Hobbs 2002). In NSW, where many politicians favour decentralization and the settling of migrants in regional centres, the aim should also be to prevent the loss of already existing farmland in the urban periphery to urbanisation. This would be an important process for urban conservation as cities tend to be located on valuable habitat because they presumably started in areas of highly fertility for horticulture and crops.

Furthermore, native animals play a major role in Australian tourism constituting some 18% of international tourists' motivation to visit Australia (Higginbottom *et al.* 2004). Higgingbottom *et al.* (2004: 23) also state:

> *"The 20 million or so kangaroos in Australia (Pople and McLeod 2000) comprise some of the world's most abundant large terrestrial mammals. These larger macropodoids are widely viewed as 'overabundant' pests or as a resource for commercial harvesting (Pople and Grigg 1998). Generally absent from the debate on how Australia should approach management of its kangaroos is discussion of their role in tourism. This is surprising given the recognised economic significance of nature based tourism in Australia (Blamey and Hatch 1998) and the potential for tourism to foster appreciation and understanding of wildlife and nature (Moscardo et al. 2001)."*

This argument is also relevant for the urban and peri-urban environment. It is likely that most tourists visit the urban centres of Australia. Yet Higginbottom *et al* (2004: pp 23) state that "...where these species (large social, kangaroo species) are most likely to be abundant mostly score poorly in terms of feasibility of tourism". This is not necessarily the case as records indicate the large social macropodoid, the eastern grey kangaroo and the more cryptic swamp wallaby do occur in the large urban centres of Melbourne (van der Ree 2004) and Sydney (NSW Wildlife Atlas), and presumably other urban centres.

Tourism with eastern grey kangaroos in a peri-urban reserve.

Urban wildlife management policies should promote the conservation of members of the kangaroo family, whether endangered or common, in the urban to peri-urban environment to achieve the economic and educational benefits of tourism for both international tourists and the 85% of Australians residing in urban centres.

The concept of 'wildlife management in urban and peri-urban national parks and reserves' needs to change to 'urban and peri-urban wildlife management'. This change in the approach to urban wildlife management implies that management plans need to account for the inherent value of urban and peri-urban wildlife species whether they are endangered or common. Furthermore, appropriate and up-to-date techniques should be utilised to assess the conservation status of wildlife that are often in remnant but fragmented habitat. Urban ecosystems include a multiplicity of anthropogenic disturbances that are both ongoing, such as road-caused fatalities, predation and mauling by pets and altered resources, and stochastic, such as human caused fires, sporadic pollution, habitat loss. Management strategies employed to address the affects of urbanisation on wildlife are typically based upon qualitative data. Given the ready availability of statistical tools for assessing conservation strategies in quantitative frameworks, an important step in addressing the effects of urbanization should be to integrate these tools into management planning. A quantitative, rather than qualitative, measure of the effect of these disturbances on urban wildlife populations would contribute to effective management strategies.

An appropriate tool for achieving this is Population Viability Assessment. PVA is currently used in conservation biology to assess minimum viable populations (Gilpin & Soule 1986) and assist in the management of both threatened (Burgman *et al.* 1993; Possingham *et al.* 1993; Brook *et al.* 2000) and abundant populations (McCarthy *et al.* 1996). It is a reliable and quantitative tool that can be used to identify environmental factors that impact negatively on a specific conservation target, predict the outcome of management strategies, and account for both anthropogenic and environmental stochastic events (Lacy 1993). It should be utilised in the urban context as well to enable managers to be proactive rather than reactive in mitigating future threats to the persistence of urban wildlife populations (Banks 2004).

Population viability assessment is usually applied for a singular species but it does not make sense to tackle all of the urban conservation issues on a species by species basis (Lunney and Burgin 2004). Lunney and Burgin (2004: 3) state: "In the long term, urban wildlife needs to be part of an urban renewal plan, a catchment plan, an overall plan for biodiversity, and urban wildlife ecologists need to be part of the integrated planning process". This seminal urban ecology book *Urban Wildlife: more than meets the eye* concludes that there is also a need for "a common strategy for managing wildlife in the urban environment" (Recher 2004).

Thus there is a need for conserving both endangered and common urban wildlife species utilising the most up to date analytical techniques, a common national strategy, and in the process involving scientists, management professionals, urban planners and community groups in both conservation and renewal of the urban and peri-urban environment. Kangaroos should be the flagship species of such programs as they immediately identify the Australian landscape and the persistence of such large and conspicuous mammals will cement our respect for our wildlife heritage.

Eastern grey kangaroo male in the rangelands showing the adaptability of this species. (Photo: David B Croft)

KANGAROOS

MISUNDERSTOOD AND MALIGNED REPRODUCTIVE MIRACLE WORKERS

By Ingrid Witte

BSc. Hons. PhD (UNSW)

Kangaroos and Humans

Sometimes I wonder whether we as a species cannot deal with another animal, like the large and abundant kangaroos, that has so far refused to submit to our human onslaught. Our response seems to be to punish these animals for their reticence to yield. Nowhere else on Earth can large mammals still roam across an entire continent in the freedom that kangaroos rightfully exercise in Australia. Do we stand in wonder and applaud? No, we seem hell-bent on letting that go and so, in a rapidly advancing future, forcing everyone to be satisfied with seeing the beautiful free creatures that we call kangaroos only in zoos. This was the attitude that a grazier angrily forced onto a friend of mine who deigned to argue for the kangaroos' value as a tourist attraction. He said: "If the f…ing. tourists want to see f…ing. kangaroos, they should go into the f…ing. zoo!" Is that what we really want? I think not.

Kangaroos are so unique on this planet in so many ways! For one, their amazing reproductive system and devoted care for their young should make us stare at them in wonder and not stare at them with greed in our eyes. The kangaroo mother's miraculous ability to rear, to us, a highly premature infant through milk and skin-to-skin contact alone, has seen us emulate this behaviour in paediatric medicine. If you search 'kangaroo care' on the internet you will not come up with the expected few descriptions from animal behaviourists of maternal care by kangaroos but rather thousands of references to the value of 'kangaroo care' to premature human babies. For example, Katie Brietbach (1993) writes the following on the *Virtual Children's Hospital: Pediatrics* -

> *Kangaroo care is a form of skin-to-skin contact between a parent and their preterm baby. The baby, wearing only a diaper, is held in an upright position against the parent's bare chest. The baby is held this way for 20 minutes to four hours a day. This is called Kangaroo Care because it is similar to the way a baby kangaroo is snuggled against its mother.*

She then goes on to describe the history of 'Kangaroo Care' and the many benefits to baby and parent.

The ancestors of today's kangaroos derived from a small possum-like marsupial, dwelling in trees about 50 million years ago. Dinosaurs had only barely become extinct. Around 30 million years ago the kangaroo ancestors had evolved to a point that they ventured down from trees of the then existing rainforests and started life on the ground – just like our own human ancestors much later in life's history on Earth. Thus we humans are less original than we may like to think, in so many ways!

We have learned many aspects of kangaroos' evolution from the work of Professor Michael Archer and his team from the University of New South Wales and their finds from the rich fossil deposits at Riversleigh in Queensland and elsewhere. The unique mode of locomotion for mammals as large as kangaroos – the energetically efficient hopping gait - developed around the time of their ancestors moving to the floor of the forests. Hugh Tyndale-Biscoe (2005) describes this as one of three steps to success of the 'consummate kangaroos'.

Hopping and the mode of reproduction are two of the three steps to the success of the 'consummate kangaroos' (Tyndale-Biscoe 2005) (Photo: David B Croft)

Many different and sometimes strange, but astonishing 'models' of kangaroos evolved from these early creatures, always adapting to ever changing environmental conditions. The blueprint must have been quite successful, because those hopping marsupials are still with us today - although one wonders at times for how much longer, given Australia's extinction record and human greed knowing no bounds. Terry Dawson (1995) tells the story of the modern kangaroos. Approximately 4-5 million years ago, we may have been able to find a little Pliocene kangaroo, not so different from today's grey kangaroos. About 1-2 million years ago, following a drying out of the Australian continent, one may have been able to encounter the most beautiful of all, the first red kangaroos. In contrast hominids, the line leading to Homo sapiens, were barely appearing on the evolutionary scene and had a long way to go to become what we are now - which is a lot of the time nothing to be proud of.

We know quite a bit about their evolutionary history – but the history of their unique reproductive system and caring behaviour for their young is much harder to unravel from fossil deposits. This fascinating story began to be told in the 1950s and 1960s when seminal scientific papers were published like 'The life history and reproduction of the red kangaroo *(Megaeia rufa [now Macropus rufus])*' by Sharman and Pilton (1964).

The basics of kangaroo reproduction were described in a book 'Kangaroos' by Frith and Calaby (1969) and significantly more detail added by Tyndale-Biscoe (1973) in 'Life of Marsupials'.
Thus I am surprised and disheartened at the ignorance about and mis-representation of kangaroo reproduction that persists today and that sanctions our mistreatment of them.

Embryonic diapause in kangaroo reproduction and the overlap of up to three generations in simultaneous care is another of Tyndale-Biscoe's (2005) three steps to success of the 'consummate kangaroos'. This is the focus of my chapter. The remaining one of these steps - foregut fermentation and its foraging advantages - will not be discussed here.

Kangaroos and me

My own story and my life with kangaroos began in Germany when I was eight years old and saw a documentary on Australia, well before the later appearance of 'Skippy' on our television. This small piece in a nature show on TV, showing these unique creatures, led to a lifelong obsession, culminating in leaving my country of birth, studying biology and working for my Honours and my PhD on the four large species of kangaroos *(Macropus rufus, M. giganteus, M. fuliginosus, M. robustus erubescens)* that overlap in their ranges in the far north-west of NSW. A dream came true (yes, sometimes they do), and working with and observing these beautiful creatures on a daily basis still amazes me and brings me great joy. I became a scientist, specialising in the behavioural ecology of the large species of kangaroos. Although it is considered a cardinal sin for a scientist to personalise, or as it is often called 'humanise' study individuals – the sin of 'anthropomorphism' – I strongly believe that I became a better scientist (and a better person!) through the fact that I got very close to my study 'subjects' (not 'objects' as they are often made out to be, to separate 'us' from 'them'). I radio-tracked almost 60 individual female red, eastern or western grey kangaroos over three years and observed hundreds more kangaroos including euros. I was able to identify a large number of individuals during my time with them in their habitat and they never ceased to challenge my understanding of their survival strategies and rich but subtle social lives. I also became a carer for wildlife, a surrogate mother for the injured and orphaned. Those little orphaned joeys provided me with additional information at close range and allowed me a far better insight into kangaroo behaviour than what I would have been able to understand without them.

I strongly believe it is not only important for everybody, but absolutely vital to raise and care for

Interaction with 'Kikkoman' a hand-raised male red kangaroo that was rehabilitated to the wild. (Photo: Jean-Paul Ferrero)

an animal at least once in a human life. Only then do we gain a good and perhaps sufficient understanding of their needs which we cannot get when watching from afar. I also believe that faithful and responsible caring for a mammal, like a dog or a cat for most people, is important for personal development and the attitude we refer to as 'humane behaviour', not only towards other animals, but towards our fellow humans. One only needs to look at the strong link between psychopathic behaviour towards humans, which often starts out with atrocious acts towards pets and wildlife during youth and culminates as adults to atrocious acts towards humans (see Eleonora Gullone's chapter in this volume). It is rare that people will treat humans callously if they have developed empathy and a good understanding of animals in their care such as pets and livestock. As for those with a special interest in animals, the zoologists, I also believe it to be vitally important to use any chance provided to raise and or care for one of the animals that they are studying. Even botanists would do well to form a close association with animals as most plants one way or another are considered a resource for animals, whether as food, for shelter or for play. Plant and animal life is closely interlinked. Raising an animal will allow us a much improved insight into our natural environment, permitting us as humans to make much more sense out what makes life on our planet 'tick'.

Dependence of young – a most important but misunderstood fact!

As the physiological basis and demographics of kangaroo reproduction were revealed in the 1960s and 1970s, Eleanor Russell conducted parallel studies of mother-young relationships with a landmark paper on tammar wallabies and red kangaroos in 1973. As knowledge expanded she reviewed the subject in 1982 for marsupials in general and again in 1989 for kangaroos in particular.

Thus let me make it clear that at the time a regulated kangaroo industry came into being in the 1970s there was a comprehensive body of published scientific knowledge on the reproduction and reproductive behaviour, including maternal care, of kangaroos. This industry, its regulators and supporters have been in denial ever since about the inherent cruelty to young-at-foot executed by 'licensed trappers' (the regulators' term, shooters in everyone else's parlance) covered by a clearly inadequate code of practice as detailed by Croft (2004).

What has happened from the 1980s to the present is that ethologists, behavioural ecologists and comparative physiologists have taken to the field to study the reproductive biology of several kangaroo and wallaby species confirming and expanding observations that were initially made in captive colonies with CSIRO in Canberra and at various Universities. One of the most important lessons I learned as a behavioural ecologist during the progression of my studies and my observations of wild animals, and my experience in raising orphans, was the length and depth (nutritional and behavioural) of dependency that young kangaroos have on their mothers, their caregivers. For kangaroos, maternal care is most certainly not restricted to life in the pouch but continues well into the juvenile phase of these animals, the time we refer to as the 'young-at-foot' stage. Even past the weaning and young-at-foot stage, juveniles still frequently accompany their mothers, a behaviour that may be vital for their survival to sexual maturity through social learning (Higginbottom & Croft 1999). Long-term studies of known individuals in populations of eastern grey kangaroos, euros and red-necked wallabies have shown that young females tend to set up home ranges around their mothers (Ashworth 1996) and hence never really leave, indicating an even stronger interdependence between these animals than we dared to think before.

So let's now examine the facts, dispel the misconceptions, expose the cruelty and advocate for a 'fair go', namely humane and compassionate treatment, for kangaroos.

Roo reproduction – What's typical?

The first misconception is that all kangaroos and their kind reproduce like a red kangaroo. The female red kangaroo has a phenomenal continuous breeding system that at full capacity has three overlapping generations – a young-at-foot permanently outside the pouch but suckling from an elongated teat in the pouch, a pouch young attached to a teat on a second mammary gland (they have four), and a diapausing blastocyst (embryonic ball of cells) in the uterus (Fig. 1). There is no breeding season but females may become synchronised following drought-breaking rain since prolonged drought may lead to a suspension of any breeding. There is a misconception that females choose to stop breeding in drought. The mechanism is somewhat more tragic. A female's young-at-foot, carefully nurtured through an 8-month pouch life, is the most energetically demanding of her offspring. It needs an energy rich milk and high-quality pasture to forage on to survive and grow up to weaning at 12 months and the latter for some years later until it grows a big enough stomach to store and ferment low quality pasture (Munn & Dawson 2003). In drought a female cannot supply the milk quantity and quality and so her young-at-foot will die. The pouch young requires a more balanced milk of protein, fats and carbohydrate. As the drought intensifies its mother will be unable to supply this and it will die. The termination of the suckling stimulus will break the dormancy of the blastocyst in the uterus and it will develop and be born around 35 days later. This newborn may or may not find a functional mammary gland to support its further development but typically it would undergo some development before it too dies. After birth a female red kangaroo would normally come into oestrus ('heat') and mate but in hard drought she does not (anoestrus). Thus breeding ceases but with the overlapping generations the female hedges her bets that the drought will break and one or more of her young will survive.

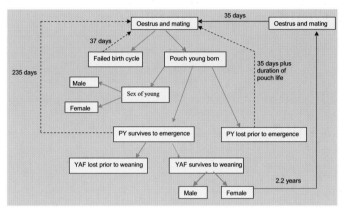

Figure 1. The timing and outcome of a reproductive attempt by a female red kangaroo. PY = pouch young, YAF = young-at-foot (Adapted from Bilton & Croft 2004)

When a long hard drought breaks, the surviving mature females will enter oestrus again, perhaps aided by the phyto-oestrogens in new plant growth, mate and about 35 days later a young will be born. Within one or two days of birth they mate again (post-partum oestrus) and this blastocyst suspends development. The same creation of two generations occurs when a female first becomes sexually mature and has her first oestrus. The onset of sexual maturity in females is variable and depends on their nutrition. Sharman & Pilton (1964) give a range of 14-20 months and I found that my orphaned females supplemented with high-quality grain-based pellets mated at the lower end of this range. In the field at the Fowlers Gap Research Station, Amanda Bilton (Bilton & Croft 2004) estimated sexual maturity later at around 26 months and Debbie Ashworth (1995) found that euros in the same site had delayed sexual maturity under poor forage conditions.

The sub-species of the common wallaroo, the euro, which shares the arid zone with the red kangaroo has a similar high fecundity through embryonic diapause and overlapping generations and continuous breeding. However, in spite of the same reproductive potential in red kangaroos and euros, they pursue different reproductive strategies. Females of both species share the remarkable adaptation that prolongs their survival in drought of a progressive shut-down of reproduction and its associated energy and water costs in lactation as I described previously. To re-emphasise, they do not choose to do this but rather the poor nutrition gained under drought conspires against their capacity to support lactation and produce the hormones necessary to sustain it. Red kangaroos attempt to evade drought by occupying more productive run-on or flood-out country in the plains than the hill-dwelling euros (Croft 1991a, b). Furthermore they emigrate to nearby areas of rainfall following patchy thunderstorm activity which is common in hotter months of the year. There they exploit grasses like the aptly named five-minute grass *(Tripogon loliiformis)* which greens up and grows with light rainfalls. During my PhD research I was alarmed to find most of the female red kangaroos I was studying disappeared from my study site under just such an event. The rain fell to the north of the study site and I was able to track their movements along a north-south gradient (Fig. 2). After later rain on my study site, they returned to their former home ranges. These dramatic but localised movements have given rise to myths about red kangaroos sweeping in hordes or plagues across the Outback.

Euro males may follow drainage channels out of the hills in dry times to exploit taller and better pastures but females endure drought in the hills. Thus in a concurrent study of red kangaroos and euros at the Fowlers Gap Research Station by Graeme Moss (1995) and Debbie Ashworth (1995), respectively, euros ceased reproduction (no young-at-foot) much sooner into drought than red kangaroos (Fig. 3).

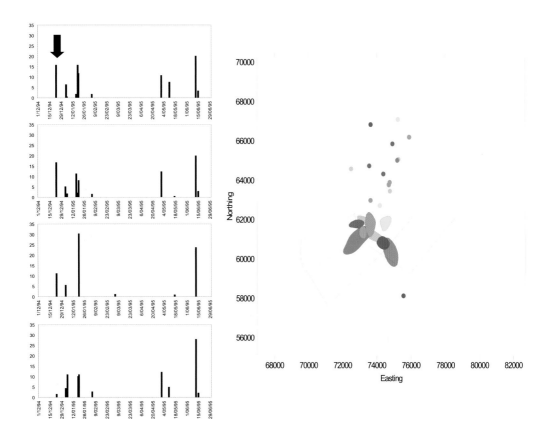

Figure 2. Rainfall (mm) pattern between 1/12/1994 and 30/06/1995 at four stations northwest, north, in and southwest of a study site on the Fowlers Gap Research Station and the movement of female red kangaroos along a north-south gradient in the same period. Each female is colour-coded and her core area on the study site is shown as a large polygon and locations outside are indicated by same-coloured filled circles. Arrow indicates start of December 1994 rainfall which triggered the movement. (From Witte 2002)

Debbie Ashworth modelled the lifetime reproductive success of female euros based on empirical data she collected over her 3-year study. Most females are expected to wean fewer than five young and most of them will not survive to produce a second generation (i.e. granddaughters) (Fig. 4).

Amanda Bilton (Bilton & Croft 2004) later modelled the lifetime reproductive success of red kangaroos on Fowlers Gap Research Station. She found an average of 3.7 offspring per female. Thus in both species replacement (≥ 2 offspring) is achieved but frequent periods of severe

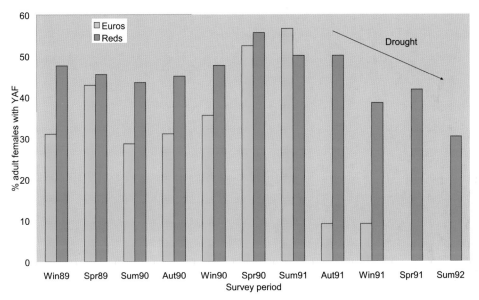

Figure 3. Percentage of adult females in euro and red kangaroo populations on Fowlers Gap Research Station between winter of 1989 and summer of 1992. (Red kangaroo data from Moss [1995], euro data from Ashworth [1995])

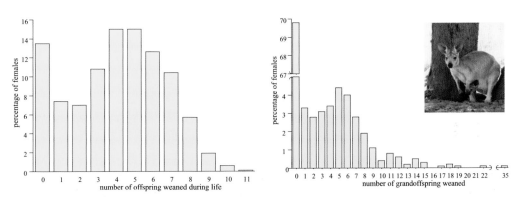

Figure 4. The estimated number of offspring and grand-offspring weaned by female euros from an empirical model of lifetime reproductive success. Most females wean fewer than five offspring in a lifetime of 18 years and very few mothers have surviving offspring in a second generation. (Adapted from Ashworth 1995)

rainfall deficiencies and drought (Fig. 5) naturally restrain population growth.

Red kangaroos and euros share relatively high annual fecundity and continuous breeding but eastern and western grey kangaroos are very different. They have much longer pouch lives and lower fecundity and generally breed once per year (Table 1). Western greys do not have embryonic diapause like the other three species and so only pouch young and young-at-foot overlap in generations.

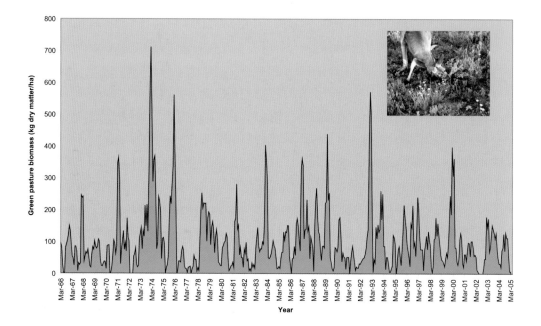

Figure 5. Estimated green pasture biomass (kg dry matter ha⁻¹) on the Fowlers Gap Research Station from mid-1966 to mid-2005. This driver of kangaroo reproductive success is highly variable and low biomass resulting from drought is frequent. Equation biomass = 1.911 x (cumulative 3 month rainfall) – 6.95 from Witte (2002).

Table 1. Reproductive biology of four kangaroo species in commercial kill.

Species	Gestation length (d)	Pouch life (d)	Annual fecundity	Overlapping generations	Birth season
Red	33.2	235	1.36	3	Continuous
Euro	33.3	243	1.32	3	Continuous
Eastern grey	36.4	319	1.03	3	Clumped
Western Grey	30.8	302	1	2	Seasonal

I concurrently studied reproductive performance in red kangaroos and western grey kangaroos on the Fowlers Gap Research Station (Witte 2002). Like the previous comparison between red kangaroos and euros, I found divergence in the species' reproductive success across a drought period in between spring 1994 and winter 1995. Western grey kangaroos maintained a positive rate of increase across this and the rest of the study period whereas red kangaroos showed a negative rate of increase which extended well through the drought (Fig. 6).

Red kangaroos showed the expected loss of young-at-foot in the drought and this trend appeared to be followed by western grey kangaroos (Fig. 7). However, in the absence of

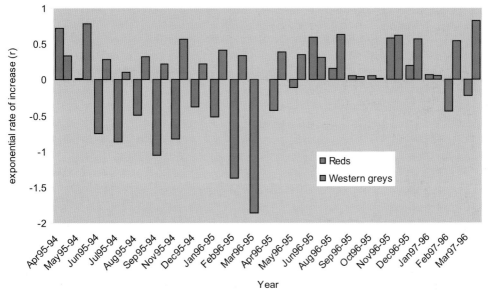

Figure 6. Exponential rate of increase in red kangaroo and western grey kangaroo populations counted by Ingrid Witte (2002) on Fowlers Gap Research Station.

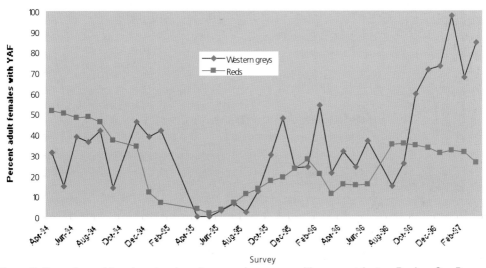

Figure 7. Percentage of female red and western grey kangaroos with young-at-foot on Fowlers Gap Research Station (after Witte 2002).

embryonic diapause western grey kangaroos tend towards a reproductive cycle with permanent pouch exit around the spring months and then a long 7-month dependency to weaning. The peaks around the spring-summer of 1994, 5, and 6 reflect this.

Grey kangaroos seemed to maintain their investment in their current offspring when red kangaroos and certainly euros had ceased. Perhaps the much longer pouch life and period to weaning spreads the cost (Table 2) and their lower fecundity makes each offspring relatively more valuable. I noted that female western greys allowed weaned offspring still associating with them to suckle for a period after they lost their pouch young in drought, seemingly re-investing rather than wasting the milk.

The red kangaroo population on my 991-ha study site fluctuated markedly suggesting a flux of individuals through immigration and emigration, variable recruitment and mortality even though my known females showed a fidelity to the site (Fig. 8). Local scale processes were also evident

Table 2. Timing of development stages in the young of the large kangaroos (Values from Dawson 1995).

	Red kangaroo	Eastern grey	Western Grey	Euro	Eastern wallaroo
1st Pouch exit (days)	185	283	298	201	213
Permanent pouch exit (days)	235	319	323	243	260
Weaning (days)	360	540	540	409	351

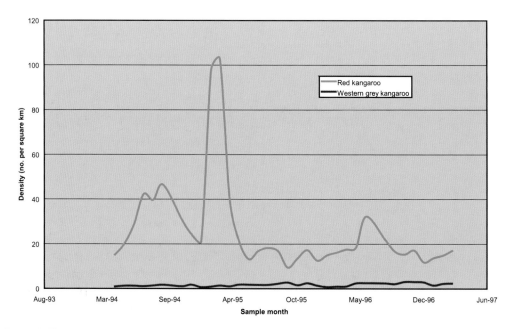

Figure 8. Populations of red kangaroos and western grey kangaroos on 991-ha chenopod-shrubland site at Fowlers Gap Research Station. Estimates were obtained by replicated monthly fixed line transect surveys stratified by land class (Witte 2002).

with a large but transient influx of red kangaroos in March 95 when a thunderstorm dumped rain on the site. In contrast the much lower population of grey kangaroos was relatively stable and showed a slight increase across the three years.

Graeme Arnold and his colleagues (1991) found similar stability in woodland fragments in the Western Australian wheat belt. They ascribed this to low rates of immigration and emigration, as expected in fragmented habitat, and high juvenile mortality. However, most remarkably they estimated that fecundity in the females declined with age (Fig. 9) and so there was in effect a self-regulating brake on population increase.

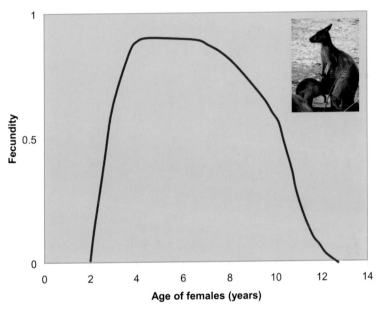

Figure 9. Projected changes in fecundity (proportion producing young) of western grey kangaroos modelled from an 11-year data set collected from Yalanbee in Western Australia (Redrawn from Arnold *et al.* 1991)

Looks can be deceiving

Pouch young in the late in-out stage of pouch life already look fairly well developed, but have no chance of survival if they should lose their mothers. Young-at-foot look like miniature versions of their kind after having left the pouch permanently, usually with 'strong' encouragement by their mothers. However, believing that those fully furred, quite well co-ordinated and foraging young-at-foot are independent after their mother has ejected them permanently from her pouch to free it up for the next occupant, is a huge misconception.

Female red kangaroo and her young-at-foot. The young-at-foot often licks its mother's lips, especially after merycism (a form of regurgitation), and probably thereby gains essential micro-organisms for its foregut digestive system. (Photo Ulrike Kloecker)

The notion that the young of kangaroos after leaving the pouch are independent and can fend for themselves appears to be very convenient when attempting to justify shooting their mothers as is done under quota provisions for the kangaroo industry. It is proclaimed predominantly by people having a vested interest in not letting this fact about the development and dependency of young kangaroos become widely known.

Or it may need to be believed by kangaroo shooters, so that compassion for the fate of the young-at-foot does not intrude on their action of killing the mother. I have heard comments from shooters of the following kind when talking about the fate of the young: "[I] usually let the bigger furred ones go to have something to shoot later on." In 'A Survey of the Extent of Compliance with the Requirements of the Code of Practice for the Humane Shooting of Kangaroos July 2002', this amongst other options was noted as follows:

"Discussions with shooters during this survey suggested that although smaller pouch young were killed immediately, young at foot were far more difficult to kill. Some shooters always let such

mobile young go free, whilst others would attempt to catch and kill these animals. Several cases were reported of shooters bringing young at foot home, to be raised by the shooter himself, or by friends. The general approach by shooters was that if it was easy to catch and kill the young at foot then this was done. However, if the young at foot were too mobile and too much time would need to be spent in killing the animal, then it was left alone."

How a professional shooter after many years in the business still understands so little about the animal he shoots remains a mystery to me. The young ones he lets go are doomed to death and will not be recruited into a population to be shot later. Regulations do not assist this matter as knowledge about kangaroo biology and ecology is not a requirement to obtain a kangaroo trappers license. All a shooter has to do is to have a valid firearms license, a TAFE Certificate for safe food handling and he has to show that he can hit a target over 80m, although shooting over 200 m is more likely what happens in reality. Regarding the target animal he only needs to be able to separate species and to estimate their weight to validate a shot. There are no other provisions.

The reality is that the young-at-foot (YAF) has very high energy and water demands that are almost equivalent to the mother who may be three times its size. Adam Munn and Terry Dawson (2001: 917) in the abstract to their paper summarise their findings as follows:

"Over a wide range of environmental temperatures (ambient temperature [T_a] – 5° to 45°C), YAF red kangaroos had a mass-specific metabolism that was generally twice that of adults, considerably higher than would be expected for an adult marsupial of their body size. The total energy requirements of YAF red kangaroos were 60% - 70% of those of adult females, which were three times their size. Over the same range in T_a, YAF red kangaroos had total evaporative water losses equal to those of adult females."

They conclude that forage must be of high quality for YAF and weaned young due to the limitations of their small gut in breaking down fibrous plant material. In a later experiment (Munn & Dawson 2003), they allowed that a YAF at 300-d age could survive on a high quality lucerne diet and water without supplementation from one of the milk substitutes (Digestelact®) uses by rearers of orphaned macropods. This was not the case with a low quality chopped oat diet. The experiment was conducted over 10 days in temperature controlled conditions in a small cage. In the wild the YAF must cope with fluctuating temperatures and expend significant energy in thermoregulation and locomotion.

Thus even if the forage were of high quality and water was freely available, milk from its mother is an efficient means of gaining an energy and water supplement. Kangaroos would have to be in an adaptive backwater if mothers needlessly expended milk on YAF for 4-7 months prior to weaning and that the species, grey kangaroos, most likely to find low-fibre high-quality forage do this for the longer period (Table 2).

What Munn and Dawson admit is that we do not know what the intake of milk in red kangaroos

Young-at-foot of female red kangaroo suckling from elongated teat in mother's pouch. (Photo: Ulrike Kloecker)

(or the other large kangaroos) is in the wild. What we do know it that suckling takes up 6-11% of the activity budget of eastern grey kangaroo YAF depending on age and sex (Stuart-Dick & Higginbottom 1989) and red kangaroo YAF suckle for about 6 minutes every 3 hours (Bilton 2004). Under favourable conditions of high-quality forage and ready water availability a mother might pursue one of two strategies: (1) scale back lactation to the YAF (which may be less demanding) and invest in own energy reserves or the pouch young, or (2) maintain or even ramp up (given her own high quality diet) milk supply to the YAF to support a faster growth rate.

Evolutionary theory regarding investment to maximise lifetime reproductive success supports the second option if the YAF is a son (Ashworth 1996). The argument, known as the Trivers-Willard effect, is that where male size gives an advantage in mating success as it does in the large kangaroos (e.g. Moss 1995), a mother may increase her reproductive success by producing a large son which she can do when energy and nutrients are readily available to her.

Debbie Ashworth (1995) found strong support for the Trivers-Willard effect in euros on the Fowlers Gap Research Station. The female euros captured in 1990 were of above average condition; i.e. the average deviation from mean body weight was significantly greater than zero (the mean) (Fig. 10a). In the same period, there was a significant bias towards male pouch young unlike other periods when females were in average or below average condition (Fig. 10b).

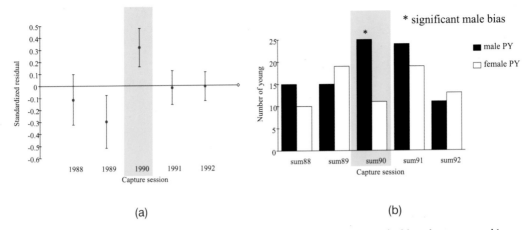

Figure 10. (a) Mean (± SEM) of deviation from average body weight (line at zero) of female euros caught and released on Fowlers Gap Research Station in 1988-92. (b) Frequency of male and female pouch young at each capture session. (Adapted from Ashworth 1995).

Young-at-foot receive additional benefits to nutrition which will facilitate their survival. Karen Higginbottom and David Croft (1999) summarise the role of social learning and the key opportunities for gaining important survival knowledge through this means in marsupials, especially the kangaroos, wallabies and rat-kangaroos. A focus on herbivorous livestock and competition with herbivorous wildlife like kangaroos has diverted our attention from the true conflict on the rangelands, that between plants and their predators – the herbivores.

Plants raise a whole battery of defences against being eaten and these include physical ones like spines and chemical ones like digestion inhibitors (e.g. tannins) and poisons (e.g. alkaloids, cyanide compounds, nitrates, terpenes). A young kangaroo can learn about what to eat and what to avoid by trial and error (e.g. does it taste bad, does it induce sickness, does it satisfy energy and nutrient requirements) and/or social learning (e.g. mimicking the foraging behaviour of its mother or peers).

This process starts at an early age as they get to do a lot of observing of the mother's diet choices in their later stages of pouch life when they push their head out of the pouch in close proximity to their mother's when she is bent over foraging. Learning what to eat is just one of a number of benefits gained from the mother and peers. Others include:

- Learning the identity, likely location, threatening behaviour and best way to avoid a predator like a dingo.
- Learning where the location of key resources are like good foraging patches, water, shelter, access ways through stock fences, escape routes.
- Learning complex behaviour used in social interactions with peers like the sparring of kangaroos which starts with young-at-foot boxing their mothers.

Process of social learning commences in the pouch with observations of the mother's behaviour, especially diet choices. (Photo: Ulrike Kloecker)

Ending the cruelty to young-at-foot

18 million females killed in the last decade

The kangaroo industry is not alone in killing females who will have a young-at-foot and abandoning the latter to a cruel death of starvation and dehydration. There are other licences to harm kangaroos and further harm may occur through collisions with vehicles (see chapter by Dan Ramp in this volume). However, the commercial kangaroo industry is responsible for most of the killing and the regulators provide statistics on its magnitude. When these figures are quoted in press releases or by supporters of the industry, the population of kangaroos is always given in millions but the quota for 'harvest' is presented as a percentage thus masking the true numeric value of the killing. On the available figures from the last decade (1994-2003), the Department of Environment and Heritage of the Australian Government reports that 30,636,941 kangaroos of four species (red, eastern and western grey kangaroos and common wallaroos) were killed by the commercial industry. From this we can estimate the extent of cruelty within the industry. The first defence that the industry and supporters will offer is that most individuals killed are males. Hacker and colleagues (2004: 37) give a value of 60% male as current industry practice for at least the Murray-Darling basin. Thus 18,383,165 females are estimated to have been killed by the industry from 1994-2003. Given the size lower limit imposed or selected by shooters it is fair to assume that all the females were sexually mature.

4.5 million young-at-foot left to a cruel death in the last decade

Under ideal conditions a female red kangaroo or common wallaroo will produce a YAF every 8 months, or 2 YAF per year, with a 4-month interval of no YAF accompanying the female in between weaning of one YAF and permanent exit from the pouch (PEP) of another pouch young. Given the general condition of continuous and asynchronous breeding at the population level, we would expect to see about 50% of mature females with a YAF. Eastern and western grey kangaroos have birth intervals of about 12 months and may breed seasonally. With a time between PEP and weaning of about 220 d (Table 2) we would expect a mature female to have a YAF about 60% of the time. Seasonality might vary this from 0 to 100% in a few months of the year. In general, this maximum potential is not reached in real and simulated populations at, for example, the Fowlers Gap Research Station (Bilton & Croft 2004, Fig. 7). Thus let's choose a conservative figure of 25% of females with a YAF. Thus the industry has left 4,595,912 YAF to a cruel and inhumane death in the last decade, sanctioned by its regulators and supporters.

The fatuous 'it would happen anyway' counter-argument

The response from the industry and its supporters is to focus on the high juvenile mortality in 'natural' populations and thus argue that such a death from starvation and dehydration is somehow normal and thus acceptable. The argument is fatuous. The cause of the cruel death by the kangaroo industry is anthropogenic and controllable. The cause of so-called natural mortality is a function of unpredictable and uncontrollable climatic conditions. Mortality under the latter conditions varies across the spectrum of years of flooding rain when it would be minimal to severe and prolonged drought when it would be close to maximal. The industry would be unsustainable if the numbers of adults shot were not replaced by recruitment from reproduction and as the industry claims to be sustainable it obvious that juvenile mortality is not the norm.

Clearly in our own moral system we would not abandon a randomly selected number of infant children to die based on the argument that infant mortality is a finite proportion of the children born. In the livestock industries, there is an economic driver to maximise production of say lambs or calves and so taking a ewe or cow to slaughter and leaving her unweaned lamb or calf would be abnormal and irrational economically. However, in drought it is conceivable that the same argument could be made. For instance, a sale of ewes or cows at a good price would be profitable even if the lambs or calves had to be abandoned as the drought is likely to cause them to die anyway. This option of abandonment of dependent offspring to a certain death is exercised every night in the kangaroo industry but would be unacceptable and branded cruel and inhumane in the livestock industry which facilitates and nurtures the former. At the extreme, the livestock industry would have to humanely put-down the abandoned lambs or cows.

Cruelty in the kangaroo industry should not be sanctioned for expediency

If the government sanctioned the routine abandonment of lambs and calves because it was simply more expedient to slaughter their mothers without concern for them, there would be a public outcry at the gates of parliament. If the offspring were foals and the mothers were mares then we might expect parliament to be burning and the politicians pilloried. If they are young-at-foot kangaroos, well who cares? The industry and supporters will say it is a lunatic fringe engaged in a conspiracy to stop Australians eating meat (most Australians don't want to eat kangaroo meat regardless of their arguments and inducements anyway!).

It is certainly not in the best interests of the pastoral industry to facilitate and sanction cruelty in the kangaroo industry.

The wool industry is in dispute with organisations claiming cruel practices in animal husbandry. Yet this industry is one of the strongest advocates of lethally controlling kangaroo populations since they are largest in the sheep rangelands. Currently it argues for more killing than current commercial quotas, not less, and for a higher quota of females in that target (Hacker *et al.* 2004). If the wool industry is to sustain this argument then it will do so condoning cruel and inhumane practices that would be unacceptable with sheep. Many graziers, their partners or their children will have raised a 'potty' lamb or calf out of compassion for its suffering under abandonment or death of its mother. How long does it think the Australian public and its international clients will be willing partners in, by its own standards, the unacceptable cruelty to kangaroos? The truth is out there!

A fair go for our fauna

It is clear that kangaroos are not 'dumb' herbivores, but perfectly and amazingly adapted to their environment, with strategies for survival in the most trying of environments. They are mammals with a high degree of individuality and like all mammals they are highly dependent on their mothers until at least weaning. It is one of the saddest experiences of my life to see how these magnificent but defenceless animals are treated by the kangaroo and pastoral industries and more sad still how their dependent young are treated, with such deliberate callousness and thoughtlessness. In all other civilised societies, female mammals accompanied by dependent young cannot be shot. The annual shooting season will not permit females to be shot that care for dependent young – only in Australia we permit that to happen, all in the name of the mighty dollar and a few jobs. And even the dollar is not that mighty considering the income from meat and hides of kangaroos in comparison to the tourism dollar. If only people are willing to open their eyes to see what a unique animal has developed on this continent – not as a primary resource for meat or hide, but what they are, part of the world that we need for our spiritual health and survival. If you feel compelled to eat their meat or wear their hide, then how many young-at-foot have to die from abandonment to satisfy you? The kangaroo is more than the symbol of our nation's carrier or lending the name to our sporting teams. It is significantly more famous and recognisable worldwide as the indomitable icon of Australia than a cultural icon like the Sydney Opera House. But while this recognition is coming from overseas, at home we are not prepared to recognise its unique value beyond that of the dollar earned by a few.

The shot to the head out of the darkness that the industry and its supporters promote as clean, green and humane; every night leaves behind abandoned young-at-foot quietly coughing in an attempt to unite with their mothers – but nobody hears!

This male red kangaroo that became known as 'Mr Perky' was found listless, mal-nourished, dehydrated and with blistered feet. The provision of the milk he was denied saw him grow into a cherished example of his kind. (Photo: Ulrike Kloecker)

IS 'CONTROL' OF KANGAROO POPULATIONS REALLY NECESSARY?

By Daniel Ramp

BSc. Hons, PhD (Melbourne)
School of Biological, Earth & Environmental Sciences, UNSW Sydney.

Prior to European occupation, kangaroos and other macropods existed within the Australian landscape and there was a balance between these herbivores and the plant communities upon which they foraged. Balance does not simply imply stasis, but reflects an ebb and flow of species abundance and distribution within a continually changing landscape. Plant and faunal communities have evolved within this changing landscape and have responded to many disturbances like fire and climate change. But the presence of humans in the landscape has seen dramatic shifts in the functioning of ecosystems. The burning of small patches of land by Aboriginal communities ('looking after country') to maintain plant diversity, and therefore game diversity, was once widespread in arid Australia (Gould 1971). This promoted kangaroo populations as they foraged on the regenerating vegetation. Yet the impact of these burning practises has been drastically superseded by land-use and modification by Europeans, dramatically shifting the natural balance of ecosystems right across Australia.

Land clearance for agriculture and habitation has been rampant in Australia, leading to an 'opening up' of the country. Even in the spinifex deserts of central Australia the land is used – in this case primarily for cattle grazing. However, land-use and modification has been most intense in the temperate environment of south-eastern Australia, as this is where we live at high population densities and build our largest cities. To conserve our plant and faunal diversity in this environment we have created a park and reserve system that provides refuge to both common and threatened species. We also protect land that is used for the collection of water. While these protected areas seek to preserve Australia's biodiversity, they also pose significant management issues as they are impacted upon by many types of disturbances and pressures from neighbouring land-use. The interplay between our native flora and fauna and human needs has seen many species bear the brunt of our history of self-interest.

If one group of species was to typify how humans have altered the natural balance in the environment and then tried to rectify the situation with short-sighted management strategies, often at the expense of the species, it is the kangaroo.

In temperate Australia it is the park and reserve system that harbours the majority of our kangaroos and other macropods. However, the frequent isolation and fragmentation of these landscapes often creates scenarios that alter the balance between our native herbivores and the plant communities upon which they subsist. Often, checks and balances on kangaroo populations are removed and this can alter the natural interactions between these herbivores and their environment. Kangaroo populations can be favoured in these isolated or enclosed areas as they benefit from human land clearance, although it should be noted that the range of most kangaroos is not thought to have changed markedly since European occupation (Barker & Caughley 1992).

Within a scientific framework the favouring of one species through an altering of natural processes and balances has been termed 'overabundance' (Caughley 1981). However, the use of this term is often misrepresented in the media as meaning 'plague' or 'pest', or in cases of extreme densities of animals. This misuse tends to focus the attention on the species that is causing the problem in the public eye, and kangaroos are often represented in this way.

As a result our response has been to implement culling and fertility programs aimed at reducing the kangaroo populations. But this type of strategy does not address the real reason why these populations might be thought of causing problems in the first place, completely ignoring the fact that human landscape alteration and use is responsible.

Most people would agree that in order to maintain Australia's unique biodiversity we need to achieve a balance between our faunal and floral communities, presumably in ways that they are adapted to through their co-evolution. We must therefore question whether culling and other short-term 'control' measures are appropriate, or whether there are alternatives that are both sustainable and ethically acceptable. *Is there really a need to 'control' populations or should we be focussed on restoring natural ecosystem processes in our park and reserve systems so that the supposed need for culling never arises?*

To explore this question this chapter will discuss the scientific framework surrounding intervention so as to demystify this concept. Using a detailed example from research I conducted at Yan Yean Reservoir Catchment in Victoria, the chapter will then provide evidence of how it is only when we examine the legacy of human disturbance on plant communities that we can truly understand why kangaroo populations are erroneously thought to have negative consequences on our flora. I will ultimately show that conservation of both plant and herbivore populations must find an appropriate balance: that is our parks and reserves should be havens for kangaroos as well as for other life forms.

With proper planning and foresight, 'control' methods like culling and fertility programs should be relegated to our unflattering past.

A lack of balance

In order to address the reasoning behind why kangaroo populations are sometimes portrayed as requiring some kind of managerial intervention, we need to look at exactly how this definition of 'out of balance' is arrived at. There are a number of reasons why we might consider a population to be 'out of balance' with the environment, and these were classified by Graeme Caughley (1981) as relating to four different criteria: (1) threats to human life or livelihood; (2) depression of the density of other favoured species; (3) decline in body condition and reproduction (i.e. too numerous for their own good); and (4) loss of equilibrium between plants and animals (i.e. population above equilibrium density/carrying capacity). The primary ingredients for any one of these four criteria occurring are when resources (food) and mortality are not limiting. Species may shift their use of habitat or resources to match the modifications resulting from human land use, and this in turn affects other fauna and the environment.

The labels 'overabundance' and populations being 'out of balance' are not restricted to kangaroos. Examples of species considered overabundant are the grey-headed flying-fox *(Pteropus poliocephalus)* that has established a large roost in the Royal Botanical Gardens in Melbourne, the Australian white ibis *(Threskiornis molucca)* that has proliferated from an escaped captive population kept at Taronga Zoo in Sydney, and the koala *(Phascolarctos cinereus)* that has populated areas like Kangaroo Island in South Australia after deliberate introduction.

But are these criteria defined by Caughley (1981) really any different to what might occur through the natural ebb and flow of ecosystems? And should the favouring of one species in the environment mean that that species be labelled as a pest? In each of the cases listed above, the real reason why populations of species increased, or that their ranges changed, is due to human landscape modification. A typical example is the galah *(Cactua roseicapilla)* in south-west Western Australia that has become a serious management issue in the wheat-belt. The range of galahs has increased and their numbers have jumped because of an abundance of food in areas where previously it was not available. Indeed, galahs were previously restricted to three isolated locations in this area but now are widespread between the 300 and 600 mm isohyets where wheat is grown (Burgman & Lindenmayer 1998). As a consequence the galah is labelled a 'pest' because it forages on the wheat crops so convenient for them, and much effort is made to get rid of the galahs that have been labelled as 'overabundant'. This example highlights how the terms 'overabundance' and 'pest' have become synonymous and clearly indicates how humans often ignore their own culpability in creating environmental problems.

Some insights on previous attempts to 'control' kangaroos

As mentioned earlier, the dramatic changes to Australia's landscape since European occupation have, in some cases, benefited kangaroos. Eastern grey kangaroo *(Macropus giganteus)* populations prosper in environments where a variety of resources are available, especially where nature reserves or protected areas lie adjacent to crops and improved pasture (Hill *et al.* 1988; Taylor 1985) and predator numbers have been reduced (Banks *et al.* 2000). Often, kangaroo populations have been suggested to be 'out of balance' in areas where the landscape has been 'opened up' and threats have been reduced. When populations have been considered by managers to require action, methods of 'control' have been instigated that have been solely targeted towards the kangaroos.

As an example of the kinds of management strategies implemented and the reasoning behind the actions taken, I will discuss two widely publicised cases of eastern grey kangaroo populations in temperate Australia and their attempted management (for more detail see Coulson 2001). These cases were Government House, Canberra, and Woodlands Historic Park, Melbourne. In both of these cases kangaroos were kept within fenced borders and the habitat was mostly comprised of open grassy woodland. As there were no predators to prey on them, dispersal was prevented, and there was an abundance of food, recruitment to the populations was not subjected to the normal measures of control of more natural environments. In both cases intervention in the form of culling was instigated because of a variety of concerns. In the Government House case action was taken because of safety concerns for staff and the public (Caughley class 1), as well as damage to the vegetation in the form of browsing on ornamental shrubs (class 2). In the Woodlands Historic Park case action was taken because of an observed decline in kangaroo body condition (class 3), an imbalance with the plant communities (class 4) and a threat to the survival of other fauna such as the endangered eastern barred bandicoot *(Perameles gunnii)* (class 2).

In contrast to these cases the issue of kangaroo management has rarely been of concern in areas where threats to kangaroo populations are substantial (e.g. predators, farmers, roads) and the landscape has retained a semblance of structural integrity. Although the threats might not be exactly what they were prior to European occupation they may indeed limit recruitment in a similar manner. This holds true for protected areas like national parks and state reserves. These areas are not solely for conservation, as most allow tourists to engage in compatible, and sometimes incompatible, recreation activities within them. Some parks even contain townships within their borders (e.g. the Royal National Park just south of Sydney). As a consequence, these parks are frequently disturbed and suffer from a range of threats. In these situations kangaroos typically become a management problem only when they interfere with the public (i.e. when they are fed at camping grounds).

In our parks and reserves native herbivore populations are often kept below carrying capacity (the number of animals that the area would hold as determined by the availability of space and other resources). This occurs because of the loss of individuals to feral predators like domestic dogs and foxes, competition from exotic herbivores like deer and rabbits, fatalities of individuals on roads through collisions with vehicles, declines in habitat suitability through the changing of natural fire regimes and an influx of exotic plant species, and general survival issues created by the isolation and fragmentation of habitat. On top of these threats are natural disturbance processes relating to climatic events like El Niño and La Niña. Management practices can also cause problems when they are implemented in a static way, a strategy that typically prevents or restricts natural community variation. As a consequence, the dynamics of these ecosystems are altered and this is a major reason why such protected areas are inherently difficult to manage.

For eastern grey kangaroo populations to prosper they require food and shelter, and this typically means open grassy areas within woodland or forest vegetation. When these kangaroo populations prosper it is often argued that grazing by kangaroos has negative impacts upon plant communities. Indeed, much effort has been made to examine just how kangaroos of various species impact on plant communities and how this differs from that of our livestock (Croft 1996; Freudendberger 1995; Griffiths et al. 1974). In many cases of intervention by managers in temperate Australia evidence for the impact of kangaroos on plant communities has been restricted to changes in biomass. However, while it is certainly true that kangaroos can graze open grassy areas down to a few centimetres, the question remains whether these plant communities, having evolved under various grazing regimes in the 16 million years of evolution of the Macropodoidea, are adversely affected by this. By adversely I mean that the floristic composition is so altered by grazing alone that the plant communities that once existed there are no longer viable. This question warrants further exploration.

Just what impact does grazing by kangaroos have on plant communities in temperate Australia?

Along with livestock and feral animals like goats, deer, and rabbits, the large kangaroos and some wallabies have been widely documented as contributing substantially to herbivore grazing across arid, semi-arid and temperate environments. A range of studies in the late 1970s, 1980s and the early 1990s observed that most kangaroo species are highly selective foragers, with foraging restricted to perennial grasses and occasionally supplemented with herbs and shrubs when grasses are scarce (e.g. Ellis *et al*. 1977; Jarman 1994; Short 1986; Taylor 1983). Grice and Barchia (1992) identified differential defoliation of species favoured by kangaroos as one mechanism that poses a significant threat to the integrity of remnant vegetation communities under heavy grazing conditions.

Yet the response of plants to herbivory is commonly thought of as following patterns of grazing intensity. Plant species exhibit a variety of responses to grazing pressure, and have traditionally been classified according to these responses (i.e. as either 'decreasers', 'increasers' or 'invaders'). However studies examining the conformity of responses to grazing have observed that consistency has been infrequent. Indeed, Hadar *et al*. (1999) observed that only small or prostrate species tended to respond similarly in different locations. Inconsistencies in the response of individual species have been recorded for different sites, times, grazing histories, environmental conditions and different species ecotypes (Noy-Meir *et al*. 1989). In examining published studies of the effects of livestock grazing on botanical composition in the Australian rangelands, Vesk and Westoby (2001) from Macquarie University found that of the 326 species that occurred in at least two response lists, 41% exhibited inconsistent responses. It is apparent that the response of plants to grazing is neither linear nor necessarily consistent between different locations. This is very important to keep in mind when thinking about how herbivore grazing, particularly from kangaroos, affects plant communities.

There is no question that kangaroos eat, but unfortunately many studies on grazing impacts prove only this.

It is important to recognise that plant communities in Australia have evolved with various levels of grazing pressure and are adapted to it. This has been observed and reported on by many of Australia's leading plant ecologists, particularly since the mid 1990s (for example Fensham *et al*. 1999; Landsberg *et al*. 1999; McIntyre & Lavorel 1994). Consequently, the response of plants to herbivore grazing should be thought of as one of a variety of directional processes, with flow of species either favoured or disfavoured. This process is spatially patchy, as plant communities vary across an alternating landscape, as does grazing pressure. It is essential to think of the grazing 'problem' as fluctuating both spatially and temporally: *it is not as simple as thinking that 'kangaroos' plus 'remnant vegetation' equals 'management problem'.*

Comparing human and kangaroo disturbance

Plant communities do not exist in herbivore-free environments and neither would they exist as they do if they did. To explore why a lack of balance occurs it is necessary to examine the one ingredient that is often responsible for creating the imbalance: landscape modification and/or alteration of ecosystem function by humans. For protected areas that exist within fragmented landscapes the variety of disturbance regimes impacting on plant communities should be recognised. The impact of human disturbance on plant communities can be severe when land is cleared for agriculture, but can also be subtle, for instance when genetic diversity is altered by the introduction of genetically-modified-organisms. It is well documented that fragmented remnants in temperate zones are susceptible to invasion by exotic and native colonising plants, particularly annuals (Prober &Thiele 1995; Tremont & McIntyre 1994).

Without a doubt, kangaroo populations are influenced by landscape modification and other anthropogenic sources of disturbance, and this should also influence how plant communities are affected by grazing pressure from kangaroos. Distinguishing between the effects of two inter-related disturbance variables on floristic composition can be difficult. Human and kangaroo disturbance remain interconnected, as human-induced disturbance has been shown to alter plant-herbivore relationships in many environments (Chaneton & Facelli 1991; McIntyre & Lavorel 1994; Noy-Meir et al. 1989). Yet it is the interaction with landscape modification that must be examined and identified so that appropriate and holistic management actions can be implemented. In the following detailed example I provide evidence of how both human disturbance and kangaroo grazing pressure affect the fine-scale patterns of dynamics in remnant plant communities in a protected area, and use the findings to show that grazing by kangaroos does not necessarily result in damage to plant communities.

An example from Yan Yean Reservoir Catchment

The cases of Government House and Woodlands Historic Park involved very public management problems. However, there are many populations of kangaroos living in larger protected areas at reasonably high densities that have not yet necessitated intervention. An example is the population of eastern grey kangaroos at Yan Yean Reservoir Catchment – an 'enclosed' water catchment (Fig. 1).

Setting the scene

Yan Yean is approximately 40 km north of Melbourne, encompassing 2,250 ha of land, including a water body covering an area of 560 ha when filled to capacity (MMBW 1989). As a southern extension of the Kinglake Plateau, the catchment forms a system of undulating hills which are surrounded by farmland. It is closed to the public, with access prevented by a 1.8 m 'Cyclone' chain-mesh security fence (Coulson et al. 2000). Since quantitative measurement began in 1961, the density of eastern grey kangaroos has varied from 1,770 to 3,000 individuals (at either 1.05 or 1.78 individuals per hectare respectively). The kangaroos are effectively competitor free, with only 20 or so swamp wallabies (Wallabia bicolor), an almost complete absence of rabbits (Oryctolagus cuniculus) and the continual removal of predators (mainly domestic dogs) by catchment managers (Ecoplan 1995). As a result, kangaroos are relatively free to select habitat that maximises their access to quality forage.

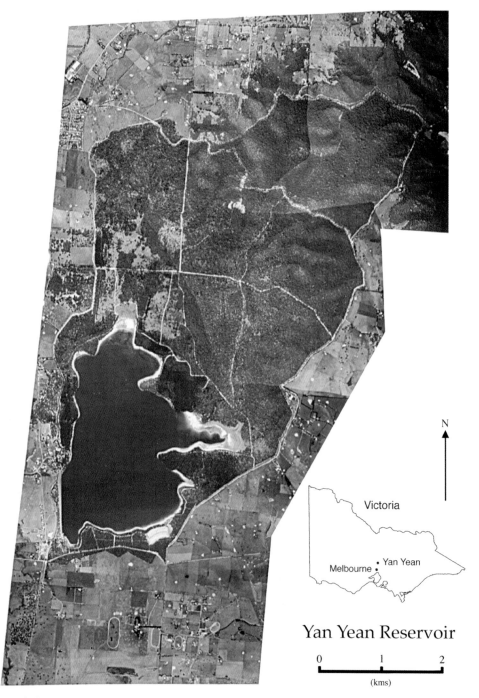

N

Victoria

Melbourne • • Yan Yean

Yan Yean Reservoir

0   1   2

(kms)

Figure 1. Aerial image of Yan Yean Reservoir Catchment, 40 km north of Melbourne, Victoria. The catchment is surrounded by farmland (mostly hobby farmers) and Kinglake National Park to the north-east. The dam itself is artificial and was once swampland. The abundance of cleared areas that act as foraging areas for kangaroos is clearly evident along the western side of the catchment.

The catchment itself has had a varied history. It was initially the land of the Wurunjerri-baluk people, but since the 1830s it has been used by Europeans for livestock grazing, orchards and vineyards, timber harvesting, and, since the 1880s, as a water source to the northern suburbs of Melbourne (Coulson *et al.* 1999; Griffiths 1992). Now managed by Melbourne Water, a mixture of disturbed and remnant vegetation situated on the undulating hills surrounding the water body characterises the catchment (Fig. 2). Eastern greys kangaroos prosper in this environment, as it is relatively protected from predators and human interference and provides an abundance of resources. Kangaroos also frequently move outside the catchment to forage in adjacent pasture, supplementing their diet with high quality grass (Coulson *et al.* 2000). Management of the population of eastern grey kangaroos has been of concern to catchment managers for a long time (Melbourne Water 1982). There was some suggestion that the kangaroos were impacting on the catchment soils and water quality, although this claim was not substantiated after rigorous investigation (Alviano 2000). The main driving force behind management concern has been the result of issues raised by landholders adjacent to the catchment (Coulson *et al.* 1999). Landholders are regularly granted culling licences to remove kangaroos from their properties that access them to forage on the fertilised pasture.

Figure 2. This north-facing slope is situated near Bear's Castle. Evidence of an old vineyard or orchard on this slope can be seen in the planting lines running from left to right at a slight angle. This location is a favoured foraging ground by kangaroos. A grazing exclosure is located on the right-hand side of the slope.

Purpose of the study

In this study I wanted to determine if grazing pressure exerted by the eastern grey kangaroo population was having a negative impact on plant communities (Caughley's 1981 class 4), and evaluate how previous land modification by humans and environmental variation combine to influence this impact. This study was conducted as part of my doctoral research at the University of Melbourne (2002).

The research – Experiment One

The spatial distribution and composition of plants within the catchment was assessed using circular sampling plots distributed throughout the catchment area. A number of environmental variables, the level of human disturbance, and kangaroo grazing pressure (estimated via faecal pellet density surveys) were recorded. A total of 186 vascular plant species were observed, bringing the total number listed as residing within the catchment to 326 (an increase of 49 on previous records). Four floristic communities were identified and labelled as Disturbed Open-Forest, Disturbed Open-Woodland, Intact-Open Forest and Aquatic Verges.

The data were analysed using a combination of non-metric multidimensional scaling (NMDS) and vector fitting. NMDS finds a configuration for which the distances between sample pairs are reflective of their dissimilarity in floristic composition (Fig. 3). Interpretation of the ordination results was achieved by vector fitting (Kantvilas & Minchin 1989), which enables the identification of variables that are significantly influencing the floristic composition of samples. The vectors for human disturbance and kangaroo grazing were similarly correlated with floristic composition, as the angle between the vectors was small (5°). The directional trends of these two variables contrasted with altitude, as angles between altitude and human disturbance and kangaroo grazing were 113° and 118° respectively. As a result we can see that there are two interpretable dimensions in the ordination, one related to altitude and one related to disturbance, with no real separation between human disturbance and kangaroo grazing.

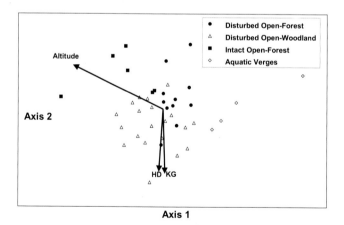

Figure 3. Two-dimensional NMDS ordination of floristic data showing the four vegetation communities identified and significant fitted vectors for environmental and disturbance variables. Vectors are labeled as follows: human disturbance (HD), kangaroo grazing (KG), and altitude (Altitude). The arrow indicates the direction of the vector gradient, pointing towards high values of the variables.

While the direct impact of human disturbance and kangaroo grazing on floristic dynamics can be considered equivalent in this analysis, differences between them became apparent when their interaction with other environmental variation was examined. By assessing how environmental variables varied at either high or low levels of human disturbance and kangaroo grazing, it was revealed that human disturbance was responsible for masking the effects of altitude and other environmental attributes on the flora. On the other hand, altitude remained significantly correlated with floristics at both high and low levels of kangaroo grazing. What this implies is that while the effects of human disturbance appear to override any natural variation in plant species distributions, the effect of kangaroo grazing does not appear to be as detrimental (see Ramp 2002 for further details).

For example, there are a number of locations in the catchment where the landscape has been modified (i.e. as timber plantations of pine trees, *Pinus radiata, or sugar gum, Eucalyptus cladocalyx)* that are not frequented by kangaroos. At these locations, the flora has been radically altered to the extent that environmental variables like altitude, slope, aspect and lithology no longer have any significant influence on plant species distributions. In contrast, at all locations measured where kangaroo grazing pressure was high but landscape modification was not major, environmental variables still retained some influence on the flora.

The research – Experiment Two

To quantify the effects of the removal of grazing on the flora at Yan Yean Reservoir I established a split-plot design of matched exclosure and grazed plots. Exclosure plots were 12 x 12 m in area and were constructed in areas frequently grazed by kangaroos and within each of the different floristic communities in the catchment. Grazed plots were situated approximately 20 to 25 m adjacent to the exclosure plots. The plots were established to monitor the short-term directional responses of plants to the removal of grazing pressure to provide an indication of potential for change within the system. It would be necessary to monitor the plots for many years to derive a more accurate picture of plant responses; however studies like these are difficult to conduct in today's funding climate that rewards quick answers to ecological problems.

(a)   (b)

Figures 4. A matched pair of grazed (a) and ungrazed (b) plots used to assess the response of plants to the removal of grazing pressure in Disturbed Open-Woodland. These photos were taken in summer during the second year of the experiment. At this time the vegetation is grazed to within a centimetre or two of the ground. On the ungrazed plot (b), while grass stems dominate, evidence of shrub and herb regeneration is evident. Species that had not previously been recorded on the site were now abundant.

No real change in species diversity in response to the removal of grazing pressure was observed over a period of 18 months, as would be expected over this time scale. Variation that was observed was attributed to environmental fluctuation, rather than grazing treatment. However, differences were observed in species responses to the removal of grazing pressure. The contribution of herbaceous species to the difference in composition between grazed and ungrazed plots increased over time, while an opposite response was observed with the grass species, declining in dominance on grazed plots. Native species were seen to increase their contribution to the total cover of plots after the removal of grazing pressure. These trends were observed in each of the habitats in the catchment area, including those considered to be heavily disturbed. From this it is possible to say that the ability of the plant communities to respond to the removal of grazing pressure was universal, despite the long disturbance history (see Ramp 2002).

Kangaroos: culprits or victims?

This grazing study has provided evidence that highlights two important points. The first is that grazing by kangaroos cannot be considered in isolation from other habitat effects, particularly that caused by human disturbance. Indeed, as the Yan Yean example shows, the long-lasting impact of human modification can remove natural environmental variation in plant communities. In addition, grazing by kangaroos is promoted by this modification and as such humans are directly implicated in any kangaroo management issue.

It has previously been recognised that disturbance can have overriding impacts on floristic dynamics in temperate communities. McIntyre and Lavorel (1994) found that when various environmental variables were compared in unison, their relative contribution to floristic composition could be considered additive, with disturbance variables superimposing themselves on natural environmental patterns. Working in the grassy white box woodlands of New South Wales, Susan Prober (1996) also found that natural environmental variation in floristic composition was superseded by disturbance resulting from humans.

The second important point identified by this grazing study is that despite a long history of human disturbance and kangaroo grazing the plant communities at Yan Yean retain the capacity to regenerate. This holds true for most areas of the catchment except where human disturbance has been severe. Certainly the plant communities of Yan Yean could never return to what they once were before European occupation, especially as the water body is artificial and the lands were once swampy marshes. Yet the evidence suggests that balance is possible with sensible management of this protected system.

In other studies I conducted at Yan Yean, eastern grey kangaroos were observed to utilise open patches within the different vegetation communities for foraging (Ramp & Coulson 2002; Ramp & Coulson 2004). They utilised this network of patches and moved between them frequently. Not all of the patches were of a similar quality as this varied among the different habitats. I showed that the kangaroos were able to assess the difference in quality and distribute themselves among the foraging patches so that on an individual level, each kangaroo received similar foraging rewards. That is, on better quality patches there were typically more kangaroos than on poorer patches. In scientific terminology this is termed 'density dependence'. It is this knowledge that adds weight to the argument that the kangaroo population is constrained by the environment and responds directly to it. It stands to reason that if the better quality foraging patches at Yan Yean were either fenced-off or had tall shrubs or trees planted on them the resultant decline in quality forage would have an impact on the environment's ability to sustain current kangaroo population levels. It is therefore reasonable to infer that the removal of access to foraging areas, either through fencing or by planting them with shrubs (i.e. habitat restoration), would result in a natural balance being achieved with the kangaroo population over time.

Kangaroo 'control' or responsible environmental management

Isolated cases like Government House and Woodlands Historic Park aside, the management of populations of kangaroos in temperate environments must be tackled somewhat differently to the approaches taken in semi-arid and arid environments. The management programs adopted in many cases have not solved the problem and are severely lacking in scientific rigour (Coulson 2001). What are needed in these situations are clear management solutions that seek to restore balance using a comprehensive adaptive management framework. Management is not easy, but it is clear that a few grazing enclosures and a culling program are not likely to result in any long-term solution, and on the basis of the scientific evidence appear completely unjustified.

So what implication does our history of management have for future cases of imbalance? What has been lacking from the many cases where intervention has been instigated is a detailed understanding of exactly what the cause of the problem was. Too often intervention was the result of political pressure that misconstrues the ecological relationships at hand, and where the needs of landholders and the public were valued higher than those of the environment.

We know that kangaroo populations are promoted when remnant vegetation exists within a matrix of agricultural lands, especially in semi-rural areas (Coulson et al. 2000). The eastern grey kangaroos at Yan Yean regularly use farmland abutting the catchment to forage (Yazgin 2000). Recently, a study by Viggers and Hearn (2005) examined the home ranges of eastern grey kangaroos at three sites with varying degrees of landscape modification, particularly where remnant habitat abutted farmland. They found that home range sizes differed among their three sites, with kangaroos at the most disturbed site (the Cotter Farm) having the largest home ranges. Resource availability was found not to influence home range size in their study, however in contrast, other studies have indicated a direct relationship between resource availability and quality with habitat use by kangaroos (Ramp & Coulson 2002; Ramp & Coulson 2004).

As an example of how the issue of kangaroos within these matrix landscapes is often focussed on the preservation of farming rights, as opposed to restoring an ecological balance, Viggers and Hearn (2005) state that the findings of their study "provide little incentive for farmers to preserve remnant vegetation, as it may be regarded as providing habitat for unwanted or 'pest' native wildlife", and farmers should expect "incursions by mobs of kangaroos" from neighbouring reserves. They acknowledge that reserves of remnant vegetation do, however, promote "the conservation of other species of wildlife".

The point that kangaroos also have a right to exist in the landscape is somehow missed.

Most managing bodies of park and protected areas throughout Australia would concede that in order to maintain a balance between plants and herbivores a total landscape approach is necessary. The evidence from the plant communities themselves, as exemplified in the Yan Yean example, is that regeneration of plant communities to an approximation of their natural structure and the protection of ecosystem functioning is the best means to successfully manage the long-term sustainability of our parks and reserves.

Rather than culling, habitat restoration provides a sustainable and appropriate means of maintaining an environmental balance in temperate Australia. Real examples enacting this type of strategy are so far lacking, but our ecological knowledge is currently sufficient to warrant nation-wide endorsement.

Eastern grey kangaroos are an adaptable species ranging from northern Tasmania to north Queensland and west to the margins of the arid zone.

REFLECTING ON LULU

AND HOW SHE SAVED MY LIFE

By Len Richards

Tanjil South Farmer, Victoria.

Just reflecting on that day in September 2003, when had it not been for Lulu alerting my wife to my plight, I might not be here today. I had been knocked unconscious by a falling tree branch following a storm, and as I lay unconscious, Lulu the kangaroo stood over me, with her big hind legs at my back 'barking' like a dog for help. My wife called an ambulance and I was airlifted to Melbourne's Alfred Hospital Trauma Centre where I was treated for head injuries. The story of Lulu's courage made headlines around the world and Lulu became a kangaroo heroine.

Following her celebrity which made Media news Internationally, Lulu's amazing act of love, intuition and courage was rewarded by an RSPCA NATIONAL ANIMAL VALOUR AWARD, the first native animal in the world to receive such an honour..

Having raised her from the time my son Luke found her, I have known that Lulu was and still is very smart. She opens our back door, comes into our house and lays around the open fire with the rest of the family. To catch her taking fruit from the fruit bowl, going to the pantry to help herself to whatever takes

**Eastern grey kangaroo 'saviour' - Lulu.
(Photo: Laura Ferguson)**

her fancy, is truly amazing. When she has filled her belly she goes back outside and hops into her own bed which we set up for her, near our dog, for a siesta. But remember Lulu is a wild kangaroo, and is free to leave us whenever she chooses. But it does show that kangaroos are smart and with a little love and kindness they will respond in a way that will surprise you.

We have not seen any kangaroos in our area since the cull, which was not long after Lulu had saved my life. Permits 'fast tracked' by the Victorian Department of Sustainability and Environment Wildlife Authorities to kill kangaroos in our area, has left their populations decimated, with few left anywhere, to be seen. Victoria's La Trobe Valley Councilors promised they would investigate providing safe habitat, in continuous, connecting safe wildlife areas to keep kangaroos free from shooters but sadly, all that is now forgotten and this promise has not been forthcoming. There is little respect for our native animals being demonstrated in our area.

Living with a kangaroo like Lulu is a beautiful experience, especially that feeling of exhilaration of watching her bounding over the fences, coming back to her home with us. The downside is getting up and finding her not there, and worrying for hours and hours, hoping that she is safe.

It is a shame that the wrong perception is out there in the community about our Kangaroos as they are truly an amazing animal to observe. Kangaroos have been wrongly labeled a pest or vermin ever since white settlers opened up the country for agriculture and slaughtered them across Australia.

Lulu's mother was killed by a logging truck outside our property in Tanjil South, Victoria, a tiny joey, left orphaned, in her pouch. I have often thought that people who thoughtlessly hit a kangaroo and just keep driving as though nothing has happened, those who take no responsibility for their action, should be penalized severely by Insurance Companies. And at the same time people who have never hit a Kangaroo, and who do their best to SLOW DOWN when they see kangaroo signs, should be rewarded by being given a much lower insurance rate or by gaining points for safe driving.

Roads impede the movement of kangaroos and they are hit by vehicles at their crossover points. No Councils or Local Governments seem to care, certainly not in our area. Young people have no standards to follow of how to treat wildlife. If they are not taught by their parents, how are children meant to learn that native animals are unique and special ; that they not only need, but deserve our protection? After all, we are the intruders and it us humans who should learn to live with them.

Kangaroos are the true spirit of Australia and the land belongs to them but they are being decimated, with no where to go. As sub-divisions for more housing and human population increases, and more agricultural land is taken for farming and grazing of stock, our beautiful native animals are trapped in smaller and smaller fragmented pockets of suburban sprawl. This has put them under enormous pressure and they are struggling to survive especially with the continuing drought over the last number of years. A great change in the Australian attitude is essential, if we are to save their dwindling populations. If we don't act soon to rectify the terrible wrongs against them, then one day we may wake up to find our kangaroos have gone, forever.

Learning to know and to love LULU has been one of the greatest joys of my life. Kangaroos are our Wildlife Heritage and Australia must save and protect this irreplaceable heritage for future generations!

'I love Lulu' sticker. (Design: Brigitte Charron)

THE FUTURE OF KANGAROOS: GOING, GOING, GONE?

By David B Croft

BSc. Hons. (Flinders), PhD (Cambridge)
Fowlers Gap Research Station and School of Biological, Earth & Environmental Sciences, UNSW Sydney.

The large kangaroos that form the basis of the commercial kangaroo industry – red kangaroo *(Macropus rufus)*, eastern grey kangaroo *(M. giganteus),* western grey kangaroo *(M. fuliginosus),* and common wallaroo *(M. robustus)* – have earned the dubious title of 'overabundant' species. Cathy Herbert (2004) discusses some of the challenges of managing such species but most pertinently notes (p. 67) "…it is very difficult to define the term 'overabundance'. It is largely defined by human interests and as such it tends to involve subjective, value-laden judgements…". Overabundance (or overpopulation) implies obviously too many individuals of a species that are either causing harm to themselves (e.g. vicious fighting, starvation), harm to their ecosystem (e.g. landscape dysfunction, endangerment of other species), harm to people (e.g. vehicle collision, monetary loss, threats to livelihood) or any combination of these (Caughley 1981). A typical kangaroo example would be a small peri-urban reserve with a barrier fence. The species will almost inevitably be an eastern grey kangaroo, the population will grow, forage will be depleted, some individuals will starve and die as they cannot easily disperse, some may break through the fence, eat the neighbour's lawn or collide with their car. The reserve will most likely be on old farmland with 'improved' pasture invaded by weeds. The exotic grasses will no longer be supported by copious application of phosphate fertiliser so the system is inherently unstable and collapse should come as no surprise. Ramp has described the causes and consequences of such a system in an earlier chapter.

Unfortunately this all too common event in eastern Australia brands the kangaroos (viz. the four species of commercially harvested kangaroos) regardless of species and location as overabundant. Thus, for instance, drought-induced mortality in the arid rangelands is evidence of too numerous kangaroos causing harm to themselves. Range expansion of western grey kangaroos, whose mallee habitat was clear-felled, is likewise evidence of a species 'out of control'. Anomalous increases in common wallaroo (euro) populations arising from over-stocking and consequent loss of forage palatable to livestock demand suppression (reviewed in Newsome 1975). The only anomaly is that the euro survived the land degradation and so it must be to blame.

The remaining two large kangaroo species, the antilopine *(M. antilopinus)* and black wallaroos

(M. bernadus), apparently do not share the sin of overabundance largely because wildlife agencies are indifferent about their numbers since conflict with pastoralism is minimal. Tony Press provided the one and only published estimate of black wallaroo abundance in 1988. There is no comparable estimate of antilopine wallaroo abundance across its range even though John Calaby and Gordon Grigg (1989) assumed that its abundance was stable or increased with pastoralism over the prior 200 years.

'Kangaroos are all alike' and 'too numerous for their own good' are two of the many myths that are used to justify commercial exploitation and killing of kangaroos to a largely ignorant or indifferent public.

Thus when an eastern grey kangaroo male scratches the face of a teenager on a Grafton golf course, a western NSW grazier can publicly proclaim all kangaroos are a danger to people and must be controlled. When yet another reserve is created from flogged out farmland or an unviable degraded pastoral lease, the advocates of kangaroo management through lethal control will proclaim that there is ongoing degradation and weed infestation caused by the uncontrolled kangaroo population. This view holds currency because managers have unrealistic expectations of vegetation recovery from more than a century of livestock grazing and expect it to happen within a few years.

Contrary evidence comes from abandoned farmlands in Western Australia, long-term studies of calcareous rangelands in central Australia, and long-term destocking of protected areas in arid NSW. Arnold and his colleagues (1999) found a similar trajectory of increased cover of cleared or cleared and cultivated farms following abandonment over 22 years but cover did not reach the level of undisturbed remnants. The landscapes (cleared, cultivated, undisturbed) had a 'memory' of the farming impacts with significant differences in native annual plant communities remaining after two decades. In central Australia, key nutrients are lost to the landscape from heavy grazing and not simply redistributed by landscape processes (Sparrow *et al.* 2003). Soil seed reserves are significantly depleted by decades of heavy grazing and this reduces the capacity of the vegetation to recover under favourable climatic conditions (Kinloch & Friedel 2005). This lack of recovery is shown in arid rangelands in Sturt National Park which was destocked in the early 1970s. After three decades chenopod shrubs have failed to regenerate around heavily grazed water points with no evidence that native herbivores are maintaining this piosphere effect (Montague-Drake 2004).

This chapter will examine these and other 'management myths' to assess their generality with the caveat that the geographical ranges of the four commercially exploited kangaroos are so large and heterogeneous that you could potentially find an example to support any argument.

We need to keep in mind that eastern grey kangaroos span the eastern seaboard from northern Tasmania to Cooktown and well into the hinterland, western grey kangaroos cross southern Australia from western NSW and Victoria to coastal WA, red kangaroos occupy the arid rangelands encompassing more than 50% of the continent, common wallaroos are pan-continental and on some offshore islands but not Tasmania. Too often, observation of an uncommon event is generalised across all individuals in all parts of the range of a species if not all kangaroos regardless of species. For instance, in the rangelands kangaroos may jump the fence and graze lawns at homesteads. The likely species is an eastern or western grey kangaroo or common wallaroo but rarely a red kangaroo, the most abundant species. The behaviour is not habitual as lawn grasses are planted for their tolerance to trampling not their palatability. In some cases the rhizomes are preferred to the blade leading to the belief that these if not all kangaroos habitually dig up grasses and thereby degrade perennial pastures. Under the same conditions I have observed western grey kangaroos and common wallaroos eating corrugated cardboard boxes but there is no suggestion that these are typical of their diet or that kangaroos are a threat to the packaging industry!

The title of the chapter is deliberately provocative and likely to draw howls of derision as there are said to be 'millions of kangaroos'.

All species have suffered some diminution and change in range through land clearance for intensive agriculture and urban development. These processes are ongoing and are likely to be compounded by anthropogenic changes to climate. Kangaroos in the wet-dry tropics like tree-kangaroos and the antilopine wallaroo will likely have much diminished ranges in a greenhouse future (Busby 1988). Being widespread and abundant is no guarantee of resilience against anthropogenic environmental change as evidenced by the boodie or burrowing bettong (*Bettongia leseur*) whose range once spanned all states except Tasmania (Fig. 1) and was in places the most abundant mammal of the 1800s (Burbridge in Strahan 1998).

Figure 1. The current distribution of the burrowing bettong (*Bettongia leseur*) is shown in green. The former distribution was across all states except Tasmania. Distribution map redrawn from Strahan (1998), illustration from John Gould's *The Mammals of Australia.*

One species or four or six or sixty one?

Administratively it is convenient to lump species together under a single kangaroo management plan.

Plans that regulate the commercial killing of kangaroos usually apply to two or more of the species – red kangaroo, eastern grey kangaroo, western grey kangaroo and common wallaroo (http://www.deh.gov.au/biodiversity/trade-use/wild-harvest/kangaroo/stats.html). Some have included wallabies: the whiptail wallaby *(M. parryi)* in Queensland (1975-2002), the red-necked or Bennett's wallaby *(M. rufogriseus)* and Tasmanian pademelon *(Thylogale billardierri)* in Tasmania (1975-1986, Flinders Island 1998-9) and the swamp wallaby *(Wallabia bicolor)* and red-necked wallaby in Victoria (1981-82). In South Australia there is research to assess the viability of a commercial harvest of tammar wallabies *(M. eugenii)* on Kangaroo Island but they are not yet part of the kangaroo management plan (commercial version). If products are used domestically and not exported then Commonwealth approval is not required.

Following agitation from organisations opposed to the commercial kangaroo management plans and challenges before the Administrative Appeals Tribunal, more regard is now given to species differences in these plans. Primarily there is recognition of differences in productivity of grey and red kangaroos and differences in accessibility and acceptability to the kangaroo industry. There is still a tendency to promote a kangaroo management plan for a kangaroo problem or resource which leaves the public ill-informed about species-level impacts.

Conflict between people and kangaroos most often arise with eastern grey kangaroos because this is the species found where most Australians live – the coasts and hinterlands of Victoria, NSW and Queensland. These are often local issues but all species get branded with the complaint through lack of clarification by wildlife management agencies and an ill-informed or mis-informing media. For instance, ABC's Landline played footage of mobs of kangaroos during the 2002 drought that flitted across species and habitats with the implication that 'overabundance of kangaroos' was exacerbating drought management for farmers and pastoralists. There was often a mis-match between the location of the supposed problem and the species and/or habitat shown. Kangaroos are kangaroos, or are they?

Recognition of species can be a challenge since in spite of common names like red and grey kangaroo. Grey colours predominate along with reds and browns. So you can have a chocolate coloured grey, a blue-grey red, and a common wallaroo with a rufous patch on the neck. However, the species have pronounced differences in their body size, reproductive biology, habitat use, diet preferences, behaviour and ecology which all have implications for conflict with peoples' interests and yield of products per unit effort if they are to be exploited for meat and hides. These differences come into play because the four states with commercial industries take different proportions of species (Fig. 2). In the decade 1994-2003, the NSW industry spanned all four species with red kangaroos marginally dominating over eastern greys. The western grey is less abundant and fewer were killed than the eastern grey. There was a minimal kill of common wallaroos. The Queensland industry is dominated by eastern grey kangaroos with a much higher proportion of wallaroos than any other state. Both South Australia and Western Australia take predominantly red kangaroos with the kill of western greys increasing westwards. Both states kill common wallaroos in lower proportions than Queensland with this kill trending opposite to western grey kangaroos. Of the 30.6 million killed in this decade, red kangaroos dominated at 43% followed closely by eastern greys at 40% and similar proportions of western greys (9%) and common wallaroos (8%).

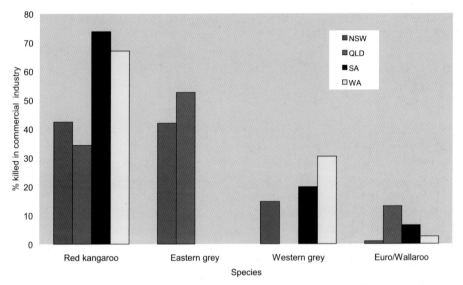

Figure 2. Percentage of red, eastern and western grey kangaroos and common wallaroos (euro or eastern wallaroo) killed between 1994 and 2003 in commercial industries of NSW, QLD, SA and WA.

Western NSW includes a zone of overlap between all four species in the commercial industry. The euro subspecies *(M. robustus erubescens)* of the common wallaroo found there is not killed under the NSW 2002-2006 management plan because only the eastern wallaroo *(M. robustus robustus)* was listed.

Of the four species, the red kangaroo and euro share relatively high annual fecundity and continuous breeding and the eastern and western grey kangaroos have much longer pouch lives and lower fecundity and generally breed once per year. Witte describes the differences in reproductive strategies and the consequences to productivity in an earlier chapter. Her research on the Fowlers Gap Research Station (Witte 2002) further showed the differences between species in how they used a typical landscape of footslopes and alluvial plains in a chenopod shrubland (Fig. 3). Density and distribution of the four kangaroo species was assessed in 33 monthly line-transect surveys stratified across land classes in 1994-97.

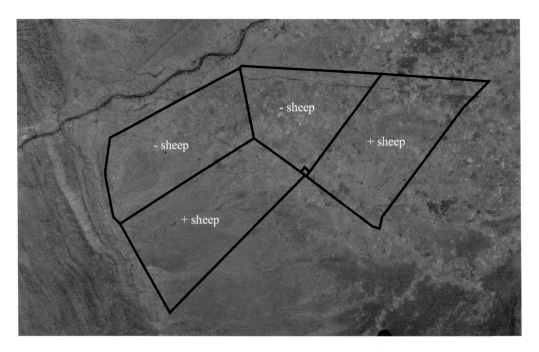

- sheep

- sheep

+ sheep

+ sheep

Figure 3. Study area on the footslopes and alluvial plains of a chenopod shrubland on Fowlers Gap Research Station. The area is demarcated by livestock fences and totals 2158 ha. Two paddocks were stocked with merino ewes and wethers and two were unstocked (10+ years).

The core habitat of the euro is the hills and footslopes of the northern Barrier Range on this site (Croft 1991). Males move out of this core habitat in dry periods and follow drainage channels down the footslopes to the margins of the plains. Their distribution (Fig. 4a) on Witte's study site reflected this behaviour and their density was relatively low – mean ($\pm$SEM) = 1.19 $\pm$ 0.12 km^{-2}. Eastern grey kangaroos prefer areas with lateral cover for shelter during the hotter days and were associated with *Eucalyptus camaldulensis* which lines Fowlers Creek running along the north-west (Fig. 4b). Thus their density on the site was very low - mean ($\pm$SEM) = 0.21 $\pm$ 0.03 km^{-2}. Western grey kangaroos were more abundant (mean ($\pm$SEM) density = 1.40 $\pm$ 0.09 km^{-2}) and associated with major drainage lines and areas of high tree density (Fig. 4c). Red kangaroos were the most abundant species (mean ($\pm$SEM) density = 21.2 $\pm$ 01.42 km^{-2}) and were distributed over most but not the entire site (Fig. 4d).

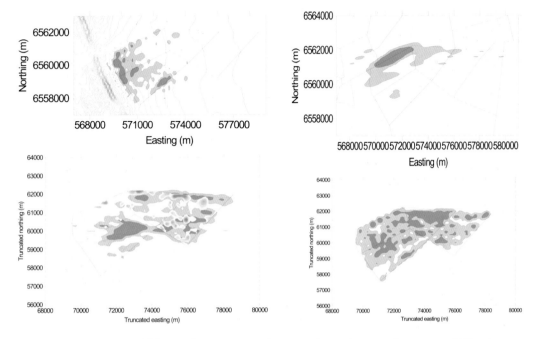

Figure 4. The distribution of (a) euro, (b) eastern grey kangaroo, (c) western grey kangaroo and (d) red kangaroo on Witte's (2002) study site (see Fig 3 for detail). The dark grey polygons represent areas of high density (core 50% of total counted) and the light grey areas the residual 45% (density contours truncated at 95% to remove misleading outliers). The black curved lines in (a) are 5-m elevation contours. The blue lines in (b) and (c) are ephemeral creeks and drainage channels. The green polygons in (c) are areas of high tree density (mainly *Acacia victoriae*). The paddock boundary fences are shown for reference.

The lesson from this study is that the species assort on the landscape in different ways and at different densities. Their interaction with livestock given that the two western paddocks were destocked varies from relatively more for western grey kangaroos, about equal for euros, relatively less for red kangaroos and minimal for eastern grey kangaroos. The terrain and relative use of covering vegetation (e.g. creeklines of *Eucalyptus camaldulensis* and thickets of *Acacia victoriae*) would affect the various species' visibility and accessibility were commercial shooting to take place on this site (note this site has had no commercial shooting since 1966). There are further differences in diet selectivity and diet niche breadth, and water, energy and nitrogen requirements (Dawson 1995) and some of these are discussed in the following sections.

Kangaroos and the blame game

The species are clearly different yet the only measure that the current commercial kangaroo management plans take account of is their density to set a quota of a fixed proportion of the estimated population with a higher offtake for the more fecund red kangaroos and common wallaroos than the grey kangaroos. This leads to a rather insensitive tool if a goal of the commercial kangaroo industry is to control grazing pressure by kangaroos as Kelly (2003: 1) states in the following:

> "Whilst the sustainability of pastoral activities in much of the Australian arid rangelands is under constant investigation, the fact remains that they are currently supporting a large population of kangaroos which, if uncontrolled, would seriously threaten the economic viability of the pastoral industry and the environmental sustainability of huge tracks of land. These are extremely fragile areas which can support a limited number of grazing animals. Allowing the grazing pressure from all animals to increase is one of the most serious environmental hazards in the rangelands. The kangaroo industry is the only tool currently available to exercise control over the kangaroo contribution to grazing pressure."

Leaving aside the fact that the kangaroo industry is not exclusive to the arid rangelands (40% of the kill in 1994-2003 was eastern grey kangaroos that are marginally present there), this kind of statement assumes that the impact of grazing by any mammalian herbivore is additive and by implication degrading to the environment. This is a fallacy as I have argued elsewhere (Croft 2000).

There are often significant differences in the diets of domestic livestock and kangaroos (and amongst kangaroos themselves) due to the lower metabolic requirements of kangaroos, their smaller mouthparts and lack of rumination, their lower water turnover and consequent greater foraging distances from water and their manipulative abilities with the forepaws.

After good rains there is usually a superabundance of food (ephemeral grasses and forbs) for both kangaroos and domestic livestock, so competition is not an issue (Edwards *et al.* 1996). High numbers of grazers is not necessarily indicative of loss of vegetation in the long-term (Fig. 5) just as mowing the suburban lawn does not kill it! Diets of kangaroos and livestock diverge where palatable shrubs are available to livestock, but converge (creating more competition) in degraded lands where kangaroos and livestock are both dependent on an ephemeral 'bounty' and sustained rainfalls. In the latter scenario the landscape is dysfunctional and needs remediation by removal of pastoralism as the major contributor to this dysfunction. This is the 'get off the land' strategy reviewed by Ludwig and Freudenberger (1997).

Kelly contends that the annual removal of some number of kangaroos from the population that is proportional to the density of each species will fix the problem or avoid it happening. The

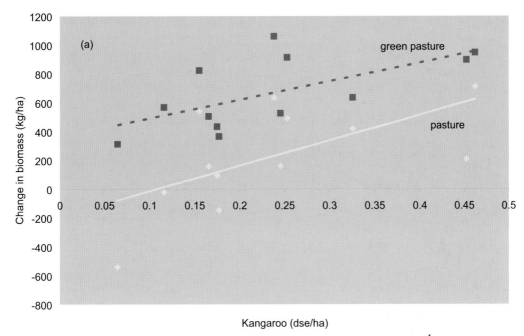

Figure 5. Relationship between the change in pasture and green pasture (kg dry matter ha^{-1}) and kangaroo density expressed as dry sheep equivalents (dse) in unstocked paddocks at the Fowlers Gap Research Station (From Witte 2002). Biomass accumulates with a higher density of kangaroos (a positive relationship) not diminishes.

capacity of the industry to do this is variable across years and species (Fig. 6). What the industry really wants is maximal yield within some economically desirable margin at minimal cost and variability (Hacker *et al*. 2004). This leads to unequal effort across management areas with those with more services and infrastructure favoured over remote ones. Furthermore the removal of kangaroo biomass is a function of the sex ratio of the kangaroos killed and this is by no means fixed.

Thus the equitability and value of the current kangaroo industry to sustainable land management and a reduction in grazing pressure that is measured in any other value than enhanced livestock production is dubious.

As Hacker and colleagues (2004: 39) note the increases in mean total standing dry matter and the proportion of time with biomass above 300 kg/ha are small with kangaroo 'harvesting' as there is "...the overriding influence of seasonal variation, rather than kangaroo density, on biomass production and total standing dry matter." Furthermore Grigg (2002: 57), an advocate of meat and hide production from kangaroos rather than sheep in the rangelands, concludes from an evaluation of field metabolic rates that "...reducing kangaroos will not bring the anticipated benefits to woolgrowers, because kangaroos at typical densities are a much smaller component of the total grazing pressure (TGP) than is generally assumed."

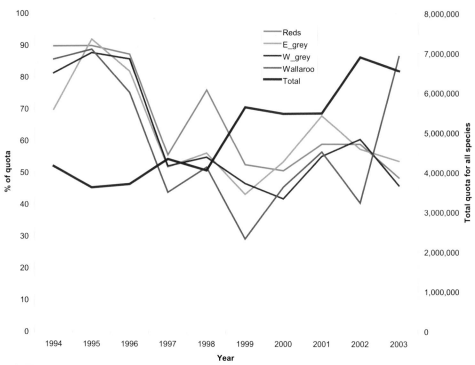

Figure 6. The relative proportion of the commercial quota of red, eastern grey and western grey kangaroos and common wallaroo killed in the last decade (1994-2003) and the total quota for all species. Data combined from NSW, QLD, SA and WA from http://www.deh.gov.au/biodiversity/trade-use/wild-harvest/kangaroo/stats.html. In some years the proportion of the quota is similar across species (e.g. 1996) whereas in others it is highly biased (e.g. 1998).

One of the main arguments for control of kangaroo numbers within the context of management of total grazing pressure is that any grazier or farmer who attempts to rest a paddock from livestock grazing will lose the benefit because kangaroos will invade and consume the standing crop of pasture. The movement patterns of red kangaroos in particular have caused much concern in land management, especially in rangeland recovery through de-stocking.

Many graziers believe that red kangaroos are nomadic and turn into plagues (see below) cutting swathes through large tracts of country over long periods and thus render the countryside useless for pastoral activity unless their populations are severely reduced.

Norbury and Norbury (1993), while not supporting such nomadic behaviour (Norbury *et al.* 1994), contend that localised population shifts are detrimental to rangeland recovery, either when paddocks are spelled from stock grazing or spelled and re-seeded with shrubs. They measured the 3-monthly accumulation of red kangaroo dung along fixed transects in a large destocked paddock (7500 ha) and a neighbouring stocked control in arid Western Australia. Their control for variation in habitat quality was to sample land systems in proportion to their availability but they did not provide any topographical detail, relating to run-on or run-off areas along their sample transects. They found a six-fold increase in the weight of kangaroo dung after 15 months of de-stocking over a period that coincided with favourable rainfalls for pasture growth (80-90 fold increase). However, the reality of this six-fold increase was that kangaroo density only reached the level of the control paddock, which also had 700 sheep and thereafter fluctuated in a similar manner to the control paddock.

Grazing pressure in the de-stocked paddock had in effect significantly been reduced by the removal of 400 sheep. The amount of kangaroo dung never surpassed that of kangaroos in the stocked paddock, despite the absence of sheep.

Furthermore, in the second pair of sites where cultivation (re-seeded with shrubs) was undertaken, pasture biomass (not re-seeded) significantly increased on the cultivated site relative to its uncultivated control, yet there was no significant difference in the mass of kangaroo dung between sites. The authors attributed some of this lack of an effect to commercial shooting with an off-take of 2300 kangaroos from the cultivated paddock in the 3-year study.

However, when the culling was most intense (July-October 1991, Norbury and Norbury 1993: Fig. 3), dung weight increased, suggesting either the method was an unreliable index of kangaroo density or the offtake was insignificant in reducing kangaroo density.

Norbury and Norbury (1993) thus showed that localised movement, as evidenced from a sample of radio-collared red kangaroos, is not necessarily detrimental to rangeland recovery. Any shift in the kangaroo population onto de-stocked pastureland was gradual and a typical response to a dramatic improvement in pasture biomass with favourable rainfall. Thereafter the population fluctuated as pasture waxed and waned like the stocked control. Cultivation did not support a large increase in red kangaroos and since the goal was to recover shrubland they are unlikely to impact on this least favoured food (Dawson and Ellis 1994). Any recovery is likely to be gradual, perhaps only sustained in 1 in 7 years (Ludwig et al. 1998), and beyond the term of Norbury and Norburys' 3-year study. Furthermore, paddocks in good condition are unlikely to be de-stocked.

The experimental paddock in Norbury and Norbury's study (1993) had a significantly lower starting pasture biomass than the control. Thus their experiments were typically poorly controlled.

The localised movement of red kangaroos, especially in response to patchy rainfall during dry periods, is a reality. However, the assumption that red kangaroos will capitalise on the removal of stock reducing the efficacy of such management for rangeland recovery is not supported by research at Fowlers Gap Research Station (Edwards 1990, Witte 2002).

Given the sedentary behaviour of mature individuals, there is no strong evidence that red kangaroos invade areas of improved pasture within a short period of time and remain there to cause long-term damage.

Furthermore, neither Witte's study nor that of Norbury and Norbury (1993) support the suggestion that red kangaroos segregate from sheep due to behavioural antagonism (Andrew and Lange 1986; Wilson 1991) if adjacent paddocks are de-stocked to the extent that grazing pressure on the latter is maintained at pre-stocking levels. Edwards et al. (1994) had an influx of kangaroos into study paddocks after a flush of green pick but it was into a 'kangaroo-free' set with sheep and not a sheep-free set. Furthermore Pople's (1996) detailed study of red kangaroo responses to various shooting pressures in western Queensland showed that numbers do not necessarily drop in heavily shot properties rather individuals were younger and smaller.

The current kangaroo industry by necessity claims something good for everyone by its actions. It claims to rid the pastoral and cropping industries of an unwanted pest and holds out promises of increased production and profitability, it claims to remove destructive mouths and saves the environment garnering support from some 'environmentalists', it claims to provide a cheap and 'healthy' red meat and attempts to seduce consumers to its cause and so on.

Believe this if you will but the reality is that the industry is captive to the farmers and graziers as they hold the means of production – the land on which the kangaroos are killed. The industry needs first to satisfy this constituency to turn a profit and the government of the day colludes to greater or lesser degrees out of its own political interests in this same constituency. Part of this collusion is to foster and promulgate the belief that kangaroos have never had it so good than since the advent of farming and pastoralism and so these industries 'own the problem' and should have a major say in its solution. The propaganda goes something like this – 'there are more kangaroos in Australia than before European colonisation', 'they are now in some place they never were before', 'high numbers of kangaroos are maintained by the water pastoralists and farmers provide', and the perennial 'kangaroos are in plague proportions'. Let us now examine the veracity of these under a suitably catchy headline.

A miracle – European farmers create kangaroos in the Antipodes

The contention that there have never been so many kangaroos in Australia until the advent of farming and pastoralism is an absurdity. Firstly, in several million years of occupancy of the Australian continent by the modern kangaroo fauna who has the time machine to know? Secondly, the kangaroo family as a whole has hardly prospered. As I reported in my previous chapter, Calaby and Grigg's (1989) accounting of 50 species showed 60% (30) had substantial declines in range and/or abundance, six species had declined to extinction and ten (20%) were extinct on mainland Australia, while 28% (14) remained stable or may have increased in the prior 200 years. In the intervening decades to now the situation has hardly improved with species like the brush-tail rock-wallaby in further decline. Newsome (1975) refers to the anomalous increase in red kangaroos and euros in the rangelands with the advent of pastoralism but the anomaly is not that they may or may not have increased but rather than they did not go extinct like so many others of their kind.

We once had a rich and balanced community of mammalian herbivores and omnivores that included macropods, wombats and bandicoots (Fig. 7a). We now have an unbalanced and probably dysfunctional community of native, feral and domestic herbivores (Fig. 7b) with all the smaller species effectively extinct.

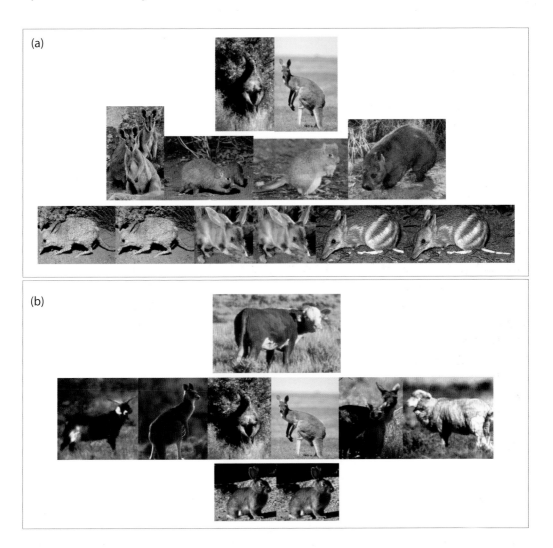

Figure 7. The community of mammalian herbivores and omnivores in western NSW once included (a) red kangaroos, euros, yellow-footed rock wallabies, burrowing bettongs, brush-tailed bettongs, hairy-nosed wombats, pig-footed bandicoots, bilbies and western barred bandicoots. The current community has (b) cattle, goats, eastern and western grey kangaroos, euros, red kangaroos, sheep, rabbits along with horses, donkeys and pigs and a remnant population of yellow-footed rock wallabies.

In 2004, we had a beef cattle herd of 22 million and a sheep herd of 105 million in Australia (ABARE 2005). In sheep and beef enterprises, the energy requirements of livestock is estimated from a standard animal, 50 kg wether sheep of constant weight, which has a dry sheep equivalent (DSE) of 1. For cattle, the standard dry stock of 450 kg has a DSE of 6 (Davies, 2005). If we assume all the sheep and cattle in the Australian herd are standard animals (a conservative estimate since lactating sheep and cows have higher DSE, an 800 kg bull has a DSE of 10) then Australia carried 237 million DSE in the beef and sheep herds (Table 1). To estimate the potential number of 'standard' kangaroos Grigg (2002) provides three estimates of the DSE – 0.7 (based on lower basal metabolic rate of marsupials like kangaroos), 0.4 (based on comparative biomass accounting from smaller mass of female kangaroos than males and estimated demographics of populations), and 0.2 (based on measured field metabolic rates and comparative biomass). From these values, the 2004 sheep and cattle herd is equivalent in energy demands to between 339 million and 1.185 billion kangaroos (Table 1)! The population of the kangaroos species in the commercial industry has been estimated at 20-50 million in recent years. So amazingly we have been clever enough to create pasture for the equivalent 7 to 24 times the more generous estimate of the number of kangaroos currently in Australia yet this supposedly excessive number was unsustainable pre-1788.

Table 1. Kangaroo equivalents of Australian sheep and cattle herd in 2004. Herd data from ABARE (2005), DSE values for sheep and cattle from Davies (2005), DSE values for kangaroos from Grigg (2002).

Variable	Cattle	Sheep	Total
Herd size (millions)	22	105	
DSE multiplier	6	1	
DSE (millions)	132	105	237
Kangaroos @ 0.7 (millions)	189	150	339
Kangaroos @ 0.4 (millions)	330	263	593
Kangaroos @ 0.2 (millions)	660	525	1185

The numbers obviously do not add up to sustain this argument. Some possible reasons are:

1. We have increased productivity by mining guano and other fertiliser sources and dumped it on the Australian landscape. The productivity gains are unlikely to be 7 – 24 times and these inputs are generally absent from the rangelands.

2. The sheep and cattle occupy a vacant niche left by the extinction of the marsupial megafauna (Flannery 1994). If this is true then sheep, cattle and kangaroos can live together as they occupy separate niches and we do not have to control the latter! If the megafaunal extinction was a result of climate change and loss of habitat then there may be no vacant niches. Either way I believe we underestimate the broadness of the

dietary niche of the large kangaroos. Based on modest body size, dentition and gut size they should be at the more specialised end of the grazing gradient than larger sheep and cattle (Croft 1996). However, in the unpredictable environment of Australia, especially the rangelands, specialisation is risky. The rangeland kangaroos do show a preference for grass and winter forbs (Dawson 1995) but variability between individuals and environmental conditions in dietary niche is quite high (Dawson & Ellis 1994, 1996). They are not exclusive grazers and the diet of western grey kangaroos, in particular, can have a high browse component. When you watch individuals eating they sample a variety of plant types and while the gerenuk grew a long neck to browse, a kangaroo simply reaches up to pull down a tasty morsel of *Acacia* foliage.

3. We are living on borrowed time and the grazing pressure from livestock is unsustainable. There is ample evidence for dysfunctional landscapes and real declines in productivity across the rangelands (Ludwig *et al.* 1997).

Finally, the evidence for a low abundance of the large kangaroos prior to European settlement and an increase with the advent of pastoralism and agriculture is based on an historical interpretation of explorers' diaries and account by early settlers (or squatters) (See Auty in this volume). However, the populations of especially the rangeland kangaroos show large fluctuations. Caughley (1987) modelled the red kangaroo population on Kinchega National Park which was the Laidley's Ponds visited by Charles Sturt (Sturt 1849). Dependent on the run of the seasons, Sturt could have seen red kangaroos at a low density of 5 km^{-2} to a high of 80 km^{-2}. Basically you could pluck out a figure to support any argument given this high variability. John Calaby who has supported the interpretation that red kangaroos have increased since settlement (Calaby & Grigg 1989) said in a seminal book on kangaroos in 1969 (Frith & Calaby 1969: 60):

> "...Red Kangaroos are not nearly so abundant as is generally thought and that they are subject to great and sudden decline in numbers due both to overshooting and to drought; where both occur together there seems to be a very real chance that the species could be reduced to a level from which it cannot recover."

Fortunately we still have red kangaroos on the rangelands but the point is made about great declines (and increases) and there is no reason to suggest this variation was not present in pre-1788 populations.

Water, water every where - Nor any drop to drink

Samuel Taylor Coleridge in these lines from *The Rime of the Ancient Mariner* was of course referring to the water in the sea. However, the proponents of the view that kangaroo abundance has increased in, especially the rangelands, due to the provision of water for livestock (and domestic use) would have us believe that pre-pastoralism a few hardy kangaroos grazed around sparse watering points in an essentially waterless landscape. The fact that water has been widely distributed over the rangelands through trapping run-off in earthen tanks and tapping subterranean sources is incontrovertible (Landsberg *et al.* 1997).

However, the interpretation that these numerous water sources are necessary to sustain the kangaroo population is a falsehood generated by looking at the landscape though the eyes of a livestock manager. This viewpoint started with the very first explorers into the inland.

Accompanying Charles Sturt on his expedition into Central Australia were 15 men, 11 horses, 30 bullocks, 200 sheep, 4 kangaroo dogs and 2 sheep dogs (Sturt 1849). He had to supply water to the equivalent of a rugby team and a small farm on a daily basis and often from a single source. No wonder he thought the Outback was dry!

Hacker and McLeod (2003: Fig. 10) produced an elegant map based on the White Cliffs 1:250,000 topographic map sheet. They populated this map with the current 407 earthen tanks and 155 bores and wells to show that a once sparsely watered landscape of some springs and semi-permanent water holes in the south and east is now blanketed with water sources.

What they failed to show was that this same landscape is populated with a vast network of drainage channels, ephemeral creeks, gilgais and clay pans. All of these can hold water for weeks to many months after a very modest rainfall.

For example, Condon (2002: 104) discusses the importance of claypans for water catchment and run-on to forage for kangaroos prior to livestock in the western division of NSW. The only water holes that would appear on the map used by Hacker and McLeod are those substantive enough to support people and livestock. The White Cliffs map also has significant areas of marshes, swamps and land mapped as subject to flooding which form persistent lakes.

If you make the effort to observe the behaviour of kangaroos in the arid rangelands, as I have done over 29 years, they will show that any water source no matter how small and fetid is acceptable and useable.

Kangaroos have a long narrow muzzle and equally long tongue with which they lap water making small ephemeral sources accessible (Fig. 8). In contrast sheep and cattle have broad muzzles and suck water and thus require relatively deep and broad water sources. If surface water is not available kangaroos will dig soaks in creeks gaining access to further water that is not available to livestock. Furthermore, all the species of kangaroos need much less water than livestock. Graziers normally budget 10 litres per day for sheep with this potentially doubling in a hot dry summer. The water turnover in summer is 97 mL $kg^{-0.71}d^{-1}$ for red kangaroos, 104 for euros and 177 for eastern grey kangaroos (Hume 1999). This translates to around 1 litre for a 25 kg red kangaroo or euro and 1.75 litres for a 25 kg eastern grey kangaroo. Not all of this is required from drinking as water taken in with plant matter and created by oxidation of foodstuffs both add to the water budget.

Figure 8. These photographs show how red kangaroos can utilise a small narrow water source which would be unavailable to a sheep or a cow. (Photo: Ulrike Kloeker)

Thus kangaroos are relatively miserly drinkers compared to livestock and certainly people. They lap with a long and narrow tongue and do not suck water. They can exploit water sources that are small and shallow, which are insufficient for livestock.

Furthermore, my observations made during a study of drinking behaviour (Croft 1985) revealed that they will readily lap muddy and algae infested water that is unacceptable to sheep. For kangaroos, light rainfalls across the hotter months will maintain adequate ephemeral water sources in the many catchments from claypans and gilgais to swamps and lakes. Many of these have been silted up by the much accelerated erosion introduced by livestock and overstocking (Fanning 1994; Condon 2002). Large water holes have been replaced but not necessarily supplemented by earthen tanks. Many of the latter lie on top of old springs or simply create deep holes in existing swamps. Kangaroos may have expanded their range into areas of central Australia where artesian bores have provided water (Newsome 1980) but equally much well-watered habitat has been lost to irrigated horticulture and crops along inland rivers.

We can take thousands of gigalitres of water out of the Murray-Darling system for people and agriculture, but apparently before pastoralism, are we to believe that kangaroos could not get a drink? Likewise we have five major rivers flowing inland through Queensland to the Lake Eyre basin and a huge grassland now supporting millions of cattle and sheep but kangaroos apparently had nothing to eat and drink until Europeans came along and settled the country!

The plague of roos – you should have been here yesterday

For much of 2002 we read, watched and listened to stories of 'plagues' of kangaroos invading drought-stricken graziers and farmers and apparently advancing the drought by six months. Interestingly in the continuing drought of 2004-5 there was little if no media comment on kangaroos imposing further hardships on landholders as the 2003 count in western NSW revealed a 50-70% reduction in population dependent on species. Kangaroos are not habitually in 'plague proportions', their populations wax and wane according to the run of the seasons. In fact, I have often been puzzled by the term 'plague proportions' – in proportion to what? I found an explanation from Frith and Calaby (1969: 60) as follows:

> "...some landholders' organisations have coined a useful phrase 'plague proportions' to cover most kangaroo populations and refer to greater local numbers than existed locally last year, last decade or, in some cases, last century, to justify further reduction in numbers."

Thus proportion simply means more than the landholder thinks he or she should have relative to some point in the past. But what about the 'plague'? Of the many definitions given in the Macquarie dictionary I think we can dismiss epidemic disease and pestilence, God or evil afflicting the landholder with a calamity and settle on 'trouble or torment in any manner'. So 'plague proportions' really means kangaroo numbers in excess of some previous arbitrary benchmark that cause trouble or torment to the landholder. I bet you were thinking Cecil B DeMille with swarms of kangaroos blotting out the horizon and devouring everything in their path!

So embedded has this notion of kangaroo and plague become that it seems that any time kangaroos aggregate in large numbers, as red kangaroos may do on the green pick sprouting after a thunder storm (see Witte in this volume), it is cause for panic and concern. Contrast this to the wonder with which we view large herds of wildebeest or zebra on the African plains or in fact the desire of most nature-based tourists to view large aggregations of any wildlife (Croft 2001).

The populations of eastern and western grey kangaroos under optimal conditions can be very dense but are remarkably stable (see Ramp in this volume). The red kangaroos and euros of the rangelands defy the ecological concept of 'carrying capacity' because environmental conditions that drive their forage are too stochastic and unpredictable so Caughley (1987) introduced the term 'centripetality' for at least red kangaroos. He describes this as follows (p. 161):

> "...the forces causing temporal variation may be so powerful, continual and multidirectional that the 'equilibrium' is seldom or never occupied. The forces of centripetality are those that dampen temporal variation; a centripetal system is one that would come to equilibrium if it were not buffeted continually."

Thus at times of good and frequent rainfall there will be a build up of the population just like the bounty of ephemeral plants that they eat. We should marvel at this great wildlife spectacle and carry plane-loads of tourists to the Outback just like those few occasions when the Lake Eyre basin fills with water and waterfowl. There is no greater sight than red backs bent into a sea of wildflowers with the young leaping and finding their full hopping stride as they cavort around their mothers. If it were the Adoni plain of Etosha National Park or the Auob River of the Kgalagadi Transfrontier Park of Southern Africa and the springbok calves were pronking, it would be a wildlife spectacle. In Australia it's just a plague of bloody kangaroos.

The stony downs of Sturt National Park are awash with green vegetation but hardly groaning under a mass of red kangaroos. Tourists would be more satisfied if there were hundreds and not tens (Croft 2002).

The search for day 1

The reasons for lethal control of kangaroos are too often based on fatuous argument in a search for day 1. This is the day the proponent of some management measure believes we should be going back to but rarely going forward to. It may be last year, last decade, last generation, last century or pre-European settlement. Thus we have ludicrous statements about what the kangaroo population should be based on fatuous argument about some past and untestable benchmark set to support the proponent's cause. We should certainly learn from the past and not repeat the persecution and wave of extinctions that followed the introduction of livestock. For that the pastoral industry certainly does own the problem. Diana Fisher and her colleagues (2003) reviewed the extrinsic (climate and range overlap with introduced foxes, sheep and rabbits) and intrinsic (body size, habitat specialisation, diet, reproductive rate and range size) factors in the decline and extinction of Australian marsupials. The introduction of a pastoral industry based on sheep was clearly the cause as the only extrinsic factor that was a consistent predictor of declines. The foxes and rabbits that often get the blame followed the sheep not preceded them. Thus it seems beholden on the current pastoral industry to take a more benign if not supportative attitude to the wildlife, especially the large and obvious members of the kangaroo family, than their predecessors. It is in their interests to ensure that any kangaroo industry that they may wish to support is scrupulous in its animal welfare or at least consistent with their own standards which the current industry and its code of practice is not. The Australian wool industry is now looking to New Zealand for marketing advice after they successfully introduced wool blend outdoor wear to a market captured from wool by synthetics. Their future consumers are likely to be those with an interest in outdoor activities, nature-based tourism and sound and sustainable environmental management. The synergy of happy sheep growing organic wool on native pastures in a functional ecosystem serving wildlife and a small imprint of people may well be the marketing tool of the future.

The promotion of an indigenous red meat resource from kangaroos to replace sheep meat and wool production in the rangelands has thus far largely failed (Grigg 2002).

Regulators claim the reason for kangaroo management through lethal control is to utilise a sustainable resource but equally allow population suppression for dubious land management benefits in the name of reduction of total grazing pressure. If you read the rural press, it seems that on one page an agri-economist is proclaiming the benefits of fewer but better quality livestock but on the next another says the only way to make more money is to run more livestock. Alternative models for commercial utilisation of kangaroos are developed but the status quo apparently best satisfies stakeholders (Hacker et al. 2004). The conservation benefit of consumption of kangaroos is lauded but the flagship of such industries, South Africa, is already corrupted by greed and the human quest for novelty. Julienne du Toit (2004: 24) reports on that industry as follows:

> "Putting a commercial value on wild animals has arguably increased the numbers, and distribution ranges of many species throughout South Africa. But greed and ignorance are putting our biodiversity at risk in unexpected ways. The case of introduced herbivores provides a good example."

The problem she is referring to is that trophy hunters and consumers of meat and hides are no longer content with utilising indigenous wildlife but seek the novelty of shooting, eating or wearing a species from somewhere else, like a cheaper and different subspecies of Roan antelope imported from West Africa, or exotic species from other continents. It is like the introduction of deer into Australia as a game meat – they have escaped, run wild and spawned a fanatical deer-hunting fraternity.

Meanwhile the commercial kangaroo industry rolls on governed by an inadequate, unacceptable and unenforceable code of practice.

It harvests meat and hides from native wildlife owned by the Crown (and thus all Australians) at minimal cost and profit for a few. It sells the meat largely for pet food with a minor proportion going to human consumption as predominantly a cheap red meat. This industry is firmly and necessarily embedded in the pastoral industry which some naively believe it will replace. The regulators model on!

If today is day 1, then let's have some forward and innovative thinking. The leadership of the pastoral industry is narrow-minded, combative and unlikely to be much help. The agencies supporting primary industries, natural resource management and conservation are inconsistent within and between themselves – read the rural press! I am unconvinced that an eat them, wear them or stuff them and hang them on the wall attitude to wildlife is forward thinking.

After all, as Jared Diamond (1997) notes we had a choice of lots of different mammals on all the settled continents to produce our meat and hides but settled on a very few tractable species to domesticate, use and ultimately spread around the world.

I don't see the need to engage with my hunter-gatherer past and appreciate an animal through killing and consuming it even if Tim Flannery (2004: 77) tells me that killing my own meat is a moral action. After all societies created the slaughterhouse to contain the spread of infectious disease from livestock whereas consumption of wildlife (or bush meat) apparently gave us HIV and SARS.

What I will take from my hunter-gather past is an appreciation and inquisitiveness about the natural world.

I think that our kangaroos and all their kind can teach us about how to use the island continent in a frugal way. After all some of them have survived us! Rangeland management is not just about maximising production from a few herbivores. Production must be married with other objectives like conservation of regional biodiversity and maintenance of indigenous peoples' rights, and other land uses like nature-based and cultural tourism (Morton et al. 1995). The capacity of the rangelands to meet these demands is finite and we have been mining resources in the form of wool, hides and meat for more than a century. Landscape dysfunction is common and resilience to drought diminished. What I don't want to see is a misguided obsession with consumptive use or population suppression see kangaroos GONE! I want to see substantive landscapes with red, brown and grey backs bent into a riot of wildflowers – and so do many other people.

The spirit of Australia - red kangaroo in the outback. (Reproduction of a painting by Rosemary Woodford Ganf)

EPILOGUE

WHAT IS THE FUTURE FOR OUR KANGAROOS?

By The Hon. Richard Jones

Patron of Australian Wildlife Protection Council

Until just over two hundred years ago, the unique wildlife in this great land had lived in relative peace and safety for hundreds of thousands of years. Aborigines scattered across the continent took only what they needed to eat for that day. The ancient forests were intact. There was no threat of extinction for the unique flora and fauna of this continent.

After the European invasion began in 1788, species after species of mammals, birds and plants quickly became extinct. Fifteen marsupials became extinct including the Tasmanian tiger, the Toolache wallaby, the Crescent Nailtail wallaby, two species of hare-wallabies, bandicoots, the Broad-faced potoroo and the Lesser Bilby.

Australia has the unenviable record of having the worst record of recent mammal extinction of any country in the world. For over two hundred years now, we have been conducting what amounts to a war on our wildlife.

Almost half of our marsupials are extinct, endangered or vulnerable.

75% of our rainforests, precious home to so many unique species, and 43% of all our magnificent old forests have been cleared. Less than 1% of the lowland and native grasslands of south-eastern Australia remains intact.

This devastation of habitat has contributed to extinctions and severe declines in populations which is especially alarming when you consider that 82% of our mammals and most of our birds, plants, fish, frogs and reptiles are found only in Australia.

After all this destruction, which is still continuing at an alarming pace, we still allow the largest land based wildlife slaughter on earth.

Kangaroos some years ago were derogatively referred to as being in "plague proportions". They had to be culled, they said.

They had no regard to the fact that kangaroo populations for millions of years had expanded during the good years and then contracted rapidly at times of severe drought. The populations stabilized themselves, according to the conditions.

Eastern grey kangaroo male cooling blood flow through the forearms after heat stress of exercise. The behaviour was once given as evidence of their primitiveness but now is recognised as a much more efficient use of water than the drooling dog that might have chased it! (Photo: Bill Corn)

The rationale then was that as kangaroos had to be "culled" they should not be allowed to be wasted. Then, without any consultation with the Australia public and without any fanfare, suddenly what had been protected animals were now merely a resource to be exploited commercially, just as the koalas were in the 1920s. Their status had been changed to de facto farm animals.

Now it didn't matter if the kangaroo populations had been shattered by severe drought, the killing had to go on, to keep shooters and processors in jobs and to fulfill export orders.

There is no recognition by government that kangaroos have a special place in the hearts of so many Australians. Our national carrier has the kangaroo proudly emblazoned on its tail. It's our most recognized symbol. It's on our coat of arms. A dramatic photo of a kangaroo is on the latest Lonely Planet Guide to Australia. Tourists come here wanting to see these amazing animals. And yet we treat them like vermin. There's no understanding or caring by governments that kangaroos live in families and have complex family and social structures. No studies have been undertaken, for example, as to how the family reacts when the lead male in the group is killed.

The killing is egregiously brutal and shameful. As the large males are killed off, the shooters concentrate on the larger females. During good times every adult female is pregnant and has another larger infant at foot.

Greys can have one young per year, Reds three every two years. The Code of Practice for the "Humane" Shooting of Kangaroos says how they must kill the young.

How can a decent human being bash a young kangaroo to death? How can a humane person leave the young kangaroo at foot to starve to death or be taken by foxes? How can it ever be "humane"?

Dependent young-at-foot - the offcuts of the kangaroo industry. (Photo: Bill Corn)

So many Australians unthinkingly, perhaps even unknowingly, condone this outrageous brutality. No one, except the most hardened and callous brute, would be able to eat kangaroo meat or feed it to their cats and dogs if they saw for themselves the shockingly cruel way the meat was obtained.

There are two possible outcomes for our amazing and unique kangaroos. One is the "koala option" where the industry, aided and abetted by government, reduce the numbers to such a low level that they don't recover.

Millions of koalas were killed for their fur in the 19th century with 300,000 skins sent yearly to London as "cheap and durable" fur. During the early part of the 20th century 500,000 skins were being sent to St Louis every year, until President Hoover, who had worked in Australia in early life, signed an order prohibiting imports. He saved our remaining koalas. The last open season was in 1927. The koalas have never recovered and still remain at risk nearly eighty years later.

The same happened to the whales. The killing of humpback whales off Australia's coast only stopped when the numbers crashed to the point of near extinction. Now forty years later their numbers are still only at a fraction of the original population and yet the Japanese want to start killing them again.

The other option is the enlightened one. We as a nation finally recognize that kangaroos are unique and special and that they deserve to live in peace, as do the koalas. We need to accept that farming and grazing in the severely drought prone area, where most of our remaining kangaroos live, has to end.

We have to come to the understanding that killing kangaroos is as unacceptable as killing whales and koalas. Just as so many Australians and overseas tourists take real delight in seeing whales pass our coast so will they take the same delight in seeing, once more, large mobs of magnificent free roaming kangaroos in our outback.

Australians, including MPs and bureaucrats, must come to the realization as to just how lucky we are to have these amazing animals here in Australia. It's time for it to be the Lucky Country for kangaroos as well as for humans.

Will the large kangaroos become a shadow in the bush like the once numerous brush-tail rock-wallabies shot out for pelts? (Photo: Bill Corn)

Maryland Wilson - American born, Maryland completed a B.A. (Hons), lived in Europe and travelled extensively before settling in Australia. She first heard in graphic detail about the suffering of kangaroos and their orphaned joeys in 1980, at a Monash University conference. Shocked that the world fame of kangaroos, a national tourist icon, a species linked inexorably to this ancient land, and the very spirit of Australia, was repaid for their fame by commercial slaughter, Maryland's waking hours have been devoted to changing attitudes. Kangaroos - Myths and Realities is a rallying call for help.

David B Croft - Director and resident of the Fowlers Gap Research Station in far north-western NSW and senior lecturer in the School of Biological, Earth and Environmental Sciences of the University of NSW. Croft's research interests are in behavioural ecology with a focus on the arid zone and native fauna, especially kangaroos. His publications include fundamental studies of the behaviour of kangaroos and wallabies and applied studies of people-wildlife interactions in nature-based tourism and encounters such as wildlife roadkill. He teaches a course on arid zone biology with a focus on rangeland ecology and management in Australia and Southern Africa.

Sir Paul McCartney - "Without reservation, I support the Australian groups fighting to save the kangaroo. The killing is a disgrace – cruel and entirely profit motivated. The kangaroo is one of Australia's original inhabitants, deserving both respect and compassion."

Steve Irwin - "It's embarrassing for Australia that we eat our own wildlife. Do you think the Americans would eat bald eagle? I'm here to tell you it's not right. I'm a wildlife warrior and I'll fight... fight to the death for our wildlife... every person can make a massive difference to global conservation. Simply do not buy use or eat kangaroo products."

Brigitte Bardot - Vive Les Kangourous! - Fondation Brigitte Bardot "I am with you all in my heart in your fight against the massacre of kangaroos. The destruction of these totally inoffensive animals is revolting and unjust. It is a matter of urgency that the Australian authorities become conscious of their elementary duty, to prohibit definitely this carnage and this deplorable trade."

BIBLIOGRAPHY

ABARE (2005) Farm survey data for the beef, prime lamb and sheep industries. Australian Government, Australian Bureau of Agricultural and Resource Economics: Canberra. http://www.abareconomics.com/ame/mla/mla.asp. Retrieved 1/6/2005

Abson RN, Lawrence RE (2003) 'Slaty Creek wildlife underpass study.' Centre for Sustainable Regional Communities, La Trobe University, Bendigo, Australia.

Abu-Zidan FM, Parmar KA, Rao S (2002) Kangaroo-related motor vehicle collisions. *Journal of Trauma-Injury Infection and Critical Care* **53**, 360-363.

Adams C (1994) 'Neither Man nor Beast: Feminism and the Defense of Animals.' (Continuum: New York)

Adams C (1995) 'The Sexual Politics of Meat: A Feminist-Vegetarian Critical Theory.' (Continuum: New York)

Administrative Appeals Tribunal (2003) Wildlife Protection Association of Australia Inc & Ors and Minister for The Environment and Heritage & Anor [2003] AATA 236 (13 March 2003). Administrative Appeals Tribunal: Canberra. http://www.austlii.edu.au/cgi-bin/disp.pl/au/cases/cth/aat/2003/236.html?query=wildlife. Retrieved 2/4/2003.

Administrative Appeals Tribunal (2004) Wildlife Protection Association of Australia Inc and Minister for Environment and Heritage and Ors [2004] AATA 1383 (14 October 2004). Administrative Appeals Tribunal: Canberra. http://www.austlii.edu.au/cgi-bin/disp.pl/au/cases/cth/aat/2004/1383.html?query=wildlife. Retrieved 14/1/2005.

AFFA (2004) Sustainable wildlife enterprises: trials of the commercial value of wildlife as an incentive to restore on-farm habitats. (Rural Industries Research and Development Corporation, Canberra)

Altman JC (1984) The dietary utilisation of flora and fauna by contemporary hunter-gatherers at Momega outstation, north-central Arnhem Land. *Australian Aboriginal Studies* **1**, 35-46.

AMBS (1997) 'Fauna usage of three underpasses beneath the F3 Freeway between Sydney and Newcastle.' Australian Museum Business Services Consulting & Roads and Traffic Authority, Sydney.

Andrew MH, Lange RT (1986) The spatial distributions of sympatric populations of kangaroos and sheep: Examples of dissociation between the species. *Australian Wildlife Research* **13**, 367-73.

Andrews A (1990) Fragmentation of habitat by roads and utility corridors: a review. *Australian Zoologist* **26**, 130-141.

Anglsea Online (2005) Living With Kangaroos in Anglesea. http://www.anglesea-online.com.au/wildLIFE/living_with_roos.asp. Retrieved 10/5/2005.

Archer M, Beale B (2005) 'Going Native: living in the Australian environment.' (Hodder Headline Australia: Sydney)

Arluke A, Levin J, Lucke C, Ascione F (1999) The relationship of animal abuse to violence and other forms of antisocial behaviour. *Journal of Interpersonal Violence* **14**, 963-975.

Arnold GW (1990) Can kangaroos survive the wheatbelt? *Western Australian Journal of Agriculture* **31**, 14-17.

Arnold GW, Abensperg-Traum M, Hobbs RJ, Steven DE, Atkins L, Viveen JJ, Gutter DM (1999) Recovery of shrubland communities on abandoned farmland in southwestern Australia: soils, plants, birds and arthropods. *Pacific Conservation Biology* **5**, 163-178.

Arnold GW, Grassia A, Steven DE, Weeldenburg JR (1991) Population ecology of western grey kangaroos in a remnant of Wando woodland at Baker's Hill, southern Western Australia. *Wildlife Research* **18**, 561-575.

Ascione FR (1993) Children who are cruel to animals: A review of research and implications for developmental psychopathology. *Anthrozoos* **4**, 226-247.

Ascione FR (1998) Battered women's reports of their partner's and their children's cruelty to animals. *Journal of Emotional Abuse* **1**, 119-133.

Ascione FR, Weber CV, Duluth MN, Heath J, Maruyama M, Kayashi K (2005) Battered pets and domestic violence: Animal abuse reported by women experiencing intimate violence and by non-abused women. *Submitted.*

Ashworth DL (1995) Female reproductive success and maternal investment in the euro (*Macropus robustus erubescens*) in the arid zone. PhD thesis, University of New South Wales.

Ashworth DL (1996) Strategies of maternal investment in marsupials: A comparison with eutherian mammals. In 'Comparison of Marsupial and Placental Behaviour'. (Eds DB Croft and U Ganslosser) pp. 226-251. (Filander Press: Fuerth)

Australian Bureau of Statistics (1999) 'Australian Year Book.' (Australian Bureau of Statistics: Canberra)

Australian Bureau of Statistics (2002) Australia's beef cattle industry. In 'Yearbook Australia: Agriculture'. (Australian Bureau of Statistics: Canberra)

Australian Greenhouse Office (2002) National Greenhouse Gas Inventory 2002. (Department of Environment and Heritage: Canberra). http://www.greenhouse.gov.au/inventory/2002/index.html. Retrieved 1/4/2004.

Baker RH (1998) Are man-made barriers influencing mammalian speciations? *Journal of Mammalogy* **79**, 370-371.

Bank FG, Irwin CL, et al. (2002) ,Wildlife habitat connectivity across European highways.' U.S. Department of Transportation, Federal Highway Administration, International Technology Exchange Program, Alexandria, USA.

Banks PB (2004) ,Population viability analysis in urban wildlife management: modelling management options for Sydney's quarantined bandicoots.' (Royal Zoological Society of New South Wales: Mossman, NSW)

Banks PB, Newsome AE, Dickman CR (2000) Predation by red foxes limits recruitment in populations of eastern grey kangaroos. *Austral Ecology* **25**, 283-291.

Banks PB, Norrdahl K, Korpimaki E (2000) Nonlinearity in the predation risk of prey mobility. *Proceedings of the Royal Society of London - Series B: Biological Sciences* **267**, 1621-1625.

Barker RD, Caughley G (1992) Distribution and abundance of kangaroos (Marsupialia: Macropodidae) at the time of European contact: Victoria. *Australian Mammalogy* **15**, 81-88.

Beaglehole JC (1962) 'The Endeavour journal of Joseph Banks. Volume II.' (Trustees of the Public Library of New South Wales: Sydney)

Beattie WA, De Lacy Lowe M (1980) 'Australia's north - west challenge.' (Kimberley Publishing: Melbourne)

Ben-Ami D (2005) The behavioural ecology of the swamp wallaby, *Wallabia bicolor*, and its response to human induced disturbances. PhD thesis, University of New South Wales.

Bender H (2001) 'Deterrence of kangaroos from roadways using ultrasonic frequencies - efficacy of the Shu Roo.' University of Melbourne, Melbourne, Australia.

Bender H (2003) Deterrence of kangaroos from agricultural areas using ultrasonic frequencies: efficacy of a commercial device. *Wildlife Society Bulletin* **31**, 1037-1046.

Bennett AF (1991a) Roads, roadsides and wildlife conservation: A review. In 'Nature Conservation 2: The Role of Corridors'. (Eds DA Saunders and RJ Hobbs) pp. 99-117. (Surrey Beatty & Sons: Chipping Norton)

Bennett DH (1991b) Animal rights and aboriginal concepts. In 'Australian People and Animals in Today's Dreamtime: The Role of Comparative Psychology in the Management of Natural Resources'. (Ed. DB Croft) pp. 53-69. (Praeger: New York)

Bilton AD (2004) Determinants of reproductive success in female red kangaroos *(Macropus rufus)*. PhD thesis, University of New South Wales.

Bilton AD, Croft DB (2004) Lifetime reproductive success in a population of female red kangaroos *Macropus rufus* in the sheep rangelands of western New South Wales: Environmental effects and population dynamics. *Australian Mammalogy* **26**, 45-60.

BioCity (2005) Animals present and extinct. http://www.biocity.edu.au/content/view/87/43/. Retrieved 27/5/2005.

Blamey RK, Hatch D (1998) 'Profiles of motivations of nature-based tourists visiting Australia.' Bureau of Tourism Research, 25, Canberra.

Brandl EJ (1980) Some notes on faunal identification and Arnhem Land rock paintings. *Australian Institute of Aboriginal Studies Newsletter N. S.* **14**, 6-13.

Brandl EJ (1982) 'Australian Aboriginal paintings in Western and Central Arnhem Land.' (Australian Institute of Aboriginal Studies: Canberra)

Breitbach K (1993) What is kangaroo care? http://www.vh.org/pediatric/patient/pediatrics/kanga/. Retrieved 28/5/2005.

Bride TF (1969) Letters from Victorian Pioneers. In. (Ed. CE Sayers). (Heineman: Melbourne)

Brook BW, O'Grady JJ, Burgman MA, Akekaya HR, Frankham R (2000) Predictive accuracy of population viability analysis in conservation biology. *Nature* **404**, 385-387.

Burgman M, Ferson S, Akçakaya HR (1993) 'Risk Assessment in Conservation Biology.' (Chapman & Hall: New York)

Burk A, Springer MS (2000) Intergeneric relationships among Macropodoidea (Metatheria: Diprotodontia) and the chronicle of kangaroo evolution. *Journal of Mammalian Evolution* **7**, 213-237.

Busby GW (1988) Possible impacts of climate change on Australia's flora and fauna. In 'Greenhouse: Planning for Climate Change.' (Ed. GI Pearman) pp. 375-386. (CSIRO Division of Atmospheric Research: Melbourne)

Calaby JH, Grigg GC (1989) Changes in macropodid communities and populations in the past 200 years, and the future. In 'Kangaroos, Wallabies and Rat-kangaroos'. (Eds GC Grigg, PJ Jarman and ID Hume) pp. 813-820. (Surry Beatty & Sons: Sydney)

Caughley G (1981) Overpopulation. In 'Problems in the management of locally abundant wild animals'. (Eds PA Jewell, S Holt and D Hart). (Academic Press: New York)

Caughley G (1987) Ecological relationships. In 'Kangaroos their ecology and management in the sheep rangelands of Australia.' (Eds G Caughley, N Shepherd and J Short) pp. 159-187. (Cambridge University Press: Cambridge)

Caughley G, Grigg GC (1981) Survey of the distribution and density of kangaroos in the pastoral zone of South Australia, and their bearing on the feasibility of aerial survey in large and remote areas. *Australian Wildlife Research* **8**, 1-11.

Chaneton EJ, Facelli JM (1991) Disturbance effects on plant community diversity: spatial scales and dominance hierarchies. *Vegetatio* **93**, 143-156.

Cheal D (1986) A park with a kangaroo problem. Oryx 20, 95-99.

Cilento R (1971) Sir Joseph Banks F.R.S. and the naming of the kangaroo. *Notes: Records of the Royal Society of London* **26**, 155-157.

Clevenger AP, Chruszcz B, Gunson K (2001a) Drainage culverts as habitat linkages and factors affecting passage by mammals. *Journal of Applied Ecology* **38**, 1340-1349.

Clevenger AP, Chruszcz B, Gunson KE (2001b) Highway mitigation fencing reduces wildlife-vehicle collisions. *Wildlife Society Bulletin* **29**, 646-653.

Clevenger AP, Waltho N (2000) Factors influencing the effectiveness of wildlife underpasses in Banff National Park, Alberta, Canada. *Conservation Biology* **14**, 47-56.

Clevenger AP, Waltho N (2005) Performance indices to identify attributes of highway crossing structures facilitating movement of large mammals. *Biological Conservation* **121**, 453-464.

Condon RW (2002) 'Out of the West: A historical perspective of the Western Division of New South Wales.' (Range Management Action Plan: Wentworth)

Conn JM, Annest JL, Dellinger A (2004) Nonfatal motor-vehicle animal crash-related injuries - United States, 2001-2002. *Journal of Safety Research* **35**, 571-574.

Conover M (2002) 'Resolving Human-Wildlife Conflicts: The Science of Wildlife Damage Management.' (Lewis Publishers: Boca Raton)

Cooke B, Kear B (1999) Evolution and diversity of kangaroos (Macropodoidea, Marsupialia). *Australian Mammalogy* **21**, 27-29.

Cooper DW (1998) 'Road kills of animals on some New South Wales roads. Report on data collected by WIRES volunteers in 1997.' Macquarie University, Sydney.

Coulson G (1997a) Male bias in road-kills of macropods. *Wildlife Research* **24**, 21-25.

Coulson G (1997b) Repertoires of social behaviour in captive and free-ranging grey kangaroos, *Macropus giganteus and Macropus fuliginosus* (Marsupialia: Macropodidae). *Journal of Zoology* **242**, 119-130.

Coulson G (2001) Overabundant kangaroo populations in southeastern Australia. In 'Wildlife, Land, and People: Priorities for the 21st Century. Proceedings of the Second International Wildlife Management Congress'. (Eds R Field, RJ Warren, H Okarma and PR Sievert) pp. 238-242. (The Wildlife Society: Bethesda, Maryland, USA)

Coulson G, Alviano P, Ramp D, Way S (1999) The kangaroos of Yan Yean: history of a problem population. *Proceedings of the Royal Society of Victoria* **111**, 121-130.

Coulson G, Alviano P, Ramp D, Way S, McLean N, Yazgin V (2000) The kangaroos of Yan Yean: issues for a forested water catchment in a semi-rural matrix. In 'Nature Conservation 5: Nature Conservation in Production Environments: Managing the Matrix'. (Eds JL Craig, N Mitchell and DA Saunders) pp. 146-156. (Surrey Beatty & Sons: Sydney)

Coulson G, Norbury G (1988) 'Ecology and management of Western Grey kangaroos (*Macropus fuliginosus*) at Hattah-Kulkyne National Park.' Arthur Rylah Institute for Environmental Research, 72, Melbourne.

Coulson GM (1982) Road-kills of macropods on a section of highway in central Victoria. *Australian Wildlife Research* **9**, 21-26.

Cowan J (1989) 'Mysteries of the dreaming: the spiritual life of Australian Aborigines.' (Unity Press: Lindfield)

Croft DB (1985) Inter- and intraspecific conflict between arid-zone kangaroos at watering points. *Australian Wildlife Research* **12**, 337-348.

Croft DB (1991a) Home range of the euro, *Macropus robustus erubescens*. *Journal of Arid Environments* **20**, 99-111.

Croft DB (1991b) Home range of the red kangaroo *Macropus rufus*. *Journal of Arid Environments* **20**, 83-98.

Croft DB (1996) Locomotion, foraging competition and group size. In 'Comparison of marsupial and placental behaviour.' (Eds DB Croft and U Ganslosser) pp. 134-157. (Filander Verlag GmbH: Fuerth)

Croft DB (2000) Sustainable use of wildlife in western New South Wales: Possibilities and problems. *Rangeland Journal* **22**, 88-104.

Croft DB (2001) 'Rangeland Kangaroos; A world class wildlife experience. Wildlife Tourism Research Report Series: No 16.' Cooperative Research Centre for Sustainable Tourism, Gold Coast.

Croft DB (2004) Kangaroo management: individuals and communities. *Australian Mammalogy* **26**, 101-108.

Cross J (1833) 'Journals of Several Expeditions made in Western Australia.' (Cross: Holburn)

CSIRO (1996) 'Australia State of the Environment 1996.' (CSIRO Publishing: Collingwood, Victoria)

Cunningham PM (1827) 'Two years in New South Wales; A series of letters, comprising sketches of the actual state of society in that colony; of its peculiar advantages to emigrants; of its topography, natural history, etc.' (Henry Colburn: London)

Czech B, Krausman PR, Devers PK (2000) Economic associations among causes of species endangerment in the United States. *BioScience* **50**, 593-601.

Darwin C (1889) 'Journal of Researches.' (Ward Locke: London)

Davies L (2005) Using DSEs and carrying capacities to compare beef enterprises. (State of New South Wales, Department of Primary Industries: Orange) http://www.agric.nsw. gov.au/reader/beefbudinfo/dse-carrying-capacity.htm. Retrieved 1/6/2005.

Dawson TJ (1995) 'Kangaroos - biology of the largest marsupials.' (University of New South Wales Press: Sydney)

Dawson TJ, Ellis BA (1994) Diets of mammalian herbivores in Australian arid shrublands: seasonal effects on overlap between red kangaroos, sheep and rabbits and on dietary niche breadths and electivities. *Journal of Arid Environments* **26**, 257-271.

Dawson TJ, Ellis BA (1996) Diets of mammalian herbivores in Australian arid, hilly shrublands: seasonal effects on overlap between euros (hill kangaroos), sheep and feral goats, and on dietary niche breadths and electivities. *Journal of Arid Environments* **34**, 491-506.

DCE (1990) 'Restoring the balance. The kangaroo control program to save Hattah-Kulkyne National Park.' Department of Conservation and Environment, Victoria.

de la Billiardiere JJ (1800) 'Voyage in search of La Perouse.' (Stockdale: London)

DEH (2002) Kangaroo Shooting Code Compliance: A Survey of the Extent of Compliance with the Requirements of the Code of Practice for the Human Shooting of Kangaroos. (Australian Government, Department of Environment and Heritage: Canberra) http://www.deh. gov.au/biodiversity/trade-use/publications/ kangaroo-report. Retrieved 14/1/2005.

Denny MJS (1980) 'Red kangaroo arid zone studies. Final report to the National Parks and Wildlife Service.' National Parks and Wildlife Service, Canberra.

Diamond JM (1997) 'Guns, germs, and steel: the fates of human societies.' (W.W. Norton & Co.: New York)

Diamond JM (2005) 'Collapse: how societies choose to fail or succeed.' (Viking: New York)

Dodd CK, Barichivich WJ, Smith LL (2004) Effectiveness of a barrier wall and culverts in reducing wildlife mortality on a heavily travelled highway in Florida. *Biological Conservation* **118**, 619-631.

Dovey L, Wong V, Bayne P (1997) An overview of the status and management of rock-wallabies (*Petrogale spp.*) in New South Wales. *Australian Mammal* **19**, 163-168.

du Toit J (2004) The buck stops here. *Endangered Wildlife* **49**, 24-26.

Ealey EHM (1967) Ecology of the euro, *Macropus robustus* (Gould), in north-western Australia - I. The environment and changes in euro and sheep populations. *CSIRO Wildlife Research* **12**, 9-25.

Ecoplan A (1995) 'Macropod and rabbit study report: Yan Yean Catchment and Reservoir Park, Plenty Gorge Park, Cardinia Catchment and Reservoir Park and Sugarloaf Catchment and Reservoir Park.' Ecoplan Australia Pty. Ltd., Melbourne.

Edwards GP (1990) Competition between red kangaroos and sheep in arid New South Wales. PhD thesis, University of New South Wales.

Edwards GP, Croft DB, Dawson TJ (1994) Observations of differential sex/age class mobility in red kangaroos (*Macropus rufus*). *Journal of Arid Environments* **27**, 169-177.

Edwards GP, Croft DB, Dawson TJ (1996) Competition between red kangaroos (*Macropus rufus*) and sheep (*Ovis aries*) in the arid rangelands of Australia. *Australian Journal of Ecology* **21**, 165-172.

Edwards R (1979) 'Australian Aboriginal art: The art of the Alligator Rivers region, Northern Territory.' (Australian Institute of Aboriginal Studies: Canberra)

Ellis BA, Russell EM, Dawson TJ, Harrop CJF (1977) Seasonal changes in diet preference of free-ranging red kangaroos, euros and sheep in western New South Wales. *Australian Wildlife Research* **4**, 127-144.

Fanning P (1994) Long-term contemporary erosion rates in arid rangelands environments in western New South Wales, Australia. *Journal of Arid Environments* **28**, 173-187.

Felthous AR, Kellert SR (1986) Violence against animals and people: Is aggression against living creatures generalised? *Bulletin of the American Academy of Psychiatry and Law* **14**, 55-69.

Felthous AR, Kellert SR (1987) Childhood cruelty to animals and later aggression against people: A review. *American Journal of Psychiatry* **144**, 710-717.

Fensham RJ, Holman JE, Cox MJ (1999) Plant species responses along a grazing disturbance gradient in Australian grassland. *Journal of Vegetation Science* **10**, 77-86.

Finlayson HH (1945) 'The red centre: Man and beast in the heart of Australia.' (Angus & Robertson: Sydney)

Fisher DO, Blomberg SP, Owens IPF (2003) Extrinsic versus intrinsic factors in the decline and extinction of Australian marsupials. *Proceedings of the Royal Society of London - Series B: Biological Sciences* **270**, 1801-1808.

Fisher P (1995) US Fish and Wildlife Service News Release. Dated 7/3/1995.

Fishman MA (1999) Predator inspection: Closer approach as a way to improve assessment of potential threats. *Journal of Theoretical Biology* **196**, 225-235.

Flannery T (1995) 'The future eaters: an ecological history of the Australasian lands and people.' (Reed Books: Port Melbourne, Vic.)

Flannery T (2004) 'Country.' (Text Publishing: Melbourne)

Flannery TF (1989) Phylogeny of the Macropodoidea: a study in convergence. In 'Kangaroos, Wallabies and Rat-kangaroos'. (Eds GC Grigg, PJ Jarman and ID Hume) pp. 1-46. (Surrey Beatty and Sons: Sydney)

Flynn CP (2000) Why family professionals can no longer ignore violence toward animals. *Family Relations* **49**, 87-95.

Flynn CP (2002a) Hunting and illegal violence against humans and other animals: Exploring the relationship. *Society and Animals* **10**, 137-154.

Flynn CP (2002b) Women's best friend: Pet abuse and the role of companion animals in the lives of battered women. *Violence Against Women* **6**, 162-177.

Forman RTT, Alexander LE (1998) Roads and their major ecological effects. *Annual Review of Ecology and Systematics* **29**, 207-231.

Forman RTT, Sperling D, *et al.* (Eds) (2003) 'Road Ecology: Science and Solutions.' (Island Press: Washington, USA)

Frith HJ, Calaby JH (1969) 'Kangaroos.' (F.W. Cheshire: Melbourne)

FSA - Environmental Queensland (2000) Alternative systems for piggery effluent treatment. http://www.environment.sa.gov.au/epa/pdfs/piggery01.pdf. Retrieved 1/6/2004.

Gellatley J (2001) Under Fire: A Viva! Report on the Killing of Kangaroos for Meat and Skin. (Vegetarians International Voice for Animals: Bristol). http://www.savethekangaroo.com/resources/KangarooReport.shtml. Retrieved 10/1/2005.

Gerritson J (1981) 'Tibooburra: Corner country.' (Tibooburra Press: Tibooburra)

Giles E (1889) 'Australia Twice Traversed.' (Sampson Low: London)

Gilpin ME, Soule ME (1986) Minimum viable populations: processes of species extinctions. In 'Conservation biology: the science of scarcity and diversity'. (Ed. ME Soule) pp. 19-34. (Sinauer Associates: Sunderland)

Goosem M (2001) Effects of tropical rainforest roads on small mammals: inhibition of crossing movements. *Wildlife Research* **28**, 351-364.

Gorecki PP, Horton DR, Stern N, Wright RVS (1984) Coexistence of humans and megafauna in Australia: Improved stratified evidence. *Archaeology in Oceania* **19**, 117-119.

Gould RA (1971a) Uses and effects of fire among the Western Desert Aborigines of Australia. *Mankind* **8**, 14-24.

Gould RA (1971b) Uses and effects of fire among Western Desert Aborigines of Australia. *Mankind* **8**, 14-24.

Gregory AC, Gregory FT (1884) 'Journals of Australian Explorations.' (Beal: Brisbane)

Grey G (1841) 'Journals of Two Expeditions of Discovery.' (Boone: London)

Grice AC, Barchia I (1992) Does grazing reduce survival of indigenous perennial grasses of the semi-arid woodlands of western New South Wales? *Australian Journal of Ecology* **17**, 195-205.

Griffiths T (1992) 'Secrets of the Forest. Discovering History in Melbourne's Ash Range.' (Allen & Unwin: St Leonards, N.S.W.)

Grigg GC (2002) Conservation benefit from harvesting kangaroos: status report at the start of a new millenium. In 'A Zoological Revolution: Using native fauna to assist in its own survival'. (Eds D Lunney and CR Dickman) pp. 53-76. (Royal Zoological Society of New South Wales and Australian Museum: Sydney)

Grigg GC, Jarman PJ, Hume ID (1989) 'Kangaroos, Wallabies and Rat-kangaroos.' (Surrey Beatty & Sons: Sydney)

Groot Bruinderink GWTA, Hazebroek E (1996) Ungulate traffic collisions in Europe. *Conservation Biology* **10**, 1059-1067.

Grumbine RE (1990) Variable populations, reserve design, and federal land management: a critique. *Conservation Biology* **4**, 127-134.

Gullone E, Clarke JP (2005) Animal abuse, cruelty, and welfare: An Australian perspective. In 'The International Handbook of Theory and Research on Animal Abuse and Cruelty'. (Ed. FR Ascione). (Purdue University Press: Purdue)

Gullone E, Johnson J, Volant A (2004) The link between animal abuse and family violence: A Victoria-wide study. In 'Welfare Conference'. Canberra. (Australian Veterinary Association)

Gunn I (1996) Preservation of Macropods: Now and in the Future. In 'Australian Wildlife Protection Society'. Canberra

Hacker R, McLeod SR (2003) 'Living with Kangaroos: A guide to their management in the Murray-Darling Basin.' (NSW Agriculture: Orange)

Hacker R, McLeod SR, Druhan JP, Tenhumberg B, Pradhan U (2004) 'Kangaroo Management Options in the Murray-Darling Basin.' (Murray-Darling Basin Commission: Canberra)

Hadar L, Noy-Meir I, Perevolotsky A (1999) The effect of shrub clearing and grazing on the composition of a Mediterranean plant community: functional groups versus species. *Journal of Vegetation Science* **10**, 673-682.

Hallam SJ (1975) 'Fire and hearth.' (Australian Institute of Aboriginal Studies: Canberra)

Hardman J (1996) The wild harvest and marketing of kangaroos. In. (Ed. DoP Industries). (Queensland Government, Brisbane)

Hawdon J (1952) 'The Journal of a Journey from New South Wales to Adelaide.' (Georgian House: Melbourne)

Hawkesworth J (1773) 'An account of the voyages undertaken by the order of His Present Majesty for making discoveries in the Southern Hemisphere.' (Becket & De Hondt: London)

Henderson J (1832) 'Observations on the Colonies of New South Wales and Van Diemen's Land.' (Baptist Mission Press: Calcutta)

Herbert CA (2004) Long-acting contraceptives: A new tool to manage overabundant kangaroo populations in nature reserves and urban areas. *Australian Mammalogy* **26**, 67-74.

Higginbottom K, Northrope CL, Croft DB, Hill B, Fredline L (2004) The role of kangaroos in Australian tourism. *Australian Mammalogy* **26**, 26-32.

Higginbottom KB, Croft DB (1999) Social learning in marsupials. In 'Mammalian Social Learning: Comparative and Ecological Perspectives'. (Eds HO Box and KR Gibson) pp. 80-101. (Cambridge University Press: Cambridge)

Hill B, Arthurson T, Challio L (2002) 'Kangaroos in the marketing of Australia: potentials and practice.' CRC for Sustainable Tourism, Gold Coast Queensland.

Hill GJE, Barnes A, Wilson GR (1988) The use of wheat crops by grey kangaroos, *Macropus giganteus*, in southern Queensland. *Australian Wildlife Research* **15**, 111-117.

Historical Records of Australia (1921) 'Series 1, VIII.' (Library Committee of the Commonwealth Government: Sydney)

Historical Records of Australia (1922a) 'Series 111, I.' (Library Committee of the Commonwealth Government: Sydney)

Historical Records of Australia (1922b) 'Series 111, V.' (Library Committee of the Commonwealth Government: Sydney)

Historical Records of Victoria (1982) '2A.' (Victorian Government Printing Office: Melbourne)

Historical Records of Victoria (1983) '2B.' (Victorian Government Printing Office: Melbourne)

Hodgson CP (1846) 'Reminiscences of Australia.' (Wright: London)

Horndage B (1972) 'It it moves, shoot it.' (Review Publications: Dubbo)

Hoyte JA (1994) 'Animals in Peril: How 'Sustainable Use' is Wiping out the World's Wildlife.' (Humane Society of the United States: Washington)

Hume ID (1999) 'Marsupial nutrition.' (Cambridge University Press: Cambridge)

Jaeger JAG, Fahrig L (2004) Effects of road fencing on population persistence. *Conservation Biology* **18**, 1651-1657.

Jarman PJ (1991) Social behaviour and organisation in the Macropodoidea. *Advances in the Study of Behavior* **20**, 1-50.

Jarman PJ (1994) The eating of seedheads by species of Macropodidae. *Australian Mammalogy* **17**, 51-63.

Jones M, Rotherham ID (1998) 'Eyes have they but they see not': changing priorities and perceptions of countryside in urban areas. *Landscape Archaeology and Ecology* **3**, 19-24.

Jones ME (2000) Road upgrade, road mortality and remedial measures: impacts on a population of eastern quolls and Tasmanian devils. *Wildlife Research* **27**, 289-296.

Kantvilas G, Minchin PR (1989) An analysis of epiphytic lichen communities in Tasmanian cool temperate rainforest. *Vegetatio* **84**, 99-112.

Kellert SR, Felthous AR (1985) Childhood cruelty toward animals among criminals and non-criminals. *Human Relations* **38**, 1113-1129.

Kelly J (2003) 'The kangaroo industry: Its image and market.' Rural Industries Research and Development Corporation, 02/166, Canberra.

Kershaw P, Moss P, van de Kaars S (2003) Causes and consequences of long-term climatic variability on the Australian continent. *Freshwater Biology* **48**, 1274-1283.

Khattak AJ (2003) Human fatalities in animal-related highway crashes. In 'Statistical Methods and Modeling and Safety Data, Analysis, and Evaluation' pp. 158-166)

KIAA (2002) The kangaroo industry is under attack and needs your help. Email. (Kangaroo Industries Association of Australia)

Kinloch JE, Friedel MH (2005) Soil seed reserves in arid grazing lands of central Australia. Part 1: seed bank and vegetation dynamics. *Journal of Arid Environments* **60**, 133-161.

Klöcker U, Croft DB, Ramp D (In Press) Factors affecting roadkill on the Silver City Highway in far western NSW. *Wildlife Research*.

Lacy RC (1995) 'VORTEX: A stochastic simulation of the Extinction process.' Chicago Zoological Society, USA.

Landsberg J, James CD, Morton SR, Hobbs TJ, Stol J, Drew A, Tongway H (1997) 'The effects of artificial sources of water on rangeland biodiversity.' Environment Australia and CSIRO, Canberra.

Landsberg J, Lavorel S, Stol J (1999) Grazing response groups among understorey plants in arid rangelands. *Journal of Vegetation Science* **10**, 683-696.

Le Soeuf AS (1928) Notes on four little-known species of kangaroos. *Proceedings of the Linnean Society of New South Wales* **53**, 397-400.

Lee E, Klöcker U, Croft DB, Ramp D (2004) Kangaroo-vehicle collisions in Australia's sheep rangelands, during and following drought periods. *Australian Mammalogy* **26**, 215-226.

Leichhardt L (1847) 'Journal of the Overland Expedition in Australia.' (Boone: London)

Leopold AS (1991) Engineering and Conservation. In 'The river of the Mother of God and other essays'. (Eds SL Flader and JB Callicot) pp. 249-254. (University of Wisconsin Press: Madison)

Liebenberg L (1990) 'The Art of Tracking: The origin of science.' (David Philip: Cape Town)

Light W (1984) 'William Light's Brief Journal & Australian Diaries.' (David Elder: Adelaide)

Lintermans M (1997) A review of the use of Swareflex wildlife reflectors to reduce the incidence of road-kills in native fauna. In 'Living with Eastern Grey Kangaroos in the A.C.T.' (Third Report, Appendix D. A.C.T. Kangaroo Advisory Committee: Canberra)

Ludwig J, Tongway D, Freudenberger D, Noble J, Hodgkinson K (Eds) (1997) 'Landscape ecology, function and management: principles from Australia's rangelands.' (CSIRO Publishing: Melbourne)

Ludwig JA (1987) Primary productivity in arid lands: myths and realities. *Journal of Arid Environments* **13**, 1-7.

Ludwig JA, Freudenberger D (1997) Towards a sustainable future for rangelands. In 'Landscpe ecology, function and management: principles from Australia's rangelands'. (Eds J Ludwig, D Tongway, D Freudenberger, J Noble and K Hodgkinson) pp. 121-131. (CSIRO Publishing: Melbourne)

Lunney D, Burgin S (2004) Urban wildlife management: an emerging discipline. In 'Urban Wildlife: more than meets the eye'. (Eds D Lunney and S Burgin). (Royal Zoological Society of New South Wales: Mossman)

Lunney D, Grigg G (1988) Kangaroo harvesting and the conservation of arid and semi-arid lands: Proceedings of a Royal Zoological Society (NSW) Conference. *Australian Zoologist* **24, Special edition**.

Lunney D, Law B, Rummery C (1997) An ecological interpretation of the historical decline of the Brush-tailed Rock-wallaby *Petrogale penicillata* in New South Wales. *Australian Mammalogy* **19**, 281-296.

Lunney D, O'Connell M (1988) Habitat selection by the swamp wallaby, *Wallabia bicolor*, the red-necked wallaby, *Macropus rufogriseus*, and the common wombat, *Vombatus ursinus*, in logged, burnt forest near Bega, New-South-Wales. *Australian Wildlife Research* **15**, 695-706.

Lunney D, O'Neill L, Matthews A, Sherwin WB (2002) Modelling mammalian extinction and forecasting recovery: koalas at Iluka (NSW, Australia). *Biological Conservation* **106**, 101-113.

Mansergh IM, Scotts DJ (1989) Habitat continuity and social-organization of the mountain pygmy-possum restored by tunnel. *Journal of Wildlife Management* **53**, 701-707.

Marlow BJ (1971) Kangaroos and men: A symposium of the Royal Zoological Society of New South Wales, 4 July 1970, Australian Museum. *Australian Zoologist* **16**, 1-100.

Maxwell S, Burbidge AA, Morris K (1996) 'Action plan for Australian Marsupials and Monotremes.' Department of the Environment and Heritage, Canberra.

McCarthy MA, Burgman MA, Ferson S (1996) Logistic sensitivity and bounds for extinction risks. *Ecological Modelling* **86**, 297-303.

McCormick SJ (2003) Parks in a new light for a new century. *Nature Conservancy* **53**, 4-5.

McDonnell MJ (1997) A paradigm shift. *Urban Ecosystems* **1**, 85-86.

McDonnell MJ, Pickett STA (1990) Ecosystem structure and function along urban-rural gradients: an unexploited opportunity for ecology. *Ecology* **7**, 1232-1237.

McIntyre S, Lavorel S (1994) How environmental and disturbance factors influence species composition in temperature Australian grasslands. *Journal of Vegetation Science* **5**, 373-384.

McLeod SR (1996) The foraging behaviour of the arid zone herbivores, the red kangaroo (*Macropus rufus*) and the sheep (*Ovis aries*) and their role in its competitive interactions, population dynamics and life-history strategies. PhD thesis, University of New South Wales.

McLeod SR, Hacker RB, Druhan JP (2004) Managing the commercial harvest of kangaroos in the Murray-Darling Basin. *Australian Mammalogy* **24**, 9-22.

McNeely JA, Harrison J, Ingwall PD (1994) 'Protecting nature: regional views of protected areas.' World Conservation Union, Gland.

Meagher SJ, Ride WDL (1978) Use of natural resources by the Aborigines of south-western Australia. In 'Aborigines in the West: Their past and their present.' (Eds RM Berndt and CH Berndt) pp. 66-80. (University of Western Australia Press: Nedlands)

Meek PD (1999) The movement, roaming behaviour and home range of free-roaming domestic dogs, *Canis lupis familiaris*, in coastal New South Wales. *Wildlife Research* **26**, 847-855.

Meek PD, Triggs B (1998) The Food of Foxes, Dogs and Cats on Two Peninsulas in Jervis Bay, New South Wales. *Proceedings of the Linnean Society of New South Wales* **120**, 117-127.

Melbourne Water (1982) 'Kangaroo Problem: Yan Yean.' Operations Division, Watersheds Department, Melbourne Water, Melbourne, Victoria.

Miller JM, Hobbs JR (2002) Conservation where people live and work. *Conservation Biology* **16**, 330-337.

Mitchell T (1839) 'Three Expeditions into the Interior of Eastern Australia. Volume 1.' (Boone: London)

Mittermeier RA, Myers N, Mittermeier CG (2000) 'Hotspots: earth's richest and most endangered terrestrial ecoregions.' (University of Chicago Press: Chicago)

MMBW (1989) 'Water for Melbourne (brochure).' Melbourne and Metropolitan Board of Works, Melbourne.

Montague-Drake R (2004) Strategic Management of Artificial Watering Points for Biodiversity Conservation. PhD thesis, University of New South Wales.

Montague-Drake R, Croft DB (2004) Do kangaroos exhibit water-focused grazing patterns in arid New South Wales? A case study in Sturt National Park. *Australian Mammalogy* **26**, 87-100.

Montgomery J (1969) Is it too late to save the Big Red? *Animals* **12**, 226-228.

Moriarty A (2004) The ecology and environmental impact of rusa deer (*Cervus timorensis*) in the Royal National Park. PhD thesis, University of Western Sydney.

Morris EE (1978) 'Australia's first century, 1788-1888.' (Child & Henry Publishing: Sydney)

Morrissey VK (2003) Wildlife-vehicle collisions in the Royal National Park, Sydney. BSc Honours thesis, University of New South Wales.

Morton J (1991) Black and white totemism: conservation, animal symbolism, and human identification in Australia. In 'Australian People and Animals in Today's Dreamtime: The Role of Comparative Psychology in the Management of Natural Resources'. (Ed. DB Croft) pp. 21-52. (Praeger: New York)

Morton SR, Stafford Smith DM, Friedel MH, Griffin GF, Pickup G (1995) The stewardship of arid Australia: Ecology and landscape management. *Journal of Environmental Management* **43**, 195-217.

Moscardo G, Woods B, Greenwood T (2001) 'Understanding visitor perspectives on wildlife tourism.' Cooperative Research Centre for Sustainable Tourism, 2, Gold Coast.

Moss GL (1995) Home range, grouping patterns and the mating system of the red kangaroo (macropus rufus) in the arid zone. PhD thesis, University of New South Wales.

Mountford CP (1976) 'Nomads of the Australian desert.' (Rigby: Adelaide)

Munn A, Dawson TJ (2001) Thermoregulation in juvenile red kangaroos (*Macropus rufus*) after pouch exit: higher metabolism and evaporative water requirements. *Physiological And Biochemical Zoology* **74**, 917-927.

Munn AJ, Dawson TJ (2003) How important is milk for near-weaned red kangaroos (*Macropus rufus*) fed different forages? *Journal Of Comparative Physiology B Biochemical Systemic And Environmental Physiology* **173**, 141-148.

Murray P, Chaloupka G (1984) The dreamtime animals: Extinct megafauna in Arnhem Land rock art. *Archaeology in Oceania* **19**, 105-116.

Myers N (1988) Threatened biotas: hotspots in tropical forests. *The Environmentalist* **8**, 178-208.

Myers N (1990) The biodiversity challenge: expanded hot spot analysis. *The Environmentalist* **10**, 243-256.

National Geographic (2005) Kangaroo Attacks in Australia Spotlight Growing Turf Wars. http://news.nationalgeographic.com/news/2005/05/0506_050506_kangaroos.html. Retrieved 28/5/2005.

Neave HM, Tanton MT (1989) The effects of grazing by kangaroos and rabbits on the vegetation and the habitat of other fauna in the Tidbinbilla Nature Reserve, Australian Capital Territory. *Australian Wildlife Research* **16**, 337-352.

Newell G-R (1999) Responses of Lumholtz's tree-kangaroo (*Dendrolagus lumholtzi*) to loss of habitat within a tropical rainforest fragment. *Biological Conservation* **91**, 181-189.

Newmark WD (1995) Extinction of mammal populations in western North American national parks. *Conservation Biology* **9**, 512-526.

Newsome AE (1975) An ecological comparison of the two arid-zone kangaroos of Australia, and their anomalous prosperity since the introduction of ruminant stock to their environment. *The Quarterly Review of Biology* **50**, 389-428.

Newsome AE (1980) The eco-mythology of the red kangaroo in central Australia. *Mankind* **12**, 327-333.

Norbury GL, Norbury DC (1993) The distribution of red kangaros in relation to range regeneration. *Rangeland Journal* **15**, 3-11.

Norbury GL, Norbury DC, Oliver AJ (1994a) Facultative behaviour in unpredictable environments: mobility of red kangaroos in arid Western Australia. *Journal of Animal Ecology* **63**, 410-418.

Noy-Meir I, Gutman M, Kaplan Y (1989) Responses of Mediterranean grassland plants to grazing and protection. *Journal of Ecology* **77**, 290-310.

NSW NPWS (2002) Cobar public urged to avoid hungry emus and kangaroos. http://www.nationalparks.nsw.gov.au/npws.nsf/Content/Cobar+public+urged+to+avoid+hungry+emus+and+kangaroos. Retrieved 1/4/2005.

NSW NPWS (2005) Atlas of New South Wales Wildlife. (NSW Department of Environment and Conservation)

O'Connell JF (1980) Notes on the manufacture and use of a kangaroo skin waterbag. *Australian Institute of Aboriginal Studies Newsletter N.S.* **13**, 26-29.

Onslow SM (1973) 'Some Early Records of the Macarthurs of Camden.' (Rigby: Adelaide)

Osawa R (1989) Road-kills of the swamp wallaby, *Wallabia bicolor*, on North Stradbroke Island, south-east Queensland. *Australian Wildlife Research* **16**, 95-104.

Oxley J (1820) ' Journals of two expeditions into the interior of New South Wales.' (J. Murray: London)

PlanetArk (2004) Australia's capital warned over aggressive 'roos. http://www.planetark.com/dailynewsstory.cfm/newsid/25909/newsDate/8-Jul-2004/story.htm. Retrieved 1/4/2005.

Plomley NJB (1991) 'Jorgen Jorgenson and the Aborigines of Van Diemens Land.' (Blubber Head: Hobart)

Poole WE (1984) 'Management of kangaroo harvesting in Australia (1984).' Australian National Parks & Wildlife Service, Canberra.

Pople A, Grigg G (1998) 'Commercial harvesting of kangaroos in Australia: overview of background information for kangaroo management. Report for Environment Australia.' Environment Australia, Canberra.

Pople AR (1996) Effects of harvesting upon the demography of red kangaroos in Queensland. PhD thesis, University of Queensland.

Pople AR, Grigg GC, Cairns SC, Beard LA, Alexander P (2000) Trends in the numbers of red kangaroos and emus on either side of the South Australian dingo fence: evidence for predator regulation? *Wildlife Research* **27**, 269-276.

Pople AR, McLeod SR (2000) Kangaroo management and sustainable use of the rangelands. In 'Management for sustainable ecosystems'. (Eds P Hale, A Petrie, D Moloney and P Sattler). (Centre for Conservation Biology, University of Queensland: Brisbane)

Possingham HP, Lindenmayer DB, Norton TW (1993) A framework for improved threatened species management using Population Viability Assessment. *Pacific Conservation Biology* **1**, 39-45.

Press AJ (1989) The abundance and distribution of Black Wallaroos, *Macropus bernadus*, and Common Wallaroos, *Macropus robustus*, on the Arnhem Land Plateau, Australia. In 'Kangaroos, Wallabies and Rat-kangaroos'. (Eds GC Grigg, PJ Jarman and ID Hume) pp. 783-786. (Surrey Beatty & Sons: Sydney)

Priddel D (1988) Habitat utilisation by sympatric red kangaroos, *Macropus rufus*, and western grey kangaroos, *M. fuliginosus*, in western New South Wales. *Australian Wildlife Research* **15**, 413-421.

Prober SM (1996) Conservation of the grassy white box woodlands: rangewide floristic variation and implications for reserve design. *Australian Journal of Botany* **44**, 57-77.

Prober SM, Thiele KR (1995) Conservation of the grassy white box woodlands: relative contributions of size and disturbance to floristic composition and diversity of remnants. *Australian Journal of Botany* **43**, 349-366.

Queensland Government Department of Primary Industry and Fisheries (2005) Zoonotic diseases - Hydatid disease. http://www.dpi.qld.gov.au/health/3893.html. Retrieved 7/5/2005.

Ramp D (2002) Dispersion of Eastern Grey Kangaroos and their Impacts on Vegetation in Semi-Rural Environments. Ph.D. thesis, University of Melbourne.

Ramp D, Ben-Ami D (In Review) The effect of road-based fatalities on the viability of an urban-fringe swamp wallaby population. *Journal of Wildlife Management*.

Ramp D, Caldwell J, Edwards KA, Warton D, Croft DB (In Press) Modelling of wildlife fatality hotspots along the Snowy Mountain Highway in New South Wales, Australia. *Biological Conservation*.

Ramp D, Coulson G (2002) Density dependence in foraging habitat preference of eastern grey kangaroos. *Oikos* **98**, 393-402.

Ramp D, Coulson G (2004) Small-scale patch selection and consumer-resource dynamics of eastern grey kangaroos. *Journal of Mammalogy* **85**, 1053-1059.

Ramp D, Russell BG, Croft DB (2005) Predator scent induces differing responses in two sympatric macropodids. *Australian Journal of Zoology* **53**, 73-78.

Ramp D, Wilson VK, Croft DB (In Review) Road-based fatalities and road usage by wildlife in the Royal National Park, New South Wales. *Animal Conservation*.

Reilly D (1999) From conservation to exploitation in South Australia. In 'The Kangaroo Betrayed: World's Largest Wildlife Slaughter'. (Ed. M Wilson) pp. 37-38. (Hill of Content Publishing: Melbourne)

Robertshaw JD, Harden RH (1986) The ecology of the dingo in north-eastern New South Wales. IV. Prey selection by dingoes and its effect on the major prey species, the swamp wallaby, *Wallabia bicolor* (Desmarest). *Australian Wildlife Research* **13**, 141-163.

Robertson D (1985) Interrelationships Between
    Kangaroos, Fire and Vegetation Dynamics
    at Gellibrand Hill Park, Victoria. Ph.D. thesis,
    University of Melbourne.
Robinson GA (1980) 'Journals of G.A. Robinson.'
    (Records of the Victorian Archaeological
    Survey: Melbourne)
Romin LA, Bissonette JA (1996) Deer-vehicle collisions
    - status of state monitoring activities and
    mitigation efforts. *Wildlife Society Bulletin* **24**,
    276-283.
Rosenfield A (1982) Style and meaning in Laura art: A
    case study in the formal analysis of style in
    prehistoric art. *Mankind* **13**, 199-217.
Rotherham ID (1994) The role of local authorities
    in conserving biodiversity through
    environmental management and land-
    use planning. *Proceedings of the Sixth
    International Congress of Ecology*, 77.
Rotherham ID (1999) Urban environmental history: the
    importance of relict communities in urban
    biodiversity conservation. *Journal of Practical
    Ecology and Conservation* **3**, 3-22.
RTA (2001) 'Road traffic accidents in NSW - 2001.'
    Roads and Traffic Authority, Sydney.
Russell EM (1973) Mother-young relationships and early
    behavioural development in the marsupials
    Macropus eugenii and *Megaleia rufa*.
    Zeitschrift für Tierpsychologie **33**, 163-203.
Russell EM (1982) Patterns of parental care and
    parental investment in marsupials. *Biological
    Reviews* **57**, 423-486.
Russell EM (1989) Maternal behaviour in the
    Macropodoidea. In 'Kangaroos, Wallabies
    and Rat-Kangaroos'. (Eds GC Grigg, PJ
    Jarman and ID Hume) pp. 549-569. (Surrey
    Beatty & Sons: Sydney)
SARDI (1999) Sex differences in nutritive value for
    broilers. (Eds B Hughes and P Zviedrans).
    (South Australian Research and Development
    Institute: Adelaide). http://www.sardi.sa.gov.
    au/pages/livestock/poultry/nutrition/sexdiff.
    htm:sectID=581&tempID=140. Retrieved
    10/1/2005.
Saville-Kent W (1897) 'The naturalist in Australia.'
    (Chapman and Hall: London)

Sharman GB, Pilton PE (1964) The life history and
    reproduction of the red kangaroo (*Megaleia
    rufa*). *Proceedings of the Zoological Society
    of London* **142**, 29-48.
Sherwood B, Cutler D, Burton J (Eds) (2002) 'Wildlife
    and Roads: the Ecological Impact.' (Imperial
    College Press: London, UK)
Short J (1986) The effect of pasture availability on
    food intake, species selection and grazing
    behaviour of kangaroos. *Journal of Applied
    Ecology* **23**, 559-571.
Short J (1998) The extinction of rat-kangaroos
    (Marsupialia:Potoroidae) in New South
    Wales, Australia. *Biological Conservation* **86**,
    365.
Short J, Milkovits G (1990) Distribution and status of the
    brush-tailed rock-wallaby in south-eastern
    Australia. *Australian Wildlife Research* **17**,
    169-179.
Shutkin WA (2000) 'The Land That Could Be.' (MIT
    Press: Cambridge)
Sivic A, Sielecki L (2001) 'Wildlife warning reflectors:
    spectrometric evaluation.' Ministry of
    Transport and Highways, Victoria, BC.
Smyth AB (1979) 'The journal of Arthur Bowes Smyth.
    surgeon, Lady Penrhyn, 1787-1789.'
    (Australian Documents Library: Sydney)
Sparrow AD, Friedel MH, Tongway DJ (2003)
    Degradation and recovery processes in arid
    grazing lands of central Australia. Part 3:
    implications at landscape scale. *Journal of
    Arid Environments* **55**, 349-360.
Spellerberg IF (1998) Ecological effects of roads and
    traffic: a literature review. *Global Ecology and
    Biogeography* **7**, 317-333.
Sprod D (1989) 'Proud Intrepid Heart.' (Blubber head:
    Hobart)
SSAS (2005) Sporting Shooters' Association of
    Australia. http://www.ssaa.org.au/graph/
    gunleg.html. Retrieved 10/1/2005.
Stevenson PM (1985) Traditional Aboriginal resource
    management in the wet-dry tropics: Tiwi case
    study. *Proceedings of the Ecological Society
    of Australia* **13**, 309-315.
Stirrat SC (2002) Foraging ecology of the agile wallaby
    (Macropus agilis) in the wet–dry tropics.
    Wildlife Research **29**, 347-361.

Stokes J (1990) Report of the Task Force enquiring into Duck Hunting in South Australia. (National Parks and Wildlife Service, South Australian Government: Adelaiade)

Strahan R (Ed) (1998) 'The Mammals of Australia.' (New Holland Publishers P/L: Sydney)

Strahan R (Ed.) (2002) 'The Mammals of Australia.' (Reed New Holland: Sydney, Australia)

Strieter Corporation (2001) 'Strieter-Lite: Wild Animal Highway Warning Reflector System. Installation Instructions.' Rock Island, Illinois.

Stuart-Dick R, Higginbottom KB (1989) Strategies of parental investment in Macropodoids. In 'Kangaroos, Wallabies and Rat-Kangaroos'. (Eds GC Grigg, PJ Jarman and ID Hume) pp. 571-592. (Surrey Beatty & Sons: Sydney)

Sturt CC (1849) 'Narrative of the Expedition into Central Australia.' (T and W Boone: London)

talkStMarys (2005) Facts. http://www.talkstmarys.com.au/talkstmarys/main.nsf/facts.html. Retrieved 28/5/2005.

Taylor BD, Goldingay RL (2003) Cutting the carnage: wildlife usage of road culverts in north-eastern New South Wales. *Wildlife Research* **30**, 529-537.

Taylor BD, Goldingay RL (2004) Wildlife road-kills on three major roads in north-eastern New South Wales. *Wildlife Research* **31**, 83-91.

Taylor RJ (1983) The diet of the eastern grey kangaroo and wallaroo in areas of improved and native pasture in the New England Tablelands. *Australian Wildlife Research* **10**, 203-211.

Taylor RJ (1985) Effects of pasture improvement on the nutrition of eastern grey kangaroos and wallaroos. *Journal of Applied Ecology* **22**, 717-725.

Tench WA (1789) 'A complete account of the settlement of Port Jackson in New South Wales.' (G. Nicol & J. Sewell: London)

Tench WA (1961) 'Sydney's first four years.' (Angus & Robertson: Sydney)

Tenhumberg B, Tyre AJ, Pople AR, Possingham HP (2004) Do harvest refuges buffer kangaroos against evolutionary responses to selective harvesting? *Ecology* **85**, 2003-2017.

Terborgh J (2004) Reflections of a scientist on the world parks congress. *Conservation Biology* **18**, 619-620.

Terry M (1974) 'War of the Warratnullas.' (Rigby: Adelaide)

The Victorian Shooter Newsletter (2004) December 2004. (Sporting Shooters' Association of Australia, Victorian Branch: Melbourne)

Tremont RM, McIntyre S (1994) Natural grassy vegetation and native forbs in temperate Australia: structure, dynamics and life histories. *Australian Journal of Botany* **42**, 641-658.

Troughton EL (1942) The truth about marsupial birth. *Australian Museum Magazine* **November 20**, 40-44.

Tyndale-Biscoe CH (1973) 'Life of Marsupials.' (Edward Arnold: London)

Tyndale-Biscoe CH (2005) 'Life of Marsupials.' (CSIRO Publishing: Collingwood)

Ujvari M, Baagoe HJ, Madsen AB (1998) Effectiveness of wildlife warning reflectors in reducing deer-vehicle collisions: A behavioral study. *Journal of Wildlife Management* **62**, 1094-1099.

United Nations Centre for Human Settlement (1996) 'An urbanising world: global report on human settlements, 1996.' Oxford University Press, Oxford, United Kingdom.

UNPD (2001) 'World Urbanization Prospects: The 1999 Revision. Key Findings.' United Nations Population Division.

UNPD (2002) 'World Population Prospects: The 2002 Revision and World Urbanization Prospects.' Department of Economic and Social Affairs of the United Nations Secretariat: United Nations Population Division.

van der Ree R (2004) The impact of urbanisation on the mammals of Melbourne - do atlas records tell the whole story or just some of the chapters? In 'Urban Wildlife: more than meets the eye'. (Eds D Lunney and S Burgin) pp. 195-204. (Royal Zoological Society of New South Wales: Mosman)

Vesk PA, Westoby M (2001) Predicting plant species' responses to grazing. *Journal of Applied Ecology* **38**, 897-909.

Viggers KL, Hearn JP (2005) The kangaroo conundrum: home range studies and implications for land management. *Journal of Applied Ecology* **42**, 99-107.

Walters B (1999) Harvesting our future. In 'The Kangaroo Betrayed: World's Largest Wildlife Slaughter.' (Ed. M Wilson) pp. 61. (Hill of Content Publishing: Melbourne)

Waring GH, Griffis JL, Vaughn ME (1991) White-tailed deer roadside behaviour, wildlife warning reflectors, and highway mortality. *Applied Animal Behaviour Science* **29**, 215-223.

Waring H (1956) Marsupial studies in Western Australia. *Australian Journal of Science* **18**, 66-73.

Watkinson BM, Kutemeyer C, Reinhold T, Werlein HD (2004) Game meat - an alternative to beef? [German]. *Flieschwirtschaft* **84**, 53-57.

Watson R (1993) No more blackberries. *Victorian Naturalist* **110**, 258-259.

Wheelwright HW (1979) 'Bush Wanderings of a Naturalist.' (Oxford University Press: Melbourne)

White J (1790) 'Journal of a voyage to New South Wales.' (J. Debrett: London)

White J (1962) 'Journal of a Voyage to New South Wales.' (Angus and Roberston: Sydney)

White ME (1994) 'After the greening: the browning of Australia.' (Kangaroo Press: Kenthurst, NSW)

Whitley GP (1970) 'An early history of Australian zoology.' (Royal Zoological Society of New South Wales: Sydney)

Williams AF, Wells JK (2005) Characteristics of vehicle-animal crashes in which vehicle occupants are killed. *Traffic Injury Prevention* **6**, 56-59.

Williams C (1998) Activitists threaten roo meat sales. again. *Food Processor* **April/May**.

Williams J, Read C, Norton A, Dovers S, Burgman M, Proctor W, Anderson H (2001) 'Biodiversity, Australia State of the Environment Report 2001 (Theme Report).' CSIRO on the behalf of the Department of Environment and Heritage, Canberra.

Wilson AD (1991) The influence of kangaroos and forage supply on sheep productivity in the semi-arid woodlands. *The Rangeland Journal* **13**, 69-80.

Wilson JA, Daub GJ (1926) The properties of shoe leather IV. Strength, stretch and stitch tear. *Journal of American Leather Chemical Association* **21**, 294-299.

Wilson M (1999) 'The Kangaroo Betrayed: World's Largest Wildlife Slaughter.' (Hill of Content Publishing: Melbourne)

Witte I (2002) Spatio-temporal interactions of mammalian herbivores in the arid zone. PhD thesis, University of New South Wales.

World League for the Protection of Animals (2003) LATEST CAMPAIGNS: St Mary's kangaroo cull. http://www.wlpa.org/index.php?fuseaction=campaigns.view&campaignID=15. Retrieved 28/5/2005.

Worster D (1973) 'American Environmentalism: the Formative Period, 1860-1950.' (Unknown: Wiley)

Yazgin VT (2000) Movements and grazing impact of eastern grey kangaroos, *Macropus giganteus*, on pasture adjacent to native woodland in southern Victoria. M.Sc. thesis, University of Melbourne.

Young L (1991) Conservationists mourn a 'courageous campaigner'. 29/4/1991. In 'The Age'. (Melbourne)